MUSIC OF
THE WESTERN
NATIONS

music of
the western
nations

HUGO LEICHTENTRITT

Edited and Amplified by
NICOLAS SLONIMSKY

Harvard University Press, Cambridge

1956

Distributed in Great Britain by Geoffrey Cumberlege,
Oxford University Press, London

Library of Congress Catalog Card Number 56–11283
Printed in the United States of America

Foreword

Hugo Leichtentritt

(1874-1951)

Hugo Leichtentritt belonged to a vanishing race of dedicated scholars. He spent his whole life searching for the artistic truth — the absolute truth according to his lights, for he countenanced no compromise. This is why his writings abound in judgments of dogmatic finality expressed with rhetorical passion. His mind was Hegelian, but his heart was romantically susceptible to human sympathies.

Leichtentritt was born in Posen, in German Poland, on New Year's Day in 1874. He received his early schooling in Berlin; in 1891 he went to America and took courses at Harvard University. He then returned to Berlin and was active there as music critic and teacher. Being Jewish, he was compelled to leave Germany after 1933. Fortunately, Harvard University extended to him an invitation to lecture on music. Leichtentritt settled in Cambridge, Massachusetts, and remained there until his death, on November 13, 1951.

Although his early photographs show a fine figure of a man, Leichtentritt partook little of the mundane joys. He had famous friends — Reger and Busoni among them — but he was not gregarious and lacked the outer graces of society. He never married. He lived all his life with his mother, who died on her ninety-sixth birthday, shortly before Leichtentritt's own death. To the end she guided him with affectionate understanding, but also with an imperious hand.

The name of Hugo Leichtentritt is familiar to professional musicians through his many scholarly writings. In 1905 he published a valuable monograph on Chopin, containing a detailed analysis of Chopin's works. In 1908 he brought out his important historical treatise *Geschichte der Motette*. He was working on an English edition of this book at the time of his death. Leichtentritt's biography of Handel, published in Germany in 1924, is still useful as a source book.

When Leichtentritt arrived in America, he was in a more advantageous position than most German scholars who found refuge here, for English was his second tongue. True, he was addicted to archaic and bookish locutions; in his writings in English, labyrinthine German constructions often asserted themselves; but, paradoxically, such stylistic infelicities enhanced the impression of earnestness of purpose and integrity of scholarship. Leichtentritt never sought to win the reader by a display of facile wit or to cajole his interest by assuming an air of affected informality. His task was to inform and to inspire; and this he undertook with all the ardor of his convictions.

Leichtentritt's first book written in English was *Music, History, and Ideas*, based on a series of lectures delivered by him at Harvard and published in 1938 by the Harvard University Press. In 1946 the same publisher brought out his monograph on Serge Koussevitzky as a champion of American music. In 1951, again under the imprint of the Harvard University Press, appeared Leichtentritt's book *Musical Form*.

Few readers of his books know that Leichtentritt was a prolific composer. He wrote two operas, an oratorio, much chamber music, several instrumental concertos, and songs. Some of these works he published at his own expense, but performances were few and far between. On the title page of the manuscript score of his cello concerto, there is an inscription in German, in Leichtentritt's hand: "Herr . . . [name of a celebrated cello player] said he would play this concerto upon occasion." The occasion never came, and the concerto remained unperformed.

There were no objective reasons for Leichtentritt's failure to establish himself as a composer. He possessed a solid technique; his style was neoromantic, with touches of impressionism. Pointing out a modernistic passage in one of his scores, Leichtentritt once remarked with undisguised bitterness: "If this were signed by Stravinsky, it would have made a sensational success."

After Leichtentritt's death, I assembled his musical manuscripts — they formed a stack five feet high — and sent them to the Music Division of the Library of Congress for safekeeping. Several of his literary manuscripts, among them an autobiography entitled *The Life of a City*, describing his experiences in old Berlin, were also included in this lot. During Leichtentritt's lifetime, the Fleisher Collection of the Free Library of Philadelphia obtained copies of all of his orchestral scores. Who knows? Some day a curious scholar may stumble upon these manuscripts and find in them interesting material for a thesis on musicologists as composers.

The present volume was prepared by Leichtentritt during the last years of his life. It is a book as panoramic in scope as *Music, History, and Ideas*, but here the distribution of material follows national lines rather than, as in the earlier volume, historical and ideational lines. National developments are examined by Leichtentritt in their relation to international, cosmopolitan music, in the light of his central hypothesis that regional traits transcend their limited significance and attain international validity only when organized in an artistic creation at the hands of a truly great national composer.

Not all music historians will agree with this thesis, but what esthetic or historic theory has ever gained universal acceptance without qualifications and exceptions? The merit of any such theory is measured by the cogency of argumentation, and by the degree of incidental illumination provided by it. This cogency, this illumination can hardly be denied to Leichtentritt.

The manuscript of *Music of the Western Nations* was not organized in final shape at the time of Leichtentritt's death. Transitional passages had to be inserted where the exposition suffered from faulty illation, that is, from lack of consequential reasoning. Substantial pruning and trimming was necessary in order to eliminate repetitious statements; factual data had to be amended in the light of recent research.

The task of preparing the book for publication fell to me. I knew Leichtentritt well, and spent many hours with him discussing the book while it was still in the making. I believe, therefore, that he would have accepted the changes that I have been compelled to make in the manuscript. I have not altered the basic plan of the book: thus national and international aspects of music intermingle; discussions of techniques common to several musical schools retain their supranational position; smaller countries are grouped according to geographical or ethnical principle. No attempt has been made to qualify Leichtentritt's personal opinions or to tone down his passionate prejudices. His somewhat truculent judgments of composers of the modern school have been allowed to stand, as well as his extravagant praise for some of his favorites, such as Max Reger, whom he compares with Bach as a master of counterpoint.

Leichtentritt was not concerned in this book with an equitable and proportionate representation of composers according to the measure of their relative fame. Often he gave more space to a minor composer than to a world-renowned figure. I have not tried to establish mechanical balance by adding material about a celebrity and cutting down discussion of a less famous personality. In fact, such preferential treatment of underestimated composers may well make the book more stimulating.

In my own additional paragraphs, dealing mostly with modern composers, I have been careful to preserve the general spirit of Leichtentritt's literary style; I even drew on his characteristic vocabulary for my interpolations, so as to avoid stylistic incongruity. In no case have I injected an estimate of my own regarding this or that composer, but have confined myself to reasoned statements of fact.

I trust that this posthumous volume will redound to Hugo Leichtentritt's fine reputation as a learned music scholar, and will give the reader a new appreciation of national music as part of universal art.

Nicolas Slonimsky

January 1, 1956

CONTENTS

CONTENTS

MUSIC OF
THE WESTERN
NATIONS

Introduction

A humble experience of everyday life has sometimes startled me, leading me to meditate on cause and effect. In the house in which I had lived for thirty years, in the rooms I had inhabited for thousands of days and nights, in the streets that I had daily walked, I was sometimes excited by suddenly noticing some detail I had never observed before. Why had I never before perceived this detail? And why did I perceive it on this occasion?

I found an answer that satisfied me. By reason of bodily structure, habit, or a certain fixed posture, every person has a certain angle from which he perceives the world around him. Sometimes, however, he happens to abandon this habitual posture for a few moments, and as a consequence, he sees the familiar objects from an unaccustomed angle. Things he imagined he knew perfectly well acquire suddenly a novel aspect. Upon reflection, he realizes that he has made a discovery: he has seen something new in an old object. The object itself has not changed, but his way of looking at it has.

This oft-repeated experience I have applied to the study of the art of music. In my book *Music, History, and Ideas*, I examined music as a part of general culture, seeking to determine how it has been influenced by political history, by social conditions, by philosophy and religion, and by other arts — poetry, painting, sculpture, architecture. In the present volume I again inspect these materials, but from another angle, hoping that they will yield new vistas when examined from the points of view of nationalism and internationalism. Here we shall look at music as an expression of the cultural status of the various nations. Although in this effort the materials — the great works of muscial art — remain unchanged, they will present a different aspect as we examine them with reference to their national and their international (or cosmopolitan) tendencies.

It will be pointed out that certain features originally peculiar to one nation have been adopted by other nations, thus acquiring cosmopolitan validity and becoming an essential part of later music. It will be shown that the great music of Bach, Mozart, Beethoven, Wagner, and others is a compound of national and cosmopolitan traits, and that an exclusively national music remains narrow and provincial in its scope, like a regional dialect in relation to a rich, fully developed language.

Some nations have impressed their seal on music so deeply that even after centuries of development it is still possible to trace these impressions back to their origin. These nations will be of particular interest for our investigation. The debt music owes to Italy, Germany, and France, and also to Greece and Palestine, is much greater than is generally assumed. England and Spain, Russia and Poland, the Scandinavian countries, Bohemia, Hungary, and finally America have all shared, through their national contributions, in the development of musical art.

The music of Africa and Asia, the continents that developed the oldest musical cultures that have preserved their primitive and alluringly exotic character, is now attracting more and more attention from the Western musical world, after nearly two thousand years of completely separate history as far as art is concerned. In this book, however, we shall deal only with the European sphere of music (to which America also belongs), not with the cultural spheres of Asia and Africa.

Although the music of the various Western nations reveals characteristic and well-defined national traits, it also contains something supranational, something fundamentally human, presenting a strong appeal to the sentiment and imagination of many distinct nationalities within a given cultural sphere. Indeed, a work of art can acquire international validity only if it possesses such universal characteristics. At the same time, some striking national trait will arouse curiosity in a stranger, unfamiliar with the essence of that particular national art. Such musical spice enhances the charm of the product.

Of primary importance in all music are the nationally circumscribed associations that are awakened in persons of the same nationality. A polonaise or a mazurka by Chopin will arouse in a listener of Polish origin a sensation quite different from an impression it will produce on an American. The sharp accents, the specific melodic turns of such compositions will vividly recall to the Polish listener the familiar dances and songs of his country, and will arouse in him a whole complex of recollections, an aura of national consciousness. For the American listener this nationalistic complex with its emotional stir will be absent; for him, Chopin's music is not specifically Polish music, but beautiful music in general. To a certain extent he may relish its Polish inflections, but only as a sort of exotic flavor. For him the main feature will be not the national traits of Chopin's music but the general, cosmopolitan musical character that transcends national frontiers. One may go so far as to assert that a Polish listener will be inclined to favor any strongly marked Polish music, even if it is faulty from a purely musical standpoint.

The same observation can easily be made with regard to the appeal of Italian music. What delights the Italian listener in his native operas cannot be fully sensed by the average American listener, because he lacks the Italian temperament, powerfully attuned to Italian strains.

To this national, racial, primitive, limited, and realistic element in music is opposed a strain that is cosmopolitan, humanistic, artistically mature, universal, and idealistic. In their extreme forms neither of these two elements is generally acceptable. Artistic value, charm, and impressive power can be achieved only in their fusion. The great cosmopolitan art of music is to the provincial idiom as spirit is to matter, as a creative idea and organized form are to mere naturalistic description. On the one hand, there is folk music, which appeals to the masses in every nation; on the other, there is art music, which attains international validity. The former is comparable to the roots and the stem of a plant, the latter to the flower, with its pleasing fragrance and delicate charm.

It will be shown, however, that art music can assume national significance only insofar as it retains elements of the preartistic stage, that is, of folk music. As soon as any considerable amount of "art" enters, the international influences become unavoidable, indeed indispensable. Music as an art of a higher type is pervaded by many currents coming from many different directions; it becomes cosmopolitan. What we call Italian, German, and French music contains a residue of numerous alien undercurrents, generally of unknown origin; though not distinctly felt, they are deep and rich; while the so-called national characteristics, easily perceptible, form but an upper stratum, a thinner layer. When this upper, national stratum becomes denser than the international residue, the music fails to acquire international validity; it is confined chiefly to home use; it remains provincial, restricted, instead of becoming cosmopolitan, universal, as the art of all our great masters is. On the other hand, music from which the distinctive national traits have almost entirely disappeared is insipid and devoid of vigor. The Spanish musical comedies (zarzuelas), for instance, are so typically Spanish in sentiment, musical idiom, plot, and treatment that they cannot be enjoyed or even properly understood in other countries, though in Spain they arouse great enthusiasm. The opposite is illustrated by that type of ultramodern, radical music which sounds almost identical in all countries, being intentionally deprived of national elements. This kind of music cannot be generally accepted; it is relished only by a limited group of musicians with more or less perverted taste.

The national or international aspect of music may be of two types: either naïve, unintentional, and natural; or cultivated, intentional, and artificial. And here, too, the pure natural product is far superior to the artificial, deliberately contrived type. The national aspect of Haydn's music, for instance, is of the first kind. His melodic and rhythmic material is typically rural Austrian. But Haydn did not set out intentionally to cultivate that sort of Austrian tonal material — it was his natural manner of speech. He could not have handled any other idiom even if he had wanted to. The rural quality of this music, however, did not prevent him from applying to it what he had learned of harmony, contrapuntal treatment, form, and orchestral color from the masters of Italy, northern Germany, France, and England. Had Haydn not applied this international, cosmopolitan technique of composition to his national material, he would never have gone beyond provincial popularity, such as was gained by Carl Michael Bellman in Sweden, Prince Michael Cleophas Oginski in Poland, Friedrich Silcher in Germany, and Stephen Foster in the United States. In the course of our investigation, the difference between national and international music and their mutual relations will be further clarified.

The oldest sources of European music are found in ancient Greek music and in the religious music of the Jews, and to these two topics we shall therefore turn our attention before inspecting the younger music of the European countries.

HUGO LEICHTENTRITT

Cambridge, Massachusetts
1950.

1

Greece

One of the strangest phenomena in the entire history of music is the immense influence issuing from Greek music, although it almost entirely disappeared more than fifteen hundred years ago. Of all the enthusiastic admirers of ancient Greek music from the fifth century of our era down to the twentieth century, hardly any have had a satisfactory acquaintance with it. But, though the music itself has not been available, the aura surrounding it ever since antiquity has been so fascinating that the imagination of artists has always been affected by ancient Greek music, and traits have been attributed to it that in reality never existed. Owing to this roundabout influence, Greek music continued for more than two thousand years to maintain a spiritual life full of activity. Imagine that by a stroke of good fortune the music to an Aeschylean, a Sophoclean, or a Euripidean tragedy should be rediscovered. It would create a sensation among musical scholars in all civilized countries. Not only mere archeological curiosity but a much deeper feeling of affinity would be gratified, for all musicians instinctively assume that ancient Greek music is our direct though distant ancestor. No such warm interest could ever be aroused by discoveries — perhaps more important — in Chinese and Japanese music, because these musical cultures are quite separate from ours.

In his previous book *Music, History, and Ideas*, the author has analyzed the few fragments of Greek music left to us and has pointed out what modern music owes to Greece. These comments were concerned with the theoretical acoustic basis attributed to Pythagoras: the ratios of the various intervals; the construction of scales, modes, tonalities; the laws of metrical and rhythmical art, derived from poetry and transferred to music; the structure of musical instruments, adapted to carry out in practice the theoretical concepts and the new insight gained by Greek genius into the nature and possibilities of music; and the first practical system of musical notation, an invention of inestimable value for the subsequent progress of music.

A few additional observations are in order here before the reader's attention is called to the indirect influences issuing from what may be called the phantom of ancient Greek music. Even before the Greeks, the older cultures of Asia and Africa, China, India, and Egypt had evolved a complex system treating the nature of intervals, scales, and tonalities; but it remained for the Greeks to modify this system of intervals, scales, and tonalities in a new and special manner adapted to the European musical mentality. The successions of intervals in the scales of Asia and Africa have never appealed to European ears, have remained foreign and enigmatic to the European musical mind, and have consequently not been adopted by European nations. The material of Greek music consisted of whole tones and semitones, and these have become the foundation of European scales. Occasionally the Asiatic quarter-tones were incorporated in Greek scales, but they always remained an exotic importation and never acquired full rights of native usage.

What we possess of actual Greek music is a small collection of a few short tunes and a number of fragments from larger works. All specimens so far discovered can easily be copied on four or five pages. Although these extant fragments are insufficient to give us anything like an adequate idea of the artistic qualities of Greek music, we have abundant indirect evidence of its flourishing state in the works of Greek writers, mathematicians, and philosophers — men like Pythagoras, Plato, Aristotle,

Plutarch, Aristoxenus of Tarentum, Claudius Ptolemæus of Alexandria, and Alypius. The Greek poets and dramatists also give us valuable information on matters of musical meter and rhythm: Homer, Hesiod, and Pindar; Aeschylus, Sophocles, Euripides, and Aristophanes; Sappho and Anacreon.

In esthetics, and in ethics too, the Greeks laid the foundation for a more profound understanding, appreciation, and interpretation of music. The Greek esthetic and ethical maxims of music are still alive, and they represent more than an antiquarian's delight. Professor Hermann Abert of Berlin University has elucidated this side of Greek music in a weighty little book, *Die Lehre vom Ethos in der griechischen Musik*. True, China and India evolved similar doctrines in advance of the Greeks. How much Greece was influenced by these earlier Oriental doctrines is an interesting question that is not likely to be easily solved. It is quite certain, however, that so far as European music in the Middle Ages and in more recent times is concerned, it is not the Indian and Chinese doctrines but the Greek esthetic maxims that became of paramount importance. In Plato, Aristotle, Plutarch, and Plotinus we find esthetic and ethical ideas on music that to some extent retain their validity even at the present time.

Plato draws a distinction among the various scales and tonalities employed in Greek music, attributing a greater ethical power to some than to others — for instance, calling the original pure Greek Dorian scale manly, invigorating, and forceful, while ascribing to the Phrygian scale, imported from Asia, a quality that is effeminate, dissolute, and orgiastic. This doctrine of the superior ethos of national music, opposed to the destructive influence of foreign elements, has been influential through the ages. Apart from the question of how much real merit there is in the maxim of superiority of national and racial traits over international tendencies, the fact remains that this Platonic maxim has, rightly or wrongly, often been applied to European music in the course of the centuries. The point here is to demonstrate the propagating power of Greek ideas, not to debate their correctness.

At the time of Christ's birth, Greek music had acquired international supremacy, being universally preferred and practiced in the vast Roman empire. Rome had deprived Greece of political independence, but Greece maintained her spiritual and artistic predominance. The Romans, little gifted musically, never evolved a music of their own, and as a consequence Greek artists had for centuries held undisputed sway among the Roman territories on three continents. Yet Greek music, with all its fascination, could not have won the universal admiration tendered to it in so many countries without the effective assistance of that practical Roman organization which carried musical culture along the far-flung highways of the vast empire.

This music, for the most part, was no longer the classical Greek music of the age of Aeschylus and Sophocles, but a somewhat debased art that had degenerated owing to the influence of Oriental practice. For centuries the contest went on between the austere Greek classical music and the sensuous and pleasing (though often vulgarized) new Greek music. In the second century of our era the Emperor Hadrian tried to bring about a renascence of the pure antique Greek music. In the fourth century Julian the Apostate launched an even more ambitious revival of ancient Greek culture, ethics, and art, seeking to reintroduce the old Hellenic sacred hymns in a special school for old Greek music at Alexandria. We read of these projects in Julian's letters; his ideas had evidently been inspired by his observation of the important part that music played in the religious rites of the young Christian church, and he probably thought he might render a similar service to the dying Roman religion, which he had readopted. But all these plans were frustrated by Julian's premature death.

The fascination of Greek music, continuing through the ages, gave rise to an extensive literature in many countries, from late antiquity through medieval times and on into the twentieth century. Johann Nikolaus Forkel (1749–1818), the earliest Bach biographer and the greatest musical scholar of his age, included in his erudite book *Allgemeine Litteratur der Musik* a descriptive catalogue of treatises (chiefly Latin) on various aspects of Greek and Roman music, embracing hundreds of books and essays. Were one to add what has been written on Greek music from the date of Forkel's book (1792) to 1950, this catalogue would be swelled to perhaps twice its size. Greek music has been the common hunting ground for historians of music, scholars of classical philology, mathematicians, physicists, philosophers, and theologians. And all this passionate speculation has been devoted to an extinct art, that exists solely in the form of vague hypotheses and surmises about its nature! A strange phenomenon, indeed, demonstrating the enduring power of these ancient ideas!

During the centuries following the fall of Rome — the period known as the Dark Ages — ancient art and culture were neglected, and with them the methods of higher education and learning. The Greek language disappeared in western Europe; medieval Latin succeeded the noble Roman speech. The original sources of Greek music were lost; even if Greek musical notation had been preserved, it could not have been easily deciphered or properly interpreted. However, in spite of these circumstances, certain essential features of Greek music did survive. For this survival, two authors especially are to be thanked: Cassiodorus and Boethius; and their literary activity deserves far higher credit for having saved Greek music from oblivion and for promoting church music in general than do the somewhat mythical accomplishments of Palestrina as a savior of polyphonic church music a thousand years later.

Magnus Aurelius Cassiodorus (who flourished in the sixth century) was a contemporary of Boethius; like Boethius, he was a minister of Theodoric the Great at Ravenna, and later a Roman consul. Eventually he retired to a life of study and meditation, founding a convent in which great importance was attached to scientific pursuits. His book *De artibus ac disciplinis liberalium litterarum* (On the Arts and Literary Studies) contains one part, called *Institutiones musicae*, which gives a synopsis of Greek musical theory and practice with special reference to Aristoxenus' teaching. This treatise of Cassiodorus was famous for many centuries and is highly important for its documentary value. It is published in Martin Gerbert's great collection of medieval writers on music.

Anicius Boethius, son of a Roman consul, was a distinguished scholar of ancient philosophy and music, as well as a statesman. He was born about 475, and beheaded for alleged treason in 524 by King Theodoric. In the great mass of his Latin writings, a treatise in five parts, *De musica*, became the most famous book on music during the early Middle Ages and constituted the chief guide of medieval church music. It outlines the evolution of Greek music from a closely confined national art to a spiritual force of wide European significance. Boethius, more than anyone else, was instrumental in the revival of interest in the theory of Greek music. Every medieval manuscript mentions his name with reverence; he is admired and looked up to as the highest authority on musical matters. The great authority of Boethius as a philosopher helped to maintain interest in his musical writings. For a thousand years his principal work, *De consolatione philosophiae*, which he wrote in prison, was held in veneration. King Alfred translated this treatise into Anglo-Saxon, with some changes and additions of his own; Chaucer rewrote it in English; and one of its later translators was Queen Elizabeth.

De musica made possible the study of the earliest Greek sources, of which quite a number had survived in manuscripts hidden in monasteries and not discovered until centuries later. These Greek treatises and fragments have been the object of study by scholars of many centuries. The history of this literature has charms of its own for one who has a feeling for the romance of tradition and for the strange adventures of books.

The earliest collection of Greek musical treatises, *Antiquae musicae auctores septem, Graece et Latine*, was published by Marcus Meibom and printed in Amsterdam in 1652 by the famous printer Elzevir. Meibom, an eminent scholar in the fields of Latin, Greek, and Hebrew, enjoyed for some time the support of the eccentric Swedish queen Christina, who took great interest in his works on Greek music. Later he was librarian of the Royal Library in Copenhagen, and he was also active in Amsterdam. His collection embraces musical treatises by Aristoxenus, Nicomachus, Alypius, Gaudentius, Bacchius, Aristides Quintilianus, and Martianus Capella.

Another important collection dealing with Greek music came out of Oxford in 1699. Its author, the Oxford mathematics professor John Wallis, published it in the third volume of his works: *Johannes Wallis operum mathematicorum: volumen tertium, quo continentur Claudii Ptolemaei, Porphyrii, Manuelis Bryennii harmonica*. Still larger inventories of old manuscripts were published, one in the eighteenth century and one in the nineteenth; but both are concerned mainly with medieval writings and have only an indirect bearing on Greek music. Two other great collections of medieval treatises are *Scriptores ecclesiastici de musica sacra potissimum*, by the German abbot Martin Gerbert, and *Scriptores de musica medii aevi*, compiled by the great French scholar Edmond de Coussemaker. The most conveniently accessible collection of ancient musical treatises is Carl von Jan's *Musici scriptores graeci* (1895).

Apart from these large collections there exist a great number of editions of individual Greek authors, some with translations and commentaries. The most important of these authors is Aristoxenus of Tarentum, Aristotle's pupil. He has always been considered the greatest authority on Greek music, and the fragments of his worsk have been published and reprinted, translated and commented on constantly, since their first publication in Venice in 1562.

Two ancient books by Aristoxenus, *Elements of Harmony* and

Elements of Rhythm, have had a strange fascination for modern scholars, and the last word on them has not yet been said. A German translation by Marquard came out in 1868; a French translation by Ruelle, in 1871. Two nineteenth-century scholars each devoted a lifetime of study to the rhythmical doctrine of Aristoxenus, in the conviction that Aristoxenus had mastered fundamental truths on rhythm in music. These two modern scholars are François-Auguste Gevaert and Rudolf Westphal.

Gevaert — one of the most cultivated musicians of his time and author of world-renowned manuals of orchestration — has based his monumental work *Histoire et théorie de la musique de l'antiquité* (1875) mainly on Aristoxenus. Elsewhere Gevaert says expressly that "a full understanding of the rhythmic complications in the music of our great classical masters is impossible without serious study of Aristoxenus' theory of rhythm; there exists no modern theory of rhythm." He confesses that his ideas on Greek music were greatly clarified by Rudolf Westphal's epoch-making *System der antiken Rhythmik* (1865). In this and a number of later books, Westphal extols Aristoxenus as the bright light illuminating the mysteries of rhythm. Both Westphal and Gevaert found it worth while to devote their best efforts to establishing a link between Greek music, as expounded by Aristoxenus, and the music of the modern world, particularly that of Bach. Both found enthusiastic followers; both encountered bitter opposition in the ranks of music scholars and philologists. This protracted debate, not yet settled after many decades, may continue indefinitely, for its solution depends on the varying interpretation of Greek technical terms.

Next to Aristoxenus, Aristides Quintilianus made the most important contributions to our knowledge of Greek musical theory. Hermann Abert writes of Aristides as one of the most significant sources of information about Greek music, and in some matters our only source. In an informative article, "Le Musicographe Aristide Quintilien," Charles Ruelle gives a summary of opinions on Aristides through the centuries; he reminds us that more than twenty modern scholars have written on Aristides' treatise *Peri Musikes* and that no fewer than fifty-four manuscripts of this treatise are known. We find references to Aristides even in Byzantine and Arabic musical literature.

In his treatise Aristides gives an interesting synopsis covering the whole field of what we today call musicology. He establishes two large divisions, *theoretikon* and *praktikon*:

A. *Theoretikon*, the theory of the art, is subdivided into:

1. *Physikon*, comprising arithmetic as applied to music, and physics proper, that is, acoustics and what relates to the process of hearing.

2. *Technikon*, what we would call theory proper, comprising *harmonike* (equivalent to our term "scale structure"), *rhythmike*, and *metrike*.

B. *Praktikon*, the practice of the art, is subdivided into:

1. *Chrestikon*, the teaching of composition, comprising *melopoeia, rhythmopoeia,* and *poesis*: the laws and rules governing the structure of melody and of rhythmical combinations, or forms and poetry.

2. *Exangeltikon*, performance, including *organike* (instrumental performance), *odike* (singing), and *hypokritike* (mimic action).

This synopsis represents the curriculum of a Greek college of music — what its student was expected to learn before being graduated to the rank of a real artist, a "master of arts."

Claudius Ptolemæus of Alexandria acquired world-wide fame by his great achievements in astronomy, mathematics, and geography. He also wrote a musical treatise in three books, called *Harmonike*, which constitutes the closing link and, in a sense, the climax of ancient theory. It simplifies and codifies the theory of scale formation. The fifteen different scales recognized by Aristoxenus and his school are reduced by Ptolemæus to seven, which, through transposition, suffice to account for practical uses. With regard to modulation from one mode to another, Ptolemæus introduces the terms *kata dynamin* and *kata thesin*, designating the function or position of a tone. (This idea was revived by Hugo Riemann in his theory of functional harmony.) Ptolemæus' treatise is historically important because it was regarded by Italian scholars of the Renaissance as the supreme authority on ancient Greek music. The leading musical theorists of the fifteenth and sixteenth centuries — Ramis de Pareja, Lodovico Fogliano, and especially the Venetian master Gioseffo Zarlino — all developed their ideas from the foundations laid by Ptolemæus.

The theories of yet another Alexandrian scholar, Alypius, who lived in the fourth century of our era, have acquired special importance, for it was thanks to the detailed tables of scales in his book *Eisagoge Musike* (Introduction to Music) that the deciphering of Greek musical notation was made possible.

The so-called *Problemata*, handed down through the ages as the writings of Aristotle, are now regarded as spurious; but they are of interest to scholars as reflections of medieval followers of Aristotelean theories. In his *Musici scriptores graeci*, Carl von Jan published the complete text of the "problems," as well as writings on music from the authentic works of Aristotle. And Gevaert, with J. C. Vollgraff as collaborator, devoted three volumes to *Les problèmes musicaux d'Aristote* (1899–1902). Among other eminent scholars who have written on the "problems" are Karl Stumpf, Théodore Reinach, and Charles Ruelle.

Plutarch, that immortal biographer of immortals, made illuminating comments on Greek music; his writings on the subject are discussed in the author's book *Music, History, and Ideas*. The unsolved problems presented by Greek music have influenced modern theories of scales and have encouraged a search for new possibilities of scale formation. Studies in this direction have been made by Busoni, Scriabin, Bartók, Alois Hába, and Nicolas Slonimsky. In these investigations the systematic theory of the ancient Greek scales not only serves as a precedent and a classical model but also suggests new intervallic progressions, through application and variation of what the Greeks called chromatic and enharmonic tetrachords.

Medieval Christian music — the so-called Ambrosian and Gregorian chant — is a mixture of Oriental, Hebrew, and Syrian elements, with Graeco-Roman traits. In *Music, History, and Ideas,* the author has analyzed the proportional manifestation of these components in the theory, form, and melodic substance of medieval music. A considerable part of the Greek theoretical system is preserved, with some modifications, in the music of the medieval Christian church service, in its intervals, scales, rhythm, and certain melodic features. Gregorian chant, though eight hundred to a thousand years younger than Greek music, thus shows again the great power of propagation, the international validity of Greek music and musical ideas. The so-called medieval church modes embody, though not without modification, the ancient Greek tonalities: the Dorian, Phrygian, Lydian, Mixolydian, Aeolian, and Ionian modes.

Music notation also goes back to the Greeks, who were the first among European peoples to develop the idea that music must not only be played or sung, not only heard and transmitted by ear and memory, but also written down in adequate and understandable notation. The designation of tones by letters is a Greek invention. Since then, the Greek idea of connecting musical tones with the alphabet and with arithmetical numbers, has been, in one way or another, maintained in European musical notation. Some curious changes deserve special notice. In Greek notation the letters of the alphabet denote the actual sounds: twenty-four letters of the alphabet correspond to twenty-four different sounds: In modern notation, however, only seven letters of the alphabet are used, and they are repeated over and over again in successive octaves to represent the sounds of recurring musical scales.

Perhaps the greatest achievement of Greek culture is the

music drama. Of the entire body of Greek dramatic music, only a mutilated fragment of choral music to *Orestes* by Euripides has come down to us. Nevertheless, Greek drama — perhaps because of this fatal lack of musical documentation — has exercised a singular attraction; time and again, it has fired the imagination of scholars and artists. This alluring fantasm of what Greek musical drama may have been like is responsible for some of the most powerful innovations, reforms, and even revolutions in the history of music. The Renaissance derives its name from a revival of ancient art and ancient poetry. When, toward the close of the sixteenth century, opera came into existence, it was regarded by its Florentine creators as the rediscovery of the choral and solo style of Greek drama.

The most characteristic feature of early Italian opera was the importance attached to what is called musical recitative or declamation. This recitative, a sort of scanning on a singing tone, is a heritage of Greek drama. No one knew at that time (or for that matter even later) just how the Greek dramatists intended to scan their recitative; the Florentine scholars of the Renaissance tried to recreate experimentally this unknown declamation. When the results proved pleasing, they became convinced that they had found the right solution, that they had actually rediscovered Greek dramatic speech.

This rather naïve conception of opera as a revival of Greek drama was based not on authentic facts but on a vague, fantastic roaming about of the imagination, unencumbered by historical research. It was believed for a long time that the early Florentine operas of Giulio Caccini, Jacopo Peri, and Marco da Gagliano closely resembled scenes from lost Greek drama. This supposed resemblance is not corroborated by the few genuine fragments of Greek music available to us. Nevertheless, opera attained universal success. Though born of an erroneous assumption, it possessed a tremendous vitality of its own, and it grew into a new form of art that has flourished for three and half centuries. The flowering of the modern opera would have been

impossible but for the ideal of Greek music drama, which provided the inspiration for the initial creative effort.

In French music, ancient classical tendencies have always
been strongly felt. In the age of Louis XVI the new drama of
Corneille and Racine took its esthetic maxims from Aristotle's
philosophy of art, its subject matter and much of its dramatic
technique from Greek and Roman dramas. Its musical counterpart is found in Lully's classical opera and, half a century later,
in Rameau's ballets and operas — the most genuinely French
theatrical music ever written, yet full of allusions to the ancient
myths. And toward the middle of the eighteenth century, the
Greek ideal led Gluck to his attempt at the purification of opera,
which had been debased by some of its practitioners. Gluck's
magnificent works — *Alceste, Orpheus and Eurydice, Iphigenia
in Aulis, Iphigenia in Tauris,* and *Paris and Helen* are directly
inspired by an idealized vision of Greek music drama.

The old Greek phantom was far from having exhausted its
vitality in Gluck's operatic reform. A generation after him, we
find Cherubini and Spontini passionately striving to extract new
beauties from it: Cherubini with *Medea* and *Anacreon,* Spontini with *La Vestale. Medea* has been called one of the greatest
achievements of opera, and it was described by Cherubini's
biographer, Ludwig Schemann, as "the most interesting operatic
phenomenon between Gluck and Wagner." Brahms wrote:
"This *Medea* is what we musicians among ourselves recognize
as the highest achievement in dramatic music." As for Spontini's
La Vestale, it held for a long time a high place on the opera
stage. Its libretto has been called the finest example of dramatic
action ever adapted for opera. *La Vestale* received the prize given
by Napoleon for the best opera produced in Paris.

Once again, in the nineteenth century, Greek drama asserted
its mysterious, demoniac power: in the music drama of Richard
Wagner. Greek drama is the central theme of Wagner's *Die
Kunst und die Revolution;* in his subsequent book, *Das Kunst-
werk der Zukunft,* Hellenic drama is the ever recurring and

ingeniously developed leading motive. Many pages in his book *Oper und Drama* are devoted to Greek dramatic art. This is not the proper place to discuss the question of whether Wagner's idea of the universal *Gesamtkunstwerk* — the union of all arts in the drama — was fully accomplished in his works, or of whether this revival of the Greek idea really has the importance he attributed to it. The essential point here is to show that Wagner's gigantic achievement was derived primarily from the ideal of Greek drama and was the product of his ardent wish to adapt this ancient ideal to the altered conditions of modern times.

In Wagnerian music drama, Greek music was of infinitely less importance than Greek dramatic action. No genuine Greek dramatic music was known to anyone in Wagner's time, but there was enough Greek poetic drama to arouse his artistic sensibility. For Wagner it was sufficient merely to know that Greek dramatic poetry was inseparably connected with music and that the chorus in Greek tragedy was assigned a definite task to perform. These two fundamental ideas inspired Wagner to the magnificent effort of his music dramas. The function of the Greek chorus was transferred to the Wagnerian symphonic orchestra, whose continuous commentary of the drama enacted on the stage corresponds to the lines uttered by the Greek tragic chorus.

In the twentieth century, a number of leading masters of musical drama have shown a strong inclination toward the Greek ideal. Among the operas by Richard Strauss, *Elektra* and *Salome* and (to a certain extent) *The Egyptian Helen* and *Ariadne in Naxos* owe a great deal to classical Greek drama. To be sure, none of these complex scores were directly inspired by Greek music, for Strauss seldom, if ever, made an attempt to simulate the ancient Greek scales or modes. Yet the problems that fascinated him, and led him to undertake the immense labor of creating his operas, are traceable to Greek theories, dramatically and psychologically. His aim was not to revive the spirit of the classic drama, as was the aim of the Florentine founders of opera, and of Lully and Gluck, but to gain new ground for modern music, to explore uncharted regions. In his search for a medium, he encountered the classical Greek ideas. He modernized these ideas, gave them a new color, even re-modeled their contents; but the ultimate source of his inspiration remains in the drama of the Greeks.

Igor Stravinsky, universally acknowledged as a leader of ultra-modern music, has in the course of a quarter of a century undergone a complete change of style, owing to the influence of Greek ideas. In his singular opera-oratorio *Oedipus Rex*, he took a famous story as dramatized by Sophocles and presented it in a new manner, halfway between opera and oratorio: a plastic, static, epic work with stage scenery but without dramatic action. In solemn Latin verse, the story is told by a speaker, while the chorus, after the classic manner, represents the voice of the people. This speaker is a character from the old Latin oratorios of the seventeenth century, as practiced by the great master Carissimi and his school, in which the recitation of the story is entrusted to the so-called *testo*. In the Passions of Johann Sebastian Bach, this speaker (called the Evangelist) is continually active.

In at least two of his other works, Stravinsky finds this approximation of the ancient Greek ideal fertile, though he never goes completely back to the original sources, preferring a curious mixture of ancient and French seventeenth-century features: in *Apollon Musagète*, where he treats a Greek theme in the manner of the French ballet of Lully; and in the melodramatic *Persephone*, whose spiritual content is derived from Greek poetry. *Persephone* also has a peculiar affinity with a work of the seventeenth century, Monteverdi's *Ballo delle ingrate*, which in its turn manifests a baroque reflection of the classical Greek action.

The spirit of elegiac and idyllic poetry of ancient Greece is reflected in such musical works by modern masters as Debussy's *L'Après-midi d'un faune* and Ravel's *Daphnis et Chloé*; the Greek tragic muse is revived in Honegger's music drama *Antigone* and in Krenek's opera *Das Leben des Orest.*

In the science of acoustics, the basic foundation of all music, modern theorists follow the tenets established by the Greeks. The Greek tonal system forms the basis of the European musical style; the Greek diatonic scales, with their various modifications, are still in common use. The Greek code of esthetics underlies the musical thinking of the present day. Greece set the standard for European music. For the first time on the European continent, the Greek spirit made music an art — a part of higher spiritual culture, a well-ordered system of esthetic maxims applied to practical experience. In poetry, drama, and philosophy, in architecture and sculpture, Greece evolved models of imperishable beauty. We can admire the other great Greek arts from the many preserved monuments; we cannot do so with Greek music, which left few, if any, authentic examples. Greek music is to us an imaginary model, an ideal. This ideal, however, has proved more inspiring for the art of music than Greek music manuscripts themselves might have been. Their destruction was a heavy loss, but this loss has been amply compensated by the self-regenerating power of Greek ideas; and this perpetual renaissance, which has continued for nearly two thousand years, is the unique bequest of Greek music to the modern world.

2

The Hebrews

In embarking on a discussion of Hebrew music we find ourselves with the same handicap that confronted us in discussing
Greek music. The written monuments of old Hebrew music,
during Biblical times and even during the time of early Christi-
anity, have perished. Of Greek music we possess some dozen
fragments and small pieces of undoubted antiquity; we cannot,
however, point to a single manuscript, not even to a single
melody, that may be indisputably called an original ancient
Hebrew composition.

This seems discouraging indeed. Yet a closer examination
gives us some hope. If we ask why the sacred music of the ancient
Hebrew service has vanished, while the sacred books — the Bible
and prayers and the Talmud — have survived, the answer is
this: the Hebrew people were able to write down their language;
they developed a finely constructed grammar and a science of
philology applied to the art of poetry. They did not, however,
possess musical notation; they had no means of transcribing
music, propagating it, and handing it down to posterity in written copies. It may seem strange that there existed such a dis-
parity between the treatment of language and that of music, but
we must recall that such has been the situation everywhere in
the Orient, prevailing even in our own time. To this day, no
adequate musical notation exists in Arab countries, although

music has flourished in Arabia, in Egypt, and among the Moham-
medan nations in general, and although this music is based on a
highly ingenious and complex theory. The lack of written
ancient Hebrew music does not prove, then, that such music
never existed, for in Oriental practice oral transmission from
teacher to pupil, from the older to the younger generation, has
been the rule.

The rediscovery of old Hebrew music was made in an indirect way, through the analysis of Hebrew elements of the so-
called Gregorian chant. But how can it be proved that Gregorian
chant contains Hebrew elements, if Hebrew music itself has
utterly vanished?

It was at this point that the research of Abraham Idelsohn
began. During several decades of residence and study in Palestine and other Oriental countries, Idelsohn made a minute and
penetrating study of the music of the Jews now living in Palestine, Syria, Arabia, Egypt, Tunis, Morocco, and other countries
of the Middle East and North Africa. He believed that in such
intensely orthodox Oriental regions the way of life stems from
ancient traditions, and that the folk music and religious music
of these peoples is similar in essence to that of a millennium ago.
Using the most advanced methods of comparative musicology,
with the aid of a phonograph to insure the authenticity of chants
preserved among the people, he collected thousands of Oriental
melodies and published them in ten volumes. He then made a
comparative study of this material and Gregorian chant. The
result was the discovery of a manifest resemblance between
Gregorian chant and the chants of the Jews in remote districts
of Arab countries in Asia and Africa. One can hardly suppose
that these Oriental Jews borrowed their melodies from Gregorian
chant, whose very existence was probably unknown to most of
them. Historical probabilities point to the opposite theory: that
the Christian church appropriated the ancient Jewish chants.
They have thus come down to us in two versions — as sung by
the Oriental Jews according to oral tradition, and as fixed in

neumatic notation in the medieval manuscripts of Gregorian chant.

The religious service of the Roman Catholic church has its roots partly in Jewish, partly in Greek and Roman cultures. The so-called psalmody — the peculiar style of reciting the psalms — is a relic of the Jewish service. The oldest form of Christian psalmody, the psalmodic solo, was taken over from the Jewish synagogal service. Psalm 135 gives us a particularly fine example of the Jewish style of psalmody. Every verse of this long psalm ends with the words, "for His mercy endureth forever." This repetition of the congregation's response to the solo recitation of the precentor — the so-called responsorial style practiced in the Catholic church and other churches to the present day — finds its origin in the Jewish temple service. The exclamations "Amen" and "Hallelujah" are directly taken over from the Jewish liturgy.

The antiphonal style of singing also goes back to Jewish traditions. The antiphonal style is a choral psalmody, two choirs participating alternately in the recitation or singing of the psalm; it is distinct from the responsorial style, which consists of a solo recitation answered by the congregation. Both the antiphonal and the responsorial styles have been adopted by composers of liturgical music for the Catholic church. Musically speaking, Jewish antiphony has been more fertile than the responsorial style because in antiphony it is not the congregation of laymen, but trained singers, who sing. To professional musicians, the great composers could entrust more difficult and complex parts. This elaborate antiphonal style led to the famous Venetian technique of double chorus, developed in the sixteenth century by Adrian Willaert and perfected by Andrea and Giovanni Gabrieli, the famous masters whose polychoral works became models for European musicians in the seventeenth century. In Rome the decorative polychoral style was carried to extreme complexity and became the musical counterpart of the pomp-loving, extravagant baroque spirit in architecture, plastic art, and painting. It attained its climax in the enormously complex

Festival Mass in 52 parts, with cembalo accompaniment, written by the Roman master Orazio Benevoli in 1628 for the consecration of the Salzburg Cathedral.

For the most grandiose manifestations of the antiphonal style we must turn to Bach's motets for double chorus (eight voices). Bach's Psalm 149, *Singet dem Herrn ein neues Lied*, has no equal in vigor of phrase, logic of construction, wealth of ideas, art of dialogue, and polyphonic cohesion. Hardly less admirable is the eight-part motet *Fürchte dich nicht*, from Isaiah, a marvel of animated polyphony, noble structure, and expressive declamation. The first chorus of the *St. Matthew Passion* also demonstrates the unsurpassable mastery of Bach's antiphonal style, this time with the accent on dramatic power: Jesus carrying the cross, and the people of Jerusalem lamenting His fate, interrupted by agitated questions.

The most important parts of the Christian liturgy are the psalms and the *cantica*, or canticles, taken from the Old and the New Testaments — lyric pieces of great beauty in poetic form. In the oldest extant liturgical songbook, the so-called Codex Alexandrinus of the fifth century of our era, we find psalms and canticles from the Old Testament. Here also is a legacy of Judaism to its offspring, the Christian church, a legacy which in the course of time has acquired the greatest historical significance.

Besides psalmody and the *alleluia*, the forms called *graduale* and *tractus* were transmitted directly from the Jewish service to the Gregorian chant. The *graduale* is a song performed by the cantor standing on the elevated step (*gradus*) of the place reserved for him; the *graduale* is also a psalm or part of a psalm. The *alleluia* is closely related to the *graduale* psalm; it became a jubilant piece of vocal virtuosity for the singer, expressing the delight of the Oriental Jewish singer in an elaborate florid style.

On days of mourning and penitence the brilliant *alleluia* was replaced in the liturgy by the more austere *tractus*. The name means "sung in one trait," that is, in one movement by the soloist, without interruption by the traditional responsorial or antiphonal phrases. Another interpretation of the word *tractus* connects it with the "protracted" character of the lamentation. Upon close examination, *tractus* melodies have been found to contain relics of ancient Hebrew music. They can be traced to the Byzantine *hyrmos* (which is the Greek equivalent of *tractus*) and thence back to the Jewish temple service. Hugo Riemann has convincingly explained the highly interesting form of the *tractus* as a chain of variations, occasionally with instrumental interludes. Such a *tractus* is, for instance, *Cantemus Domino* from Exodus, the canticle of Moses after the crossing of the Red Sea. Indeed, the resemblance of this *tractus* to Jewish cantillation, even that of recent times, is quite striking.

We should also remember that the Latin text of the Mass represents in several instances a Latin translation of Hebrew prayers still in use in the Jewish synagogue. To this Hebrew base the originators of the Mass text added new prayers derived from the Christian religious creed, with references to Jesus Christ as the Son of God and the Redeemer of sin by His death. Even the *Agnus Dei* is based on the Jewish idea of the scapegoat, sent into the desert on the day of atonement (Yom Kippur) to carry away the sins of the people accumulated during the past year. By recent evidence we are justified in claiming an Oriental origin for all music of a recitative character transmitted to modern times through the Jewish psalmody and the Gregorian chant.

In Gregorian chant this declamatory, recitative manner is called accentus, in contradistinction to concentus, which is applied to a formally self-contained, rhythmically well-defined, but simple melodic substance with little ornamentation. The concentus was derived not from Hebrew models but from Greek hymns, representing a songful melodic line quite different from the recitation of the metrically complicated choral sections of Greek tragedy. In early Christian music, the texts of the hymns were rarely taken from the Bible, but were specially written religious poems. The Apostle Paul mentions as a distinct species of Christian music the psalms, hymns, and what he calls *odai pneumatikai*, a term not yet clearly understood.

For the ordinary recitation of the psalms there were established in Gregorian chant nine so-called psalm tones, brief formulas of recitation consisting of an intonation, a recitation on the dominant, a middle cadence, and a final cadence. All the verses of a psalm are chanted according to the same psalm-tone formula. Eight of these melodies correspond to the eight church modes, while the ninth psalm tone, used in special cases — the *tonus peregrinus* (foreign tone) — is a compound of two other tones. Two other kinds of psalmody, responsorial and antiphonal, have already been discussed in this chapter. Attention may be called here to Idelsohn's discovery that the Babylonian and Yemenite Jews are still using traditional psalm-tone melodies, which are probably traceable to the pre-Christian period. This makes it quite evident that the Gregorian psalm tones are direct descendants of the ancient Hebrew psalmodic formulas.

In 1922 a significant discovery was made in the town of Oxyrhynchus in Egypt: a papyrus was found, containing on one side a business transaction in grain and on the other side a Greek hymn in Greek musical notation, dating from the latter part of the third century of the Christian era. In its poetry, as well as in its music, this hymn constitutes one of the earliest specimens of Christian church music. Compositions like it show that a connection existed between the ancient Greek religious songs and the early Christian hymns. The Egyptian Christians seem to have cultivated these hymns very successfully. For western Europe they became of especial importance with the creation of the so-called Ambrosian hymns, introduced into the western church in the fourth century by St. Ambrose, Bishop of Milan. A number of these Ambrosian hymns are now in use in the Catholic church — sublime melodies such as *Aeterne rerum conditor* and *Aeterne Christi munera*. The novel feature of these hymns, as well as of the somewhat older Syrian hymns of St. Ephraem, consists in their metrical treatment. The ancient prosodic principle of long syllable and short syllable is here replaced by the principle of accented and unaccented syllables, which governed the prosody of medieval Latin poetry and still governs that of modern European languages.

An epoch-making step in the evolution of church music was the practice of recitation not by one voice only but by several voices singing together, in the so-called faux-bourdon style. This term denotes a series of homophonic chord progressions, mainly in what is described in modern harmony as chords of the sixth or inverted triads — hence the name "false bass." The celebrated *Miserere* by Allegri, for centuries sung at the Papal Chapel at St. Peter's, illustrates a masterly application of the faux-bourdon in the antiphonal style.

The development of Flemish polyphony, which began about 1500, added the motet to the musical resources of the psalm. Great Flemish masters elevated the motet style to a superb art. Josquin de Près, perhaps the earliest to explore the motet technique in psalm-writing, and his great contemporaries in several countries — Palestrina, the Venetians Adrian Willaert and the two Gabrielis, the English master, Byrd, the German musicians Senfl, Stoltzer, Gallus; and the Dutchman Sweelinck — all of them enriched the psalm-motet literature with admirable works. In 1565, or thereabouts, Orlando di Lasso composed his series of seven psalms, *Psalmi Davidis poenitentiales*, unsurpassed masterpieces of this type. Psalm composition acquired a new aspect in the Calvinist Reformed church, when simplicity and melodious attractiveness were stressed more than the abstract contrapuntal art. The French psalter, in the poetic version of Clément Marot and Théodore de Bèze, and in the unassuming settings of Léon Bourgeois and Claude Goudimel, strikes a new note, akin to the *Souterliedekens*, the "little psalm songs" of the great musician from Antwerp known as "Clemens non Papa."

Among Jewish musicians who were pioneers in psalm-writing, the name of Salomone Rossi (1587–1628) stands high. On the printed title pages of his works, he proudly affixed to his name the word "Ebreo" (a Hebrew). He wrote psalms and madrigals in the then current style. Monteverdi himself did not disdain to be associated with Salomone Rossi at the Mantua festivities in 1608, when Guarini's comedy *Idropica* was performed, with a prologue and intermezzi composed by Monteverdi, his brother Giulio Cesare, Salomone Rossi, and others. However, Rossi's music had little Jewish substance. True, he published his psalms in two editions, one with the Italian text, the other in Hebrew; but even the edition with the Hebrew words sounds more Italian than Jewish.

A contemporary of Rossi, the Italian composer Orazio Vecchi, utilized in his interesting madrigal comedy *L'Amfiparnaso* the peculiar jargon of the Italian Jews for a brilliantly grotesque scene, describing the Jewish pawnbrokers refusing to do business on the Sabbath day. This is the earliest known specimen of Jewish musical caricature.

After Rossi we have to wait nearly two hundred years before we again meet Jewish composers of real stature. Meantime a famous Venetian composer, a good Catholic, had written music for a number of the Psalms of David, and in order to acquire the proper accent and expression had gone to the Jewish synagogues and studied the Jewish chant of the Hebrew psalms. This Venetian was Benedetto Marcello. His collection *Estro poetico-armonico: Parafrasi sopra i primi 50 Psalmi, Poesia di Girolamo Giustiniani* (Venice, 1724–1726) is one of the most important musical anthologies of the time. We cannot call Marcello's paraphrases Jewish compositions; yet their recitative and their melody are noticeably influenced by the inflections of the Jewish chant.

To appraise Jewish influence on music, we must not neglect to mention Lorenzo da Ponte, the Venetian Jew, without whom Mozart's *Figaro* and *Don Giovanni* might never have come into existence. Though he became an *abbé* of the Catholic church, this dignity did not prevent him from leading an adventurous life, in some ways resembling that of his friend Casanova. The culmination of his fantastic career was reached when the Emperor Joseph II appointed him court poet for the Vienna Opera and Court Theater. It was while he held this position that he wrote for Mozart the incomparable libretti of *Figaro, Don Giovanni*, and *Così fan tutte*. In later years, da Ponte tried his fortune in many places: Trieste, Holland, London, and finally America. He was appointed professor of Italian literature at Columbia College in New York and wrote an interesting book of memoirs. In 1838 he died in New York, at nearly ninety years of age.

Following the French Revolution, the emancipation of the Jews in several countries gradually gave them access to the arts and sciences. And in 1825 or thereabouts a number of eminent Jewish musicians made their appearance in Europe. The first that we may mention was Ignaz Moscheles. In Vienna, Moscheles won the favor of Beethoven, and in 1814 he was privileged to prepare the piano score of Beethoven's *Fidelio*. Some of Beethoven's last and most touching letters of 1827 were addressed to Moscheles, who at the time was in London helping to negotiate financial assistance magnanimously tendered to the dying master by the London Philharmonic Society. Moscheles was the first Jewish musician to win European fame as both pianist and composer. He was highly esteemed and honored in Vienna, Paris, and London; he taught at the Leipzig Conservatory, where he was summoned by Mendelssohn. The piano studies by Moscheles are still very much in use; his edition of Beethoven's sonatas was highly regarded until it was superseded by modern editions.

The careers of two Jewish musicians, Giacomo Meyerbeer and Felix Mendelssohn, both of whom spent their youth in Berlin, were phenomenal. Meyerbeer leaped into fame when, in 1831, his French opera *Robert le Diable* conquered the fickle Paris public. Meyerbeer's glory as an opera composer was not dimmed until the final triumph of Wagner's music drama. In Paris, Meyerbeer long enjoyed an exceptionally distinguished social position. Then King Frederick William of Prussia made this Jewish composer chief conductor and *General-Musikdirektor* of the Berlin Royal Opera House, the highest official distinction a musician could reach at that time. For more than twenty years he retained this position, until his death in 1864. His funeral in Berlin was officially celebrated in the grandest style, with honors usually accorded only to princes—and this in spite of the fact that throughout his life he had remained faithful to the Jewish community and that he was buried in the old Jewish cemetery of Berlin.

Felix Mendelssohn's life reads like a fairy tale. Surely no composer ever had a more brilliant career than this grandson of the celebrated Jewish reformer Moses Mendelssohn, this son of the wealthy banker Abraham Mendelssohn. He grew up in a period that saw the fabulous rise of wealthy Jewish society in Berlin, with brilliant Jewish hostesses presiding over literary and artistic salons frequented by cultured Germans. Though many of these leading Jewish families, the Mendelssohns among them, were converted to Protestantism or Catholicism, their Jewish blood, their racial intellectualism, could hardly be altered by baptism. In Vienna as well as Berlin, the influence of Jewish ideas and sentiments, philosophy of life, and artistic taste was profound, all the more so because this influence was masked by a Christian exterior. To this culture Felix Mendelssohn contributed generously. As a boy of twelve he visited Goethe in Weimar, introduced by his teacher Zelter, Goethe's close friend and musical adviser. Goethe was delighted with the boy's prodigious talent and remained in frequent contact with him. As a young man, Mendelssohn was recognized as one of the leading European musicians in Germany, France, Italy, and particularly in England, where he became a prime favorite as composer, conductor, and pianist. The Gewandhaus concerts in Leipzig owe their great renown to Mendelssohn, and the Leipzig Conservatory, founded by him, has for a century maintained a foremost place in musical education.

There can be no doubt that Mendelssohn left a deep imprint on German music and on European music in general. It seems paradoxical that this Jewish musician should have also been one of the leading exponents of typical German romanticism. Yet quite a number of analogous cases, not only in music but also in other arts and sciences, can be cited to show the peculiar flexibility of the Jewish mind, its power of assimilation with the cultural environment. Many distinguished Jews have become Germans in the best sense of the term; many have also become Frenchmen, Englishmen, Dutchmen, and Americans. Jewish conductors, pianists, violinists, and singers have won fame as the leading interpreters of the greatest German music and, at their best, have surpassed their German colleagues.

The most respected German masters of the time — Spohr, Marschner, Loewe, Schneider, Nicolai, and Schumann — all hailed Mendelssohn as their companion, even their leader. The greatest of them all, Robert Schumann, had a sincere admiration and affectionate love for Mendelssohn, and the alliance of Mendelssohn and Schumann created that romantic tradition which dominated German music in the nineteenth century. The strongholds of this tradition were the Leipzig Conservatory and the Royal High School for Music in Berlin. The author of the present book was nurtured in this tradition during his student years, before 1900, at the Berlin High School. From its director, the great violinist Joseph Joachim, he received the most impressive and enduring artistic lesson of his life. Joachim, a Hungarian Jew, had as a boy been in close personal contact with both Mendelssohn and Schumann and had become their spiritual heir, transmitting to posterity their ideals. No pure "Aryan" musician in all Germany even approached the Jew Joachim in reverence for and penetrating understanding of the imperishable heritage of Bach, Haydn, Mozart, Beethoven, Schubert, Schumann, Mendelssohn, and Brahms. Bach's violin music was disclosed in its full meaning for the first time by Joachim; his interpretation of Bach's gigantic *Chaconne* set a standard for other violinists to follow. The grace and warmth of his playing of Mozart was enchanting. And his matchless performances of Beethoven's violin concerto and the "Kreutzer" sonata can never be forgotten by those who heard them. Richard Wagner himself had to acknowledge Joachim's artistic greatness.

As we consider the extraordinary success, the international influence, and the artistic significance of Jews like Moscheles, Meyerbeer, Mendelssohn, and Joachim (to whom might be added Ferdinand Hiller of Cologne as a lesser light) we begin to understand why some German musicians grew fearful lest German music should slip entirely into Jewish hands, and why anti-Semitic propaganda seemed to them opportune. Richard Wagner embraced anti-Semitism only after the revolution of 1848, when he lost his influential and profitable position as chief conductor of the Dresden Opera and went into exile in Switzerland, without regular income, dependent upon the financial help of Liszt, the Wesendonks, and other friends. In view of the difficult position Wagner was in, the anti-Semitic pamphlet he wrote in 1850 appears to be a gesture of self-defense, though one neither noble nor chivalrous; and it may be assumed that in his later years Wagner himself did not take that anti-Semitic outburst too seriously, since he was by then not averse to accepting the help of Jewish friends and artists — among them the great pianist Carl Tausig, to whom he entrusted the piano arrangement of his most thoroughly German opera, *Die Meistersinger von Nürnberg*, and the Jewish conductor Hermann Levy, whom he selected as conductor for the *première* of his most Christian work, *Parsifal*. We are confronted here with one of those enigmatic contradictions that abound in the life of Wagner.

In Germany and Austria, Jewish musical activities were more important and numerous than in other countries. But in France as well, Jewish musicians attained high rank in the nineteenth and twentieth centuries. The internationalist Meyerbeer cleared the way at the Paris Opera. Close to him stands Jacques Fromental Halévy. Though Halévy's music is basically French, it includes more elements specifically "Jewish" than are found in the works of either Meyerbeer or Mendelssohn. In his most famous opera, *La Juive*, the action takes place in a medieval Jewish environment, and Halévy makes use of Hebrew ritual motives in the scene of the Passover. He was the first Jewish musician to gain eminence in France, to be awarded the Prix de Rome, and to be admitted to the Académie française.

As Halévy was the father-in-law of Georges Bizet, the famous composer of *Carmen*, it was for a time erroneously believed that Bizet also was Jewish. Saint-Saëns, too, is often said to have been of Jewish descent, probably owing to the world-wide success of his biblical opera *Samson et Dalila*. In his case, again, the assertion is untrue.

No doubt exists about the Jewish origin of Jacques Offenbach, the son of a synagogue cantor at Cologne. As a young man he settled in Paris, studied violoncello at the Conservatoire, and then entered upon a career that carried him to the pinnacle of fame. His graceful, melodious operettas, spiced with amusing satire in an Aristophanic vein, reflect like a mirror the life and the pleasures of the great Babel that was Paris during the closing years of the Second Empire. Offenbach's vivacious parodies on classical opera, *La Belle Hélène* and *Orphée aux enfers*, brought to all Europe and to America a particle of this Parisian gayety. But their composer chose to close his career on a somber note with his last work, *Les Contes d'Hoffmann*. Its theme is a fantastic modernized dance of death, an apotheosis of human frustration and the futility of love.

Offenbach's success aroused the competitive spirit of the Viennese composers of light music. Johann Strauss, Franz von Suppé, and Karl Millöcker opposed to the Parisian operettas of the Jew Offenbach a Viennese product, different from Offenbach's but just as gay and entertaining in its own fashion. The masterpieces of this new Viennese genre are *Die Fledermaus* and *Der Zigeunerbaron*, by Johann Strauss. In the generation following Strauss, the Viennese operetta was largely taken over by the Jewish heirs of Offenbach. Leo Fall and Oskar Straus dominated the field, with Franz Lehár as their Christian brother-in-arms, and the Jew Emerich Kálmán as their Hungarian cousin.

It has often been observed that in the music of Mendelssohn and Meyerbeer there are few Jewish elements, and that really Jewish-sounding music by Jewish composers did not make its mark until the twentieth century. It has also been said that non-Jewish composers, such as Max Bruch, Mussorgsky, Rimsky-Korsakov, Busoni, Ravel, and others, have written pieces that appear much more Jewish in character than does most music of the racial Jews. Both observations call for comment.

When Mendelssohn and Meyerbeer made their appearance as the earliest Jewish composers intent on attaining a respectable position in society, they entered a highly competitive field. Had they chosen specifically "Jewish" music as a medium, they would not have found any market for their product outside the limited Jewish communities. They would have had to use traditional melodies of the synagogal service, for in nineteenth-century Germany, Jewish folk music, songs, and dances were completely unknown. Music based on the temple melodies and the rich national folk tunes of the Polish Jews would not have excited any interest in the German public; they would have been at best a passing curiosity. Meyerbeer and Mendelssohn had no choice: they had to accommodate themselves to the prevalent German classical ideal or to the internationally established models of Italian and French opera. They had to demonstrate that Jews could master the complicated technique of European symphonic and operatic music. For the first time, they proved that Jews could successfully compete in music with their Christian contemporaries, and even win a place near the most exalted masters of the art.

Their triumph paved the way for the Jewish musicians of

later generations. Beginning about the year 1850, we observe the advance of a valiant little army of highly talented Jewish composers and performers, not only in Germany and Austria but in all of Europe: Anton Rubinstein, Karl Goldmark, Ferdinand Hiller, Joseph Joachim, Moritz Moszkowski, Gustav Mahler, Charles-Henri Alkan, Paul Dukas, Arnold Schönberg, Ernst Toch, Erich Korngold, Kurt Weill, Leo Blech, Mario Castelnuovo-Tedesco, Vittorio Rieti, Darius Milhaud, and many others; while in America we find Ernest Bloch, Lazare Saminsky, George Gershwin, Louis Gruenberg, Frederick Jacobi, Aaron Copland, David Diamond, William Schuman, and Leonard Bernstein.

Most of these composers do not write racially Jewish music, but are content with assimilating whatever style they have chosen as their idiom. They try to be cosmopolitan musicians, either in the older romantic, or in the impressionist, neoclassic, polytonal, or atonal style. Some, like Schönberg, have evolved techniques of their own. Others show their Jewish affiliation at least in the themes they choose for treatment. Mendelssohn wrote *Elijah*; Rubinstein wrote *The Maccabaeans, Sulamith, The Tower of Babel*. In such works, one occasionally finds an episode with an Oriental Jewish melodic turn, in the midst of international music. But it took World War I, it took the Balfour Declaration on Palestine as a national home for the Jews, and finally the formation of the independent state of Israel, to arouse the racial consciousness latent in these cosmopolitan Jewish composers and to inspire in them an earnest effort to give expression to their Jewish soul not only by chance and instinct but by deliberation and intention.

In this sense the Geneva-born Swiss Jew, Ernest Bloch, is the first truly Jewish composer of the twentieth century. His music reverberates with dark Jewish pathos, the picturesque, forceful, passionate speech of the Old Testament prophets; it is rich in roving, asymmetrical, recitative-like arioso melody, the exotic color suggestive of the Near East. His *Trois poèmes juifs* for orchestra, his psalms for solo voices and orchestra, his *Schelomo* for cello and orchestra, his *Israel Symphony*, and his Jewish pieces for violin are remarkable for their deep penetration of the Jewish racial consciousness.

In contrast to the racial music of Ernest Bloch, the compositions of another celebrated Jewish composer, Arnold Schönberg, represent the cosmopolitan side of the Jewish mind. Bloch's music is permeated with the passionate wrath, the exaltation of the Old Testament prophets and the psalms. Schönberg's music reflects the systematic, persevering, profoundly inquisitive Talmudic spirit, with its scientific rationalism and its logical acumen. The contrast between these two states of mind may be put succinctly in the formula "sentiment versus intellect," even though both occasionally trespass into the opposite camp.

What has prompted so many non-Jewish composers to write music of a pronounced Jewish type? The answer lies in the exotic attractiveness of Jewish melodies to outsiders. Chopin wrote a mazurka (Opus 17, No. 4) that in Poland is nicknamed "The Little Jew." Its wailing melody, its lamenting sighs, its mixture of pathetic and grotesque elements, its nostalgia and melancholy, and its colorful chromatic harmony conjure up a realistic vision of a Jewish dance scene, such as Chopin may have watched in any Polish town. Mussorgsky, in his *Pictures at an Exhibition*, includes a piece representing an animated dialogue between a rich and a poor Jew, which brings out the contrast between pompous self-content and despairing supplication — a caricature, to be sure, yet fascinating. Of quite a different type is the noble Hebrew lamentation in Mussorgsky's cantata *Josua Navine*. Rimsky-Korsakov's beautiful and genuine-sounding "Hebrew Love Song" and Prokofiev's tuneful *Overture on Hebrew Themes* for chamber orchestra should also be mentioned. Busoni, in his opera *Die Brautwahl*, portrays with evident affection a demoniac old Jew, the mysterious sorcerer from one of Hoffmann's fantastic tales. In his orchestral suite from *Die Brautwahl*, Busoni has the "Hebrew Piece," a somber symphonic fantasy on synagogue melodies, which is followed by an episode depicting the sorcerer — an exciting piece of music, full of soft murmurings and savage outcries. In his opera *Salome*, Richard Strauss introduces a realistic quintet of Jews, passionately debating the advent of the Messiah.

When we come to Max Bruch's version for violoncello and orchestra of the solemn and venerable chant *Kol Nidrei*, we find ourselves in a more temperate zone. The Germanic, civilized, euphonious, but uncharacteristic accompaniment supplied by Bruch (he was not Jewish) is not compatible with the Oriental agitation of the theme. Ravel's version of the *Kadish*, the Hebrew prayer for the departed, is much more authentic. Fully congenial to the noble religious tone of the old melody, Ravel's harmonization gives the proper spiritual background of the Jewish prayer, enhancing its Oriental flavor.

A glance at the liturgic music of the synagogue seems appropriate at this point. Here, if anywhere, one might expect to find a source of true Jewish music. Yet there exists no written or printed literature earlier than the nineteenth century, and owing to the lack of documentation it seems impossible to narrate the history of Jewish religious music with any degree of accuracy. We do not know what kind of music the Jews of the fifteenth, sixteenth, and seventeenth centuries used in Spain, Italy, Germany, Poland, and Holland. We do not even know exactly when and where choral singing was introduced into the service.

The traditional religious music includes the cantillation, that is, recitation of the five books of Moses according to a system of vocal formulas marked by signs similar to the medieval neumes. It is believed that these hooks, curls, and curved lines were invented during the early part of the Exile, in order to preserve the traditional manner of reciting the Bible. This is the only type of notation that has ever been used in Jewish music. The music for the psalms and for the vast collection of Hebrew prayers was never written down, but for thousands of years was transmitted by oral tradition. It was not before the nineteenth century that attempts were made to collect the traditional music of the synagogue and to preserve it in written notes. This mass of melodies contains remnants dating as far back as the Babylonian Captivity, and reaching to the Middle Ages and to the modern era. Mixed with it are fragments of Italian, German, Slavic, and Moorish melodies. A critical analysis of this material to determine its age and origin has hardly begun.

Perhaps the finest extant collection of Jewish synagogue music in manuscript is now preserved in the library of the Hebrew Union College in Cincinnati. This collection, comprising several thousand pieces assembled from Jewish communities in many countries, represents the lifelong labors of the eminent Jewish musical scholar Eduard Birnbaum, former cantor of the synagogue in Königsberg. The oldest piece in the Birnbaum collection is the Eulogy on the Death of Moses, dating back to the thirteenth century.

Another comprehensive collection of Jewish music was gathered by Arno Nadel of Berlin, eminent poet, musician, painter, and philosopher, who perished in a Nazi concentration camp. ·It must be regarded as irretrievably lost, in all probability destroyed by the Nazis. Nadel's last and dearest project was to compile a Jewish Chorale — similar in scope to the Gregorian Chorale — a codex of the oldest and finest liturgical melodies, to serve as source material for future composers. In the eastern congregations of Poland, Lithuania, and Russia, the precentors (*chasonim*) felt freer than elsewhere as regards their music; they liked to embellish the traditional chants with all sorts of improvisations, often approaching the popular Yiddish songs and dance tunes in character. The Chasidic sect especially, once thriving in Poland, held that the religious service should be joyful and jubilant, and favored a hybrid art of mixed melodies, both Hebrew and Yiddish (the peculiar German-Hebrew dialect of the eastern Jews). Until recent times only the solo singing of the cantor and the responses of the congregation were admitted in the orthodox Jewish services. Sometimes a chorus of boys and young men was introduced into the synagogue; some congregations acquired fame for their excellent singing, as did, for instance, the synagogal chorus in Vilna. A number of eminent opera singers of the nineteenth century started their careers as cantors or choral singers in the Polish and Lithuanian synagogues.

Not until the nineteenth century was some semblance of organization brought into German synagogue music. The beginning was made at Vienna, where the eminent singer and teacher Salomon Sulzer (1804–1890) was cantor of the new synagogue. His collection of liturgical chants, *Schir Zion* (Hebrew Hymns), the first of its kind, was widely used all over Germany and Austria as well as in Italy and America. Schubert contributed to it a fine setting of Psalm 92 for baritone solo and vocal quartet. A generation later, Louis Lewandowski (1823–1894) published an arrangement of the entire Jewish service music for the Jewish community of Berlin. This extensive collection for solo, chorus, and organ dominated for half a century the services in the synagogues of central Europe, and it was also adopted in England and America. Its fine vocal writing contributed to its popularity.

Lewandowski's smooth Mendelssohnian harmony and symmetrically balanced melodic patterns seemed too Germanic to Jewish musicians of the twentieth century; they craved music of a more pronounced Jewish character, set with more potent harmonies. Interesting experiments were made in this direction, culminating in Ernest Bloch's magnificent Sacred Service. Heinrich Schalit in Munich, Oskar Guttmann and Arno Nadel in Berlin, Jacob Weinberg, Frederick Jacobi, Lazare Saminsky, and Herbert Fromm in America have contributed remarkable compositions to this neo-Hebrew liturgy.

The youngest branch of musical science, comparative musicology, has contributed greatly to a deeper understanding of the essence of Jewish music and of its relationship to the music of other Oriental nations. The investigation begun by Ellis, Stumpf, Hornbostel, and others has opened new horizons to Western musicians. Earlier generations regarded the art of music as a European prerogative, and treated Oriental music as the product of primitive folklore. This attitude could not be maintained for long, however. It was found, as a result of scientific research, that among Orientals, vocal sound is a primary activity, natural to everyone. Oriental man sings because nature has given him a voice; as he intones musically differentiated sounds, his body begins to swing to the rhythm of the song; bodily motion is followed by mimic action. The desire to enlarge the activity of the body led to the construction of primitive musical instruments. In the Orient singing came first, instrumental music last, and their respective positions never changed; in the Occident, instrumental music acquired through the centuries a dominant position. It was when its development reached its peak, in recent times, that European musicians, satiated with the complex instrumental music that they had created, turned to the predominantly vocal Oriental music for new inspiration. Jewish musicians, whose racial destiny was to serve as mediators between the Orient and the Occident, found themselves once more a people divided, Oriental by ancestral instinct, Occidental by education. The newly recovered spirit of ancient Oriental music was a vitalizing infusion; Jewish artists were the predestined surgeons for this operation. It is too early to predict the outcome, for we are still in the critical period during which mortal collapse or regeneration are equally possible.

The Orient was not introduced to European music solely by the Jews. Influences from the Far East were strongly felt in Russian music. The vast Russian empire gradually extended to absorb Asiatic nations; thus Oriental music became much more of an influence in Russia than in Germany or Italy. The great Russian masters of the nineteenth century were not slow in perceiving and exploiting the opulence of this music. And as Russia had her direct connections with Asia, France in her African empire could draw on African-Arab music, while the Jewish composers of Vienna, a gateway to the Near East, infused Austrian music directly with Oriental color, rhythm, and sentiment. We find Oriental ideas flowing into St. Petersburg and Moscow, Paris and Vienna, and spreading far into the periphery. It may be confidently asserted that no composer in any country who is really interested in modern musical development can escape Oriental influences. Most modern musicians, indeed, absorb them without being conscious of their origin.

Let us briefly inquire into the Oriental influences on European music. Major and minor scales have often been replaced by new ones, either taken over directly from the Orient, or assimilated. Thus, the ancient pentatonic scale is revived in modern music for special effects. New scales have been constructed to impart the Oriental flavor. The Russian master Alexander Scriabin based much of his later music on a new scale of his own. By experiment and speculation, Busoni ascertained that more than a hundred scales of seven notes can be constructed within an octave, and that of these possible scales only a small number had so far been practically employed in music. Finally, the recently revived medieval church modes and ancient Greek and Asiatic tonalities also belong to the category of Oriental influences, as does the experimentation with quarter-tones and third-tones, which are mainly derived from Arabic music. The eminent Czechoslovak composer Alois Hába is the internationally acknowledged champion of this movement. The twelve-tone method of Arnold Schönberg and the atonal system of the Viennese composer Josef Mathias Hauer are extreme consequences of the new Asiatic influences in ultramodern music.

The alliance of European and Oriental music is a historical process of prime importance. The music of the near future must possess cosmopolitan, and universal character, in order to survive. Will the marriage of Oriental and European genius create a healthy and vigorous intercontinental offspring? This question must be left for future generations to answer.

Jewish music has had a glorious rebirth in the young state of Israel. Jewish composers from Germany and other European countries have settled in Palestine and organized a school of national and racial music. Of these composers, Erich Sternberg is one of the strongest. He was the most gifted pupil in composition taught by the author of this book. His symphonic work *The Twelve Tribes of Israel* has enjoyed significant success.

Among other important composers now working in Israel are Marc Lavry, a native of Latvia, Ödön Partos of Hungary, and Robert Starer of Vienna. Some Israeli composers dropped their original German names and adopted Hebrew patronymics: Paul Frankenburger, for example, is now well known as Paul Ben-Haim. Another Palestinian composer, Mahler-Kalkstein, a native of Poland, has changed his name to Menahem Avidom. To these should be added Joseph Tal, whose former name was Grünthal.

A vigorous folk music is at present growing in the young state of Israel, consisting to a large extent of Palestinian folk songs that have come into existence in the last twenty years and, more important, have acquired popularity and maintained their validity. A descendant of the Polish and Russian ghetto song in Yiddish, this new Palestinian folk song, to words in revitalized modern Hebrew, often possesses melodic breadth and power, rhythmic swing, and youthful, healthy joy, in contrast to the prevailing melancholy of its ancestral ghetto songs.

The number of Jewish artists, conductors, and musical scholars active in the United States is proportionately very great. Among them are such illustrious men as the famous conductors Pierre Monteux, Bruno Walter, Georg Szell, and Eugene Ormandy. Serge Koussevitzky spent a quarter of a century as conductor of the Boston Symphony Orchestra. Top-ranking Jewish pianists who make their home in America include Alexander Brailovsky, Vladimir Horowitz, Arthur Rubinstein, and the great Paris pedagogue Isidor Philippe, who continued to teach in New York even when he was past ninety years of age.

The list of celebrated Jewish violinists in America is especially impressive: Mischa Elman, Jascha Heifetz, Yehudi Menuhin, Nathan Milstein, Joseph Szigeti, Efrem Zimbalist. No less eminent are the great Jewish masters of the violoncello: Gregor Piatigorsky, Maurice Eisenberg, Nicolas Graudan. Among Jewish-American singers are Alexander Kipnis, Jan Peerce, and Emanuel List. Many Jewish musical scholars have found a haven in America and have introduced in the great American universities and other institutions the methods of modern musicological research. Among them are Alfred Einstein, Curt Sachs, Joseph Yasser, Eric Werner, Joseph Schillinger, and a number of younger men, whose ability and devotion to the art of music have contributed greatly to American musical scholarship.

3

Supranational Polyphony

The creation of polyphonic art was not the act of a single nation; it was the result of collective European labor. Polyphony, like harmony, owes its origin to human curiosity, to experimentation in sounding different tones simultaneously. In music history books, the beginning of polyphony is usually identified with the emergence of "organum," that is, the singing or playing in two voices moving in parallel fifths or parallel fourths. Its invention is attributed to Hucbald, a monk of the Monastery of St. Amand in Flanders, who flourished about A.D. 900. But modern research in comparative musicology indicates that such progressions of fifths and fourths are of a much more ancient derivation. Folk singers practiced organum thousands of years ago in the most remote regions, and the remnants of this usage are still in evidence among primitive peoples.

There was, however, a material difference between such usages in the Orient and in Europe. Orientals sang in parallel intervals by instinct, without attributing peculiar significance to it, while the Europeans regarded such singing as a conscious art. Further elaboration of singing in parallel intervals led to the inception of polyphony.

The earliest polyphonic methods are described by the terms organum and discant. Organum lies at the foundation of what we now call harmony; discant is the earliest application of what we call counterpoint. While organum employs parallel motion, discant introduces the revolutionary idea of contrary motion. Comparative musicology reveals that primitive peoples made use not only of organum but of discant as well. A rudimentary variety of discant is a device known as heterophony, that is, "other sound." In heterophonic singing, a melody is accompanied by a drone, a constant repetition of the same note in the bass. Thus we have a contrast of a fixed, stable voice, with a freely moving voice in the melody.

The next logical step was the use of two voices moving partly in parallel, partly in contrary, motion: counterpoint. The art of counterpoint assumed a recognizable shape about the year 1200; it constitutes the greatest collective achievement of European music. From that time on, music in Europe departed more and more from its ancient traditions, and set out boldly to navigate uncharted seas, in the course of time discovering new musical continents of extraordinary grandeur and beauty.

Many European nations participated in the creation of the art of polyphony and the technique of contrapuntal writing. In the twelfth and thirteenth centuries, France — the "school of Paris" — was in the lead. Masters like Leoninus and Perotinus, theorists and teachers like Franco of Paris and Franco of Cologne, made the University of Paris the most celebrated school of music in Europe. That cosmopolitan city attracted musicians from all Europe — from England, the Netherlands, Germany, Italy, and Spain. Having absorbed the musical culture of the Paris school, they returned to their native lands. Thus within a few decades polyphony found its way to many nations. The history of polyphony shows us how its distinctive traits were further developed in England, Italy, the Netherlands, and Germany, assuming different forms according to local requirements and conditions.

The early type of polyphony as practiced by Leoninus and Perotinus in Paris became known as "ancient art" — *ars antiqua*. The more ornamental type, developed internationally, was called "new art" — *ars nova*.

The conception of musical structure was formulated by the foremost masters of the *ars antiqua* of the twelfth and thirteenth centuries. To France we owe the introduction of *discantus* and of certain well-defined forms, vocal as well as instrumental, such as the *motetus, conductus, estampie,* and *faux-bourdon.* These forms reflected the new social order created by the gothic mind. Music had outgrown the church, which had fostered it for centuries. During the age of the Crusades, the knightly cult and the rise of lyric and epic secular poetry had produced a type of music at once popular, chivalric, and erotic: the songs of the troubadours, trouvères, and minstrels. In the old French motet a union is effected between the solemn, ascetic church modes and the sprightly dance tunes and love songs of the people; the austere scholastic spirit is merged with a graceful, often frivolous manner. In *discantus*, a melody from the Gregorian chant, set in strict meter, unadorned and grave, is selected as a fundamental theme in the lowest voice, while in the upper two voices appear countermelodies of quite a different character, in different measures and rhythms. The whole was sung to a French text. This complicated combination of antagonistic elements was produced boldly and with a rough hand; it lacked the softer charms of harmonic chord-writing, which was as yet unknown. The sucessful union of totally divergent melodies, each with complete rhythmic freedom, was certainly one of the most singular phenomena in music history.

Midway between the organum and the motet stands the form called *conductus*. Like the organum, the *conductus* is written mostly in parallel motion, note against note. Occasionally, however, contrary motion and a slight diversity of rhythms are applied, suggesting the motet. The *conductus* is a nonliturgical form, based not on Gregorian chant but on a freely invented melody in the tenor.

The epic and lyric literature of the later Middle Ages in France, Italy, Spain, Germany, England, and Scandinavia is full of allusions to instrumental music. Manuscripts of the twelfth, thirteenth, and fourteenth centuries are adorned with miniature pictures illustrating musical scenes, often including instruments. Musical subjects appear also in the murals and other paintings of this period preserved in European museums and cathedrals; from these pictorial representations we learn that instrumental music was part of the everyday life in those times. The instrumental literature of the thirteenth and fourteenth centuries was practically unknown until 1900, and it is only recently that these treasures of old music have been brought to light.

How is this long neglect to be explained? During the Middle Ages the art of music was the monopoly of the church. Vocal music, which served ecclesiastical purposes, was encouraged and sanctioned, while instrumental music, with its frivolous tunes and rhythmic exuberance, bore the stigma of sinful licentiousness. Lacking the sanction of the church, instrumental music was not deemed worthy of being collected, written down, and transmitted to posterity.

A certain change of attitude took place in the fourteenth century. Musicians began to emancipate themselves from the exclusive patronage of the church. Secular music, along with lyric poetry, entered upon its first springtime and produced its first flowering. Even now the songs of the troubadours and the minnesingers retain their fragrant freshness and melodic charm. These amorous lyric songs, in which the noble knight glorified the virtues of his lady, were usually accompanied by some instrument, such as the viol or the harp. Wagner's opera *Tannhäuser* vividly reflects this age of chivalry, with its poetry and song and its contests among singers, though of course *Tannhäuser* is in the musical language of the nineteenth century. Thousands of troubadour songs are preserved in manuscript, but the accompanying instrumental music is lacking; probably the accompaniment was improvised and not written out. Many jongleurs — professional musicians in the service of noble lords

— enjoyed great fame, and their names have come down to us in contemporary poetry and historical tales and chronicles; it seems probable that a skilled player, not content to accompany his master, must occasionally have distinguished himself by playing an instrumental solo. More or less detailed descriptions of these earliest forms of instrumental music — *estampies, estampitas,* or *stantipes* — are found in Latin treatises of the fourteenth century.

At the threshold of the twentieth century important research in early instrumental music was done by the eminent French scholar Pierre Aubry and his German colleague Johannes Wolf. Aubry's little volume, *Estampies et danses royales* (Paris, 1907), justly claims to contain "les plus anciens textes de musique instrumentale au moyen âge." Aubry discovered this music by transcribing the previously unnoticed interpolations in a famous collection of medieval manuscripts kept in the Bibliothèque nationale of Paris, and the discovery refutes the ordinary notion that early instrumental music was primitive in character. It consists chiefly of music for one performer without accompaniment, an ancestor of the Bach suites for solo violin or violoncello. Like Bach's masterpieces, the medieval French *estampies* expressed the "linear gothic spirit," which is the soul of all contrapuntal art. This spirit was already present in the oldest specimens of Gregorian chant (especially the more ornate type); its full revelation, the *estampie,* appeared, probably in France, about 1300 and thence passed to Italy and England, and also to Spain. The *estampie* is an ornate Gregorian melody transferred from voice to instrument, from the ecclesiastical to the secular realm, from the solemn religious procession to the gay dance. The gothic spirit is manifested in the delicacy, the charm and expressiveness produced by the changing inflections of the melodic line; the alternation of ascending and descending phrases introduces the all-important elements of equilibrium, effective preparation, plastic presentation of climax, and contrast between the plain melody and its embellished variation. All these attributes of linear art have since become integral parts of music, and it is to the French masters of *ars antiqua* of the twelfth and thirteenth centuries that we are indebted for the first clear and detailed presentation of linear writing.

The early *estampie* is a suite of little dance tunes, anticipating the graceful eighteenth-century minuet in its symmetrical eight-bar structure, with regular repetitions of a pleasing melody. In its clear melodic line and latent harmony, the *estampie* represents an oddly attractive mixture of church modes and modern major and minor tonality, the former showing the influence of the scholastic theory of church music, the latter reflecting the practice of secular folk song and dance.

The Italian *estampitas* in a manuscript in the British Museum, described and deciphered by Johannes Wolf in 1921, constitute the highest and most skillful examples of this form. They possess the structural variety, flexibility, and rhythmic and melodic interest of the French *estampies* discovered by Aubry; in addition they contain elements of virtuosity and remarkable freedom in the use of chromatics and modulation, as well as capricious changes of metrical periods. These fourteenth-century pieces often bear fanciful titles — *Cominciamento di gioia* (Beginning of Joy), *Tre fontane* (Three Fountains), *Principio di virtu* (The Principle of Virtue), and so on. These names have hardly anything to do with the character of the music; they seem to be merely pretty, eye-catching labels. From then until the time of Couperin and Rameau in the eighteenth century, composers of instrumental music loved to invent ingenious titles. In the nineteenth century Schumann and other romantics revived the old practice. One of the most beautiful and striking *estampitas* is called *Lamento di Tristano*, showing that as long as six centuries ago the romantic name "Tristan" was connected with music.

It has recently been pointed out that the Arabian musical form called *bashrav* is very like the *estampie*, that both the Arabian and the French pieces may be late descendants of lost ancient Graeco-Roman models, and that Byzantine music may represent the liaison between antiquity, Arabian practice, and French usage. Such a hypothesis may appear untenable, but it gives direction to modern musicological research and suggests some fascinating correlations.

In Gregorian chant and the instrumental *estampies*, this linear virtuosity is confined to one voice or one instrumental line only. The French masters went further. They combined the newly invented linear art with contrapuntal technique, so as to brighten melodically each of the several voices of a three-part composition. The result was not wholly adequate, however: although each line was beautifully constructed, the feeling of musicians for the harmonic effect of all three lines together had not yet sufficiently developed. This problem was left to a later age; its solution was a Flemish achievement. But in spite of harmonic imperfections, the French development of linear art in solo and ensemble, of planned architectural construction, was a precious legacy to all later music. As in the case of Greek and Hebrew music, we observe that the ultimate product of a fertile new idea may prove to be something quite different from its original form. The music of the age of *ars antiqua* was lost for six or seven centuries; yet its ideas lived on in the works of musicians who had never even heard of *ars antiqua*. In time, the old French linear and structural ideas became the basic precepts of musical art.

Faux-bourdon, or *falso-bordone*, has already been mentioned. This device, dating back to about 1200, enjoys the distinction of being the oldest form of polyphonic music still performed today. No other species of chordal music can boast an uninterrupted life of seven hundred years. Literally, faux-bourdon means "false bass," or in today's terminology, an inverted bass: a succession of triads in inversion — chords of the sixth, consisting of the intervals of prime, third, and sixth sounding together. This chain of inverted triads is in structure a variation and continuation of the more primitive organum, which consists of fourths, fifths, and octaves in parallel motion, progressing simultaneously in all voices. Faux-bourdon is a simultaneous progression in parallel motion of several parts — akin to organum in principle, but different in intervallic structure.

This variation of the old organum indicates a variation also in the philosophy of sounds and intervals. The original ecclesiastical organum recognized only the intervals of the fourth, fifth, and octave as legitimate consonant sounds, avoiding the third and sixth as being too vulgar for church music. But in the meantime the music of the common people, their dance and march tunes, had found its way into the church and could no longer be forbidden by restrictive rules. In England the so-called "gymel" was now officially accepted by the church. The word "gymel" is a corrupt form of the Latin *cantus gemellus* (twin song); it denotes a song in parallel thirds. From parallel thirds it was but a short step to parallel sixths, since the sixth is the inversion of the third. Faux-bourdon is but another aspect of gymel; both faux-bourdon and gymel are akin to organum in their adherence to parallel motion.

Another structural principle established for the first time in the thirteenth century was repetition (or imitation) in the form of a canon. Ideas of imitation were, of course, latent in the musical mind in antiquity and applied by instinct at the earliest stages of human civilization, but imitation became an artistic factor only when it was applied with a full understanding of its purpose and effect. In music, as in architecture, repetition is a means of obtaining continuity, coherence, order, and symmetry. It is a factor of primary importance and, of all structural principles, perhaps the simplest for the mind to comprehend. Repetition may be exact or approximate; it may be applied to one voice or to several; it may enter either after or before the close of the original musical phrase.

In canon we see an advanced form of repetition. The same tune is repeated by two or several voices. The different voices participating in the canon do not, however, sing the same tune simultaneously, nor does one of them wait until its predecessor has finished the tune. Instead, the repetition of the tune is started by the second voice somewhere in between. Expressing the same thing in musical terms, one might say that a canon is an organum or faux-bourdon pushed a little sideways, with melodic lines sounding not simultaneously but successively. This type of repetition was an entirely new idea in the thirteenth century, and so powerful was its impact that for at least three centuries canon was one of the chief forms of polyphonic music. For its earliest cultivation as an art form, we are indebted mainly to England. The earliest classical masterpiece of canonic art known to us is the charming English six-part canon, *Sumer is icumen in.*

The practice of canonic imitation infused new life into polyphony. The older forms — organum, conductus, faux-bourdon — were much more limited in variety of application, being based on simultaneous parallel motion in all parts. But canon, because of the principle of successive entry in the voices, led to novel and ingenious devices. For two centuries the originality of composers was taxed to the utmost in discovering further potentialities of canonic technique.

We have no certain knowledge of the way the great Flemish masters of canonic art developed their astounding skills; their solutions of immensely complicated problems appear to us to be feats of magic. Recently some efforts have been made toward rediscovering these lost techniques. Bernhard Ziehn, the German-American theorist, made a promising beginning in his book on canon, which is full of ingenious practical specimens of canonic writing but unfortunately is deficient in the analysis of the problems involved. And the present writer, in his older book, *Geschichte der Motette,* took pains to reconstruct at least some of the lost canonic formulas. But we are still far from a satisfactory solution of these old problems.

While England can claim priority in the initial use of the canon, the era of *ars nova* in France and Italy evolved new applications of the technique, and the Netherlands produced an unexcelled flowering of this new art of music.

We may pass quickly over the interesting and ingenious use

made of canonic writing in the *caccie* of the Florentine composers. The word *caccia* — in English a chase, a catch — suggests a *fuga* (fugue), a flight as observed by the fugitive; in every hunt, one party is chasing, the other party is fleeing. But in those times *fuga* meant what we now call canon, and the fugue proper did not exist. A remarkable early specimen of elaborate and skillful canon occurs in Francesco Landino's *De! dim-mi tu che se' così fragiato*. Here is found a rather extended and melodious two-part canon in the fifth, with a freely moving third voice. In the ritornello (the last two lines of the stanza) a triple canon is attempted, with an unorthodox harmony of freely entering fourths, seconds, and sevenths, which gives the piece something of a twentieth-century flavor.

In our review of novel features important in the later growth of music, we meet one that was introduced for the first time by the Florentine school of the fourteenth century: the vocal solo with an elaborate instrumental accompaniment. Gregorian chant had no accompaniment at all. The songs of the troubadours were usually accompanied by a viol or a psaltery, but these accompaniments were always improvised, and from the very fact that they were never written we may infer that they were of a crude nature, not requiring accurate notation. However, the masters of the Florentine *ars nova* were no longer satisfied with improvised accompaniments. In the Florentine madrigals of the early Renaissance, we find, for the first time in the literature of music, elaborate and ornamental instrumental accompaniments, with preludes, interludes, and postludes. The famous painting "Trionfo della Morte" in the Campo Santo (the cemetery of Pisa), attributed to Orcagna, depicts a musical scene: a little company of young ladies and gentlemen, fastidiously dressed, are singing and playing on various instruments, while grim Death stands ready to cut them down with his enormous scythe. This fourteenth-century picture shows the combination of solo singing with instruments that was typical of Florentine music of the period.

Another epoch-making achievement of the *ars nova* was the

improvement in music notation that we call "mensural notation." The neumes of Gregorian chant had not yet become a precise system of notation; they were merely a collection of melodic formulas, set down to aid the memory in singing various pieces that had already been learned by oral tradition. A method of fixing the pitch by utilizing the lines of the staff had been developed by Guido of Arezzo in the eleventh century and improved later. Yet this notation, which had precise signs for the various intervals, indicates only vaguely the comparative length of single tones, the meter, and the rhythm. Mensural notation, perfected toward 1300, represents a great advance. It consists of an ingenious system of symbols, indicating not only the precise pitch but also the metrical and rhythmical properties of a piece of music.

Mensural notation was born from the needs of polyphony, or, turning the proposition around, one may say that polyphonic art depended for its progress on the precise notation of the time value of single tones. Mensural notation is the indispensable auxiliary of higher polyphonic music, and as such is one of the most vital discoveries in music history. For more than three hundred years it was responsible for the truly astounding growth in the art of music. It is the direct ancestor of our present musical notation, which is a more rational treatment of the mensural principle.

The chief authorities for earlier mensural notation were the famous musical scholars of the Paris school and several learned English monks. In the *ars nova*, Italy developed its own theory and practice of mensural notation, which in certain essential points differed from the older French system. But after the return of the papacy to Rome in 1377 from the exile at Avignon, the French style of notation established itself more firmly in Italy, pushing into the background the attempts which had been made to create a special Italian notation.

4

The Netherlands

Having described the international character of early polyphony and its gradual growth, we now turn to that nation which was endowed with the genius needed for integrating the contributions of various countries, finding a common factor for them, and forming the unified style that became a model for all Europe and dominated European music everywhere for at least one hundred and fifty years, from about 1450 to 1600.

This was the age of "Netherlandish" polyphony. Its history traverses three phases. The first, the gothic phase (from about 1450 to 1500) embraces the music of the leading masters: Guillaume Dufay (c. 1400–1474), Johannes Okeghem (c. 1420–1495), Heinrich Isaak (c. 1450–1517), and Jacob Obrecht (1453–1505).

The second phase (about 1500 to 1550) is dominated by the great master Josquin de Près (c. 1450–1521). Other prominent names of this period are Pierre de la Rue (d. 1518), Nicolas Gombert (c. 1505–c. 1556), Antoine Brumel (flourished c. 1500), Jean Mouton (c. 1475–c. 1522), Ludwig Senfl (d. 1555), and Adrian Willaert (1490–1562).

The third phase (from about 1550 to 1600) is introduced by Clemens non Papa of Antwerp (c. 1500–c. 1556). The origin of this curious name is uncertain; it is possible that he styled himself in such a manner to avoid confusion with a contemporary musician who was known as Père Clemens. The theory that he wished to dissociate himself from Pope Clement VII is refuted by the circumstance that Clemens non Papa began to so designate himself only after the death of the Pope. The culmination of the third phase is reached in the artistic products of Orlando di Lasso (1524–1594). The great art of Netherlandish polyphony produced only one more eminent master before its decline: Jan Pieters Sweelinck (1562–1621).

The term "Netherlandish" as applied to the school of these great masters is not accurate. In reality "Netherlandish art" comprises four distinct schools: Burgundian, Flemish, northern French, and Dutch music. For our present purposes, however, it is more convenient to speak generally of Netherlandish music, leaving the subtler regional distinctions to students engaged in special research.

The imprint of Netherlandish style on all European music is so deep that it is hardly possible to tell, from the style of polyphonic writing, whether any given motet or Mass of the first half of the sixteenth century is of English, French, Spanish, German, or Italian origin. All national features had become so thoroughly assimilated that they all seem Netherlandish. Masters such as Dufay, Okeghem, Isaak, Josquin de Près, Obrecht, and Pierre de la Rue enjoyed European celebrity as composers, teachers, and conductors of cathedral choirs, and their superiority was so manifest and so universally recognized that they had no serious rivals as candidates for important positions. Toward 1500 the Papal Chapel in Rome was more and more dominated by Netherlandish musicians; Lorenzo de' Medici in Florence called to his court the most renowned masters of Netherlandish music; and in 1526 the proud republic of Venice entrusted its musical culture and the leading post at St. Mark's Cathedral to the Netherlandish master Adrian Willaert.

Netherlandish polyphony contains no trace of the crude and harsh harmonies that marked the old French motets of 1200. For the first time, the problem of making three and four voices sing or play together with faultless purity and beauty of sound was solved. The acoustic properties of intervals were identified, studied, and logically formulated by the early Netherlandish masters. No longer were the parallel fifths and fourths of the old organum tolerated, or the piercing dissonances of parallel seconds and sevenths. By 1500 Netherlandish musicians had already clearly formulated laws of intervallic progressions, parallel consonances, and passing dissonances, which retained their validity in art music down to the nineteenth century.

The new beauty and purity of concord is generally associated with the art of Guillaume Dufay (*c.* 1400–1474), the earliest internationally acknowledged master of the rising Netherlandish craft. Dufay, the head of the famous Burgundian school, shows full command of the intricate counterpoint of *ars nova* and of its isorhythmic structure — its employment of a reiterated scheme of time values. His powers are demonstrated in the monumental motet *Nuper rosarum,* which he wrote for the consecration of the Florence cathedral in 1436.

After Dufay's death, Loyset Compère (*c.* 1455–1518), canon of St. Quentin Cathedral, wrote a famous motet, *Omnium bonorum plena,* in which the Holy Virgin is implored to give comfort to musicians, enumerated by name. Dufay, who heads the list, is here aptly called "Luna totius musicae atque cantorum lumine" (the moon of all music and light of singers). Indeed, for Dufay's austere and soft music no better comparison can be found than the light of the moon.

When we come to Dufay's pupil Johannes Okeghem, new aspects of Netherlandish polyphony begin to appear. Okeghem spent the greater part of his career in Paris as leader of the Royal Chapel. The development of the artful complexity of Netherlandish counterpoint was once credited to him; but other features of his art have lately been revealed that lift him far above the rank of a mere virtuoso of contrapuntal technique.

The essence of Okeghem's art, as of Netherlandish polyphony in general, is structural ingenuity combined with the exquisite melodic shaping of each single part. In its purest state, before its modification by Italian influences, Netherlandish counterpoint, decidedly gothic in character, is strictly an art of structure and of musical design in black and white — a linear art in which little attention is paid to picturesque or coloristic effects.

These structural developments were manifested in the establishment of three new forms that have dominated music for centuries: the Mass, the motet, and the polyphonic chanson. All three are based on the idea of a *cantus firmus*, a selected melody taken over from Gregorian chant, from ecclesiastical hymns, or even from a folk song. Virtually all compositions of the gothic age are built on a *cantus firmus*, designed as an inner support for the music, somewhat like the framework of a building. In contrapuntal works, the *cantus firmus* was not meant to stand out, any more than the skeleton in a human body is to be seen through the flesh. It is in the dialogue between the contrapuntal voices that the composer's art is demonstrated. This method is diametrically opposite to the homophonic modern arrangements of a folk song, in which the melody constitutes the principal feature and is meant to be heard distinctly. In the Mass, the Gregorian *cantus firmus* serves as the repository of the thematic material. From it the composer collects small particles, or motives, as building stones for each movement of the Mass.

Another essentially gothic trait in Netherlandish music is the predilection for structural problems of an almost mathematical nature. Great attention is paid to the subtleties of canonic art, the most extraordinary example of which is a thirty-six part canon attributed to Okeghem, probably designed as an instrumental piece. By constant overlapping of the many voices, the four themes of the piece gradually lose their melodic identity, and the music is transformed into an undulating mass of recurrent musical waves. This spectacular canon reminds one of the prelude to Wagner's *Rheingold*, where canonic technique is applied to an arpeggio theme successively played by eight horns. Here, too, the overlapping melodic lines lose their melodic individuality, and the desired effect of an undulating mass of water is attained with striking realism.

Still another type of Netherlandish musical intellectualism is the co-called "riddle canon." The riddle does not concern those who listen to the canon; it is a game invented by the composer and played by the performers, who have to solve the riddle. The composer attempts to write a complicated canon in a very abbreviated manner, in a kind of shorthand. He may compose an elaborate four-part canon and write it all on a single line, leaving it to the performers to find out at what particular place and interval, in what meter and rhythm, the canonic imitations are to enter. As a clue, the composer exercises his ingenuity and his mastery of Latin by devising a more or less elegant Latin motto, often in verse, which indicates cryptically the hidden plan of the piece. Sometimes these "explanatory" verses increase the difficulty of the solution. For special effects of augmentation, diminution, and rhythmical changes, the subtleties of the difficult mensural notation are exploited to their fullest extent.

Brief definitions of the three basic forms of Netherlandish music, the Mass, the motet, and the chanson, are opportune at this point. The Mass is a polyphonic setting of the text of the Latin Mass, as distinguished from the older Gregorian treatment of the Mass text for a single voice. The motet is a short piece of ecclesiastical music set to a Biblical text or to a sacred poem. The Netherlandish motet differs from the older motet of the Parisian *ars antiqua* in that the earlier form represents a combination of liturgical and secular elements, whereas the Netherlandish motet is a liturgical piece of music written in polyphonic style for use in the church. The chanson is a polyphonic setting of a popular folk tune. In the sixteenth century, this Netherlandish style of writing was utilized in other countries as well, notably Germany, France, and England, in artistic settings of folk songs.

In both *ars antiqua* and *ars nova*, three-part writing was customary, but early in the sixteenth century the standard setting in polyphonic writing was increased to four voices. A century later, in the Italian madrigal, five-part writing became fashionable, but four-part settings have since proved to be the most practical in harmonic writing. Bach, Handel, Haydn, Mozart, Beethoven, and most of the nineteenth-century composers used four-part writing par excellence. The creation of the string quartet established it as the basis of instrumental music. This preference for four-part harmony points to the fine esthetic judgment and artistic intelligence of the great masters. Three-part writing insures clarity and grace of linear motion, but it lacks power, fullness, and climactic effect. Five-part writing produces full sonority at the expense of clarity and grace of linear motion. Four-part writing of the Netherlandish type is a happy medium, producing sufficient fullness of sound without obscuring the harmony and the distinctive component voices.

Further experimentation by the Netherlandish masters led to an ingenious contrapuntal discovery, namely, double, triple, and quadruple counterpoint, in which the individual voices alternate their melodies. This produces six different permutations in three-part writing, twenty-four in four-part writing, and one hundred and twenty in five-part writing.

Another Netherlandish innovation is the device called free imitation, to distinguish it from the strict imitation of canon. A rather short phrase is imitated more or less accurately by several voices in succession. The result is not a canon but a dialogue based on similar thematic material, which insures coherence. This device of logical dialogue in free mutual imitation of independent voices has become one of the most fertile elements in many musical forms. Motet, madrigal, fugue, part song, sonata, quartet, and symphony, all apply the principle of free imitation. Its most concentrated type is found in the fugue, which may be compared to an animated conversation on a chosen topic between three or four people. The conversation is never dominated by any single speaker; the participants discuss the theme on equal terms, none being inferior to another in the delivery of his part, and each trying to speak logically without deviating from the main subject.

The rhythmic freedom of Netherlandish music is significant. All European music from 1600 to about 1900 is constructed in successive measures, with rhythms derived from the march and the dance. Netherlandish motets and chansons, however, reveal a much subtler play of rhythms, for which it is difficult to find a common metrical division. The soprano may sing in 4/4 time, the alto in 3/4, and the tenor in 6/4 or even 5/4; 7/4 measures may also appear. The result is a delightfully free rhythmic motion, for which today we do not possess adequate means of notation. The masterpieces of Netherlandish music were originally written in mensural notation, without bar lines. In modern editions, conventional bar lines have been added. These artificial divisions disrupt the free rhythmic interplay of the original music, irregular and fanciful like the shifting formations of clouds in the sky with sudden changes of light and shade.

Another remarkable characteristic of Netherlandish music is the use of noncoincident accents. An accented note in one voice is set against an unaccented note in another; the rhythmic line is broken temporarily; then two, three, or four voices combine in the same rhythm, bringing a relaxation, particularly while coming to a cadence.

It is clear that such complexity of rhythm and accent requires a special method of leading a performance, with metronome-like precision, and yet without emphasis on artificially placed strong beats. Properly instructed, the singers and instrumentalists ought to be able to count the number of notes in each musical phrase rather than to rely on the conductor to indicate a unified measure.

During the Renaissance, classical poetry was rediscovered and passionately studied by scholars. Musicians were attracted by these literary treasures, and eagerly selected suitable lyrical texts for their settings. The earlier school of Renaissance composers subordinated the text to the music; as the understanding of classical literature increased, composers made a profound study of Latin prosody, and began to illustrate the words by appropriate musical figures. Even thematic invention was made to serve the rhetorical effect of the text, particularly in the vocal music of Josquin de Près. German scholars coined a special term to describe this device of musical illustration: *Wortgezeugte Motive* (word-engendered motifs).

The search for greater musical expressiveness was continued during the later period of the Netherlandish school. The concepts of color, chromatic harmony, and picturesque interpretation of the words began to possess the minds of Netherlandish masters; dramatic considerations began to affect the structure of their music. The process is culminated in the motets of Orlando di Lasso. He wrote more than nine hundred motets, in which he achieved a fusion of gothic, humanistic, and Renaissance characteristics; he even anticipated some salient points of the baroque period.

To give at least a glimpse of Lasso's artistic achievement, we shall briefly describe two of his motets. The five-part motet *Tristis est anima mea* translates into tones the speech of Christ to His disciples: "My soul is exceeding sorrowful, even unto death: abide ye here, and watch with me." This is music of overpowering grandeur, the intensity of expression heightened by free imitation of the individual phrases; a musical motif announces itself tranquilly and then surges onward like a majestic wave. Such passages as "vos fugam capietis" especially the regal "et ego vadam immolari pro vobis" possess an inspired quality. In 1575 his five-part motet *Domine Jesu Christe qui cognoscis* was accorded a unique honor at the famous cathedral of Evreux in France. For a number of years an international contest of composers had taken place there in honor of St. Cecilia, the patron saint of music, and at one of the contests Lasso was awarded the first prize, a silver organ, for this motet. It is a striking piece of emotional incantation. What fearful shouting at the words, "ut poenitens clamem, peccavi"! What a climax at the closing "miserere"!

With Orlando di Lasso the broad stream of Netherlandish polyphony reaches its estuary. After having traversed many lands, and having received many tributaries, it emptied its waters into the mighty ocean of European music. Philippe de Monte (1521–1603) stands as the most eminent master of Netherlandish music of this period. His Masses and many hundreds of madrigals and motets are gradually emerging from the oblivion of the centuries.

Netherlandish music reached its high point in the music of Jan Pieters Sweelinck (1562–1621). Old biographers of Sweelinck stated that he traveled to Venice and studied there with Zarlino; the assumption was then made that Sweelinck acquired his contrapuntal skill from the Venetian masters. The examination of the registers of the Old Church in Amsterdam, where Sweelinck served as organist, has proved, however, that he never left the Netherlands, and that he established his great reputation in Europe by his virtuosity as an organist and by his compositions. Organists from Germany went to Amsterdam to study with him; his influence as a teacher lasted through his disciples to the time of Buxtehude and Pachelbel, indirectly affecting the organ style of Bach himself.

Sweelinck's claim to eminence as a composer rests on his mastery of the newly developed form of the fugue, the successor to the older types of *ricercare, canzone,* and *fantasia*. Sweelinck's fugue had a principal subject and several countersubjects; thanks to his masterly treatment of the technical elements, these fugues became virtuoso pieces for the organ. Sweelinck also made skillful adaptations of the English form of variations in organ music.

With Sweelinck, the great era of Netherlandish polyphony came to a close. Italian musical genius asserted itself in a spectacular and aggressive manner. The creation of opera, the rise of the instrumental forms of sonata, sinfonia, and concerto, the emergence of the theoretical concepts of thorough bass and homophonic chord accompaniment, the influx of popular rhythms into serious music — these Italian innovations challenged the supremacy of Netherlandish contrapuntal art. Yet this art, perfected by the common effort of French, Netherlandish, English, Italian, Spanish, and German creative minds, was too grandiose an achievement to be repressed. After a temporary eclipse, it rose to its greatest glory in the supreme revelation of polyphonic genius of Bach.

A minor successor to Sweelinck's fame in Netherlandish music was Constantin Huygens (1596–1687), a diplomat, author, and poet. As secretary to William of Orange, Huygens traveled a great deal and made friends in many countries in Europe. His correspondence, preserved in the Amsterdam Royal Library, comprises some nineteen hundred autograph letters, including about a hundred letters in French dealing with various musical topics. Huygens was a fine performer on several instruments; he composed nearly eight hundred airs for lute, clavecin, viola da gamba, and guitar. His only published musical work, the *Pathodia sacra et profana*, is available in the edition of his letters. It contains twenty Latin, twelve Italian, and seven French psalms. Christian Huygens, Constantin's son (1629–1695), who gained fame as an astronomer, left some writings dealing with music.

In the eighteenth century Amsterdam produced few compositions by native masters, but it continued to serve as an important musical center. In 1696 Estienne Roger established there a music-publishing firm, which gained high distinction by its fine engraving and printing from copper plates. Roger's edition of Corelli's sonatas and concertos is an example of his best work. Corelli's pupil Locatelli, the greatest violin virtuoso of the eighteenth century, lived in Amsterdam for many years, until his death in 1764.

D. F. Scheurleer, Holland's most magnanimous and cultivated modern patron of music, published in 1909 a magnificently printed and profusely illustrated book, *Het Muziekleven in Nederland in de 18ᵉ eeuw*, which describes in detail Holland's musical life in the eighteenth century, mainly at The Hague and Amsterdam. From this book we gather interesting information about many foreign artists of international fame and about the works of Pugnani, Gossec, J. C. Bach, Haydn, Cimarosa, Paesiello, Viotti, Cherubini, and others that were performed by the Amsterdam society, the Felix Meritis. Locatelli, Hurlebusch, Vivaldi, Carlo Tessarini of Rimini, Lolly, Stamitz, Dussek, La Mara, and Todi were some of the famous virtuosos who delighted Amsterdam music lovers of those days. Several chapters of Scheurleer's book are devoted to the visit to Holland of the young Mozart with his father Leopold in 1765–66. Other chapters deal with ballet performances by Flemish, French, Italian, and German opera companies.

During the nineteenth and twentieth centuries Amsterdam maintained its importance as a musical center. But the art that has occupied the foreground has remained imitative. Two Dutch institutions have contributed signally to the national cultivation of music, one in the past, the other in the present. The Vereeniging voor Noord-Netherlands Muziekgeschiedenis (Society for North Netherlandish Music History) has since 1869 published more than fifty volumes, including Sweelinck's collected works in twelve volumes, the works of Obrecht, and many other works of historical value. The other institution is Amsterdam's Concertgebouw Orchestra, one of the world's finest and largest. Under the leadership of its eminent conductor Willem Mengelberg it achieved first-rank status, not only at home but also throughout Europe. More than any other conductor, Mengelberg was the champion of modernism in music. His attitude meant, from 1900 to 1914, a systematic and continuous fight on behalf of the music of Richard Strauss, Gustav Mahler, Debussy, Ravel, Reger, Schönberg, and Stravinsky. Those who, like the author, were fortunate enough to attend the memorable Mahler festival at

Amsterdam in May 1920, under the direction of Mengelberg, recall it as one of their most cherished artistic experiences. All the works of Gustav Mahler — ten symphonies, plus choral works and song cycles — were heard in authoritative performances. That the great musician Mengelberg should in his closing years have sullied his name by Nazi affiliations is a matter of profound sorrow to those who had known him previously.

During the last fifty years there has been no lack of excellent creative musicians in Holland, but few of them have acquired international importance. The best known are Julius Röntgen (1855–1932), an admirable musical expert in many fields; Johan Wagenaar (1862–1941), director of the Royal Conservatory at The Hague, a composer of rank in the field of orchestral music, opera, and cantata; Cornelis Dopper (1870–1939), assistant conductor of the Amsterdam Concertgebouw Orchestra, composer of symphonies and operas; Bernard van Dieren (1884–1936), a composer of highly complex polyphonic music of distinct individuality, who settled in London; Sem Dresden (born in 1881), and Willem Pijper (1894–1947), the leaders of Dutch modernism. Alphons Diepenbrock (1862–1921) is highly esteemed in Holland for his fine choral works. Among others, Willem Landré (1874–1948) is well known in Holland as a composer of romantic music in all genres; his son Guillaume Landré (born in 1905) has written several symphonies in an advanced modern idiom. Hendirk Andriessen (born in 1892) has distinguished himself as an opera composer; Alexander Voormolen (born in 1895) writes in an impressionist manner. Henk Badings (born in 1907) is the composer of six symphonies and many other important scores. Of the younger generation of Dutch composers, Marius Flothuis (born in 1914) has made significant contributions to the literature of chamber music.

A great impact to the promotion of modern native music in Holland has been made by the formation of Donemus (Society for the Documentation of Netherlandish Music). This organization has integrated the contemporary musical productions of

Dutch composers in a central agency; it serves as a distributor of unpublished works and issues complete catalogues of individual composers.

A musical specialty of the Netherlands for centuries has been the construction and playing of carillons. In the fifteenth and sixteenth centuries, the great Flemish cathedrals competed with each other in building elaborate carillons. The great eighteenth-century historian, Dr. Charles Burney, in his *General History of Music* writes with admiration of the skill of the Netherlandish carillon players and the brilliant effect of their playing. There were even composers who specialized in carillon music; a pioneer in this art was Matthias van den Gheyn in Louvain (1721–1785). Many Netherlands carillons have been exported to other countries, and at present America possesses some of the finest sets made by Dutch craftsmen.

5

Italy

Italy, daughter of ancient Rome and granddaughter of Greece, inherited from her ancestors in music a scanty fortune, which, as we have seen, was almost completely destroyed during the Middle Ages. Some elements of Greek and Roman music were, however, incorporated in the services of the Christian church, and that great creation of Rome, the Gregorian chant, was an imperishable heritage for the following centuries.

Gregorian chant expresses the Romanesque spirit, as do the glorious cathedrals of Italy, France, and Germany, whose harmonious arrangement of spatial attributes approaches perfection. A purely melodic art, the Gregorian chant represents the first of the three dimensions of space: length, width, and depth. Translated into musical terms, these three dimensions are linear extension, or melodic line (length); harmonic or contrapuntal accompaniment (width); and dynamic effects and tone color (depth). The first dimension, the linear element, is represented by monophonic music, such as Gregorian chant. The second dimension, width, is represented by contrapuntal music, with chordlike filling-in that adds the element of breadth to the melodic linear structure. Although Italy contributed little to the initiation of counterpoint, in the *ars nova* she greatly enhanced its development. The third dimension, depth, is achieved in music through dynamic variation and contrast in tone color. It was latent in the polyphonic music of the Netherlandish school and became evident in the Italian music of the late sixteenth and seventeenth centuries.

The early authorities on polyphonic writing, counterpoint, and musical theory were learned monks from the monasteries in France, England, and Germany. Among them there is only one Italian name, but this name is a glorious one, that of Guido of Arezzo, who flourished in the first half of the eleventh century. Although modern research has put in doubt several of his reputed achievements, the few that are unquestionably his works fully justify his legendary fame. Guido's invention of the musical staff of four lines whose pitch is fixed in distances of thirds was an immense advance over the vague notation of rudimentary accent marks, or neumes. For the first time music could be written and performed correctly and precisely in respect to the pitch of every note. Our modern notation is a direct descendant of Guido's music staff.

Another innovation of far-reaching importance introduced by Guido of Arezzo is solmization, a system of music nomenclature by syllables. It was taught by means of the so-called "Guidonian hand," a sketch of the human hand with various tones inscribed on it. The fourteen joints of the five fingers each represented a syllable: ut, re, mi, fa, sol, la, etc.; to these fourteen were added five more points located on the palm of the hand, and one soaring in the air above the tip of the middle finger. Thus all twenty tones of the system of music employed in Guido's time found their place somewhere on the Guidonian hand. Solfeggio, as it is taught in Italy, France, Spain, Portugal, and Russia, is the last relic of Guido's solmization. In these countries, the notes of the scale still bear the original syllables selected by Guido (representing the initial syllables of the successive lines in a Latin hymn), with the first note, "ut," replaced by the more euphonious syllable, "do."

Though the initiation of polyphony is a French achievement, to which Italy contributed but little, the second phase of polyphony belongs to Italy: the *ars nova* of the fourtenth century, the music of the early Renaissance, which followed the old contrapuntal music (*ars antiqua*) of the famous Parisian school of Leoninus and Perotinus in the twelfth and thirteenth centuries. In *ars nova* we find a felicitous marriage of music with poetry of the highest artistic refinement. The newly created and polished Italian poetry of the early Renaissance — the sonnets, *canzone,* and madrigals of Dante and Petrarch — provided texts for the new music. The study of *ars nova* has been greatly advanced by the publication of the collected works of the Italian master Francesco Landino (1325-1397), the blind organist of the Florence Cathedral. The main source of this edition is the Codex Squarcialupi, preserved in the Laurentian Library of Florence. This fourteenth-century manuscript is doubly precious on account of the beauty of its calligraphy and its profuse illumination. It transmits to posterity the music of twelve masters of *ars nova,* together with a portrait of each; Francesco Landino is represented by no fewer than one hundred and forty-five pieces. Both his portrait in the Codex and his tombstone in San Lorenzo show him playing an *organetto* with a keyboard of hardly more than two octaves.

The highly cultivated *ars nova* did not dominate Europe, however, owing to the victorious emergence of Netherlandish music. The century between 1450 and 1550 witnessed a vital struggle for supremacy between Italian and Netherlandish music. Toward 1500, the triumph of the latter seemed inevitable, and it soon became an accomplished fact. The native features of Italian music gradually vanished. One after another, Flemish artists came southward to take leading posts at the Papal Chapel, at San Marco in Venice, at the Medici court in Florence, and at other brilliant and luxurious princely courts of Italy — Ferrara, Mantua, and Milan. Netherlandish music reigned supreme; in Italy, France, England, Germany, and Spain, one style of high artistic standing prevailed, the Netherlandish; the various other national schools had sunk to the level of narrow provincialism.

This state of affairs, however, could not persist for long. The innate Italian genius, though subdued by the Netherlandish invasion, eventually began to assert itself. The most fascinating phase of this struggle was its finale: the conquest of the Netherlandish victors by their Italian subjects. In Rome, the art of the great Palestrina (1525-1594) marked the climax. Brought up from earliest youth in the discipline of Netherlandish art, Palestrina became a consummate master of that technique. The music of the Catholic church, long under Netherlandish influence, was gradually emancipated by Palestrina's creative work and acquired a melodic animation and dynamic expressiveness that are characteristically Italian.

Palestrina's music constitutes one of the noblest achievements of Italian art. He conquered the great Netherlandish masters on their own ground; yet, paradoxically, it is principally through Palestrina that the main tenets of Netherlandish music have been preserved. Moreover, his work is the greatest contribution that Italy has made to ecclesiastical music, incarnating the Catholic religious spirit in the most completely satisfying form ever achieved. His music breathes seraphic mildness and dignity, and at the same time it possesses an ecstatic eloquence.

In Venice the Italian genius asserted itself in a different way. Here the great Netherlandish masters Adrian Willaert and Cypriano de Rore gave the benefit of their knowledge to native musicians; these magnificent teachers succeeded in a surprisingly short time in making Venice a great center of music. At the same time they were captivated by the charm of the Venetian art, so that they learned from their pupils as much as they taught. The result of this felicitous synthesis was an art that possessed both Netherlandish structural mastery and Venetian exuberance of color. Whatever was achieved in color effects by harmony, through vocal or orchestral means, in subsequent centuries by Gluck and Mozart, or by Chopin, Berlioz, Wagner, Strauss, or Debussy, can ultimately be traced to the innovations made by Venetian masters during the sixteenth century.

One of the signal Italian accomplishments of that period is the madrigal. Its significance extends beyond the exquisite works of art produced in its homeland, for the Italian madrigal style was taken up in other countries. It took root in England and became thoroughly assimilated with the spirit of Elizabethan poetry, blossoming forth with flowers of a new fragrance. Though the season of flowering was short, barely exceeding half a century, the madrigal was the highest achievement of English music. Germany, too, was captivated by the Italian madrigal and by the coloristic art of Venice. It was flooded by a wave of Venetian double-chorus motets and madrigals, for which an entirely new school of German poets furnished verses in the Italian style.

The rise of the new Italian madrigal marked the growing resistance to the Netherlandish artistic hegemony. This form of madrigal began roughly about 1550. One hundred and fifty years earlier — during the period of Florentine *ars nova* — madrigals had been written mostly for solo voice. By the middle of the sixteenth century Italian musicians felt independent enough to assert their own ideas; after absorbing the art of their Netherlandish teachers, they had at last become masters in their own right. Familiar with all the contrapuntal refinements of the Netherlandish motet and polyphonic part song, they applied their technique to the prodigiously flourishing Italian lyric poetry of the Renaissance. The new madrigal was no longer confined to linear melody; it was polyphonic, in accordance with the trend of the times.

The classical Italian madrigal of 1550 was not merely an imitation of the Netherlandish chanson, whose polyphonic texture and form it retained. No longer did it use a folk tune as a *cantus firmus*. The thematic material was invented, and great care was exercised in making the musical motives, phrases, melodies, and rhythms fit the words. Italian lyric poetry was quite different in style from the vernacular French verses used in the Netherlandish chansons. The euphonious Italian language, full of poetic symbolism, gave new inspiration to the native composer.

Thus the classical Italian madrigal, though retaining the structural, formal, and polyphonic features of the motet and the part song, differs from these earlier art forms considerably in mood, coloring, and atmosphere.

For the international promotion of these new Italian ideas, the work of Claudio Monteverdi (1567–1643) was of the greatest importance. He consolidated, with the sovereign power of genius, the novel musical forms that sprang forth so abundantly in Italy around 1600. The madrigals of Luca Marenzio (1553–1599), with their subtle and colorful harmony and their lyric charm, as well as the new Florentine monody and the operas of Caccini and Peri, challenged Monteverdi to an artistic contest. He succeeded so well that his madrigals rank with Marenzio's. His dramatic music surpasses by far the dry and barren efforts of the founders of Florentine opera. He penetrated deep into the interior of a new continent of music, whose shores only had been approached before him. The music of the entire seventeenth century elaborates the ideas of structure, style, and expression first formulated by Monteverdi.

A few representative works of this great master are described briefly here in order to illustrate the nature of his achievement. Though the madrigals are among his earliest works, they represent his most finished productions. Furthermore, they mark the loftiest height attained by the combined efforts of Marenzio and Monteverdi, supported to some extent by that bizarre and erratic genius, Gesualdo, Prince of Venosa. In these madrigals the accumulated experience of several generations achieved classical perfection.

Let us examine here two of the madrigals. *Era l'anima mia già presso a l'ultim'hora* expresses the anguish of a soul close to death, recalled to life by the sympathy of a loving heart. The three lower voices sing the first section in the manner of the fauxbourdon litany of a Requiem. This darkly tinged, monotonous muttering is followed by sudden rays of light at the words, "A beautiful soul turned her eyes to me with so compassionate a glance that it restored me to life." At this point the two higher voices enter; then all voices sing in their best registers, producing a most effective contrast of color and expression. The middle section of the madrigal is distinguished by supple declamation. Following that, the ensemble of all five voices is heard in the impressive apostrophe of the loving heart: "Alas, why do you consume yourself? My own life is not so dear as you, my love, are to me!" And then comes the conclusion: "Woe to me! If you pass on, you do not die alone — I also die." In this polyphonic dialogue we hear the bittersweet dissonant harmonies that were used by Monteverdi with such a magical effect.

The second madrigal, *Ecco mormorar l'onde*, expresses a different mood. The first part of the poem is an idyllic tone painting that depicts the murmuring brook, the rustling tree branches, the joyful twittering of the birds at dawn, the morning glow of the sky reflected in the sea, the rising sun gilding the mountains with its rays. Monteverdi paints this landscape with enchanting musical colors. The pastoral mood of the first part is maintained by the deliberately economical use of only a few chords. This peaceful calm is abandoned as the music progresses, acquiring a more energetic character at the words, "Behold, the dawn appears," soaring upward in elastic rhythms, in joyful, radiant sounds. The announcement "The sky brightens," leads to a fine climax, as a resonant theme is rushed successively through all five voices. The close, with its long chain of parallel fifths and octaves and its gay dance rhythm, is of an electrifying vigor and brilliance. This is not the only instance of Monteverdi's employment of the device of parallel fifths and octaves, but nowhere else in his work does it occur with more telling effect than in this masterpiece of madrigal art.

A number of attempts have been made in various countries to revive Monteverdi's opera *L'Incoronazione di Poppea* and his ballet-opera *Combattimento di Tancredi e Clorinda*. Though both works abound in fine music, their revivals have had but limited success. The reason for this is that in their scenic action, poetry, music, and style in general, Monteverdi's operas are too remote from our conception of operatic spectacle to be impressive. Yet, when properly presented for a historically-minded audience, they provide an esthetically satisfying experience.

Monteverdi's scenic dialogue *Ballo delle ingrate* likewise merits revival. The story is this: Amor questions his mother Venus about the punishment meted out to the *anime ingrate,* the souls of those who have spurned the power of love. Venus makes a personal plea to Pluto, lord of the lower world, to release these souls from their dark abode. Pluto gallantly grants her wish; the souls then perform a dance for the guests from Olympus — and for the court society of Mantua, where the *Ballo* was presented for the first time in 1608.

The *Lamento* from Monteverdi's opera-ballet *Arianna* has exercised an almost legendary power over generations of musicians. The score of the opera was destroyed by fire and only this *Lamento* and a few more fragments survived; yet these few pages are worth more esthetically than many volumes of music by Monteverdi's rivals. The Italian master Ottorino Respighi made a valiant attempt to introduce this noble piece of music into the concert hall, in his interesting arrangement of it for voice and orchestra.

In the seventeenth century Monteverdi's influence in Italy, France, England, and especially Germany was so powerful that the best music in these countries bore his stamp. Heinrich Schütz (1585–1672), the greatest figure in German music before Bach, was proud to call himself a friend, disciple, and admirer of Monteverdi, and everywhere in his music we can see how much he profited from the example of the great Italian master — in harmony, declamation, treatment of instrumental accompaniment, and melodic freedom.

In another direction, too, Italian art made a profound impression on German musicians. In the eighteenth century, works for organ were composed almost exclusively by Germans; this was the period when Buxtehude and Pachelbel, Handel and Bach, by their power and brilliance surpassed all their predecessors. But this German art could not have flourished without the preceding accomplishments of the two great Italian organ schools: the Venetian school, with Claudio Merulo (1533–1604) and Giovanni Gabrieli (1557–1612) as its chief proponents, and the Roman school, guided by the mighty Girolamo Frescobaldi (1583–1643), the world-famous organist of St. Peter's Cathedral.

Frescobaldi fully deserves to be called the earliest classical master of organ composition. His music has endured through the centuries not merely as a historical curiosity but as a pleasurable art for its own sake. When we hear the older Venetian organ works of Giovanni Gabrieli and Claudio Merulo, we treat them with the reverence due to pioneers, but purely as music they fail to appeal to us. Not so with Frescobaldi. His *canzone*, toccatas, capriccios, and *partitas* are of a polyphonic magnificence without a parallel in organ music. The grandiose structures, the exciting chromatic harmony, the wealth of plastic thematic invention make these works stand out as supreme examples of the art of the period, and compare favorably with the masterpieces of later times.

In the polyphonic art of Venice, as perfected in the works of Willaert, Gabrieli, and their disciples, characterized by chromatic harmony and contrasting color, we find the earliest expression of the baroque style in Italy. A somewhat related trend becomes manifest in the new monodic music, the Florentine opera that arose about 1600. Here in the instrumental accompaniment to melodic lines the principle of background and perspective, of plastic appearance, is discovered in music, through the contrast in color and rhythm between the vocal solo and the instrumental *basso continuo* accompaniment. In the dramatic recitative, dynamic accents, crescendo and diminuendo, ritardando and accelerando contribute still further to the impression of depth and perspective.

All these momentous developments mark the rapid evolution

in music effected in Italy between the years 1575 and 1600. The leading masters of this period were Luca Marenzio, Andrea and Giovanni Gabrieli, Gesualdo, Prince of Venosa, Frescobaldi, Giulio Caccini and Jacopo Peri (the creators of the Florentine opera), and the great Monteverdi. The principles introduced by these artists are valid even now. They have proved sufficiently flexible to undergo modifications without losing their essential characteristics.

The revolutionary ideas generated in Italy about 1600 may be summarized as follows:

1. Monody, declamatory solo singing, recitative with instrumental accompaniment,

2. The evolution of major and minor tonality, replacing the medieval church modes,

3. The evolution of new forms appropriate to instrumental music — the suite, sonata, concerto, fugue, toccata, and overture,

4. The emergence of several new forms combining vocal and instrumental music, opera, oratorio, and cantata.

To these ideas, still valid in the twentieth century, may be added two items of a more limited significance:

5. The system of abbreviated harmonic, improvised accompaniment known as *basso continuo* or thorough bass,

6. The technique called *concertante* style.

Recitative came into being as a result of the desire of a group of scholarly citizens in Florence to revive Greek drama with music. The declamatory style, already used in Gregorian chant, seemed the most suitable model. Instances of the use of recitative are found in Lasso's motets and Marenzio's madrigals. The first attempts at extended recitative were made in the early Florentine operas: Peri's *Dafne* of 1594 and the settings made by Peri and by Caccini of Rinuccini's dramatic poem *Euridice* in 1600. Systematic treatment of the declamatory style in its various aspects is found for the first time in Caccini's collection of monodies — solo songs with figured-bass accompaniment — entitled *Le nuove musiche* and published in 1601 in Florence. This collection comprises "arias," or, properly speaking, strophic songs, and "madrigals," in this case monodic through-composed pieces rather than polyphonic works. In these monodies, songlike melody is mixed with declamatory style; ornamental coloraturas add a virtuoso touch. The style that was later called *bel canto* is clearly outlined. Only faint traces of the old church modes are left; major and minor tonalities, derived from the popular dance tunes, predominate. The instrumental accompaniment is given to the harpsichord and is written in the *basso continuo* style, which had been explicitly used for the first time by Lodovico Viadana (1564–1645) in his *Cento concerti ecclesiastici* (1602).

Basso continuo is a practical abridgement of notation — the bass part is marked with numerals that indicate what chords should be played. This Italian invention proved so useful in playing on keyboard instruments that it was adopted throughout Europe and became standard for most music from about 1600 to 1750. Bach and Handel made extensive use of the *basso continuo*. It fell into disuse about 1770, when the music of Haydn and Mozart effected a change of taste.

An important corollary of the method of the *basso continuo* is the *concertante* style, which combines plain chordal and homophonic accompaniment with traditional polyphonic linear treatment. The artistic objective is to write a second theme that will be in contrast with the dominating melodic theme. This second, or "obbligato," part has the function designated as *concertante*: it differs melodically from the theme, but the two must form together a euphonious ensemble. This elegant display of supple and elaborate melodies is set in a fixed frame of harmonic accompaniment.

Sometimes the solo and the obbligato part constitute a thematic duet, a dialogue with identical motives in each voice. In other cases, the obbligato part presents a fanciful arabesque, woven around the solo, encircling and embracing it. Sometimes the obbligato part is assigned an illustrative function, as in the aria in Handel's opera *Giulio Cesare*, when Caesar compares his strength to the irresistible power of the torrent rushing down the mountainside: the obbligato part in its restless motion strikingly suggests the flow of the waters. Bach's obbligato parts abound in symbolic significance that can be fully appreciated only after a thorough study of his unique system of symbolism.

An Italian opera may be described as a succession of cantatas. The cantata, a piece to be sung, and its sister the sonata, a piece to be played, are both Italian creations. The Italian cantatas of the seventeenth and eighteenth centuries are brief lyric or dramatic sketches, to be performed with the accompaniment of the cembalo. They contain recitatives, arias, and duets, sometimes with chorus and orchestra added. Many thousands of these cantatas lie in manuscript among the great European libraries, still awaiting historical study and publication.

While the Italian cantata resembled a sketch for an operatic scene, the German cantata became an entirely independent form. This transformation was achieved by Bach. Even the most lofty Italian cantatas are somewhat playful in character. The church cantata of Bach, however, possesses profundity and grandeur, besides presenting a multitude of innovations in structure, expression, sentiment, and sound.

Italy created not only the cantata and the sonata but also the sinfonia and the concerto, the musical forerunnners of all modern instrumental forms — in solo playing, chamber music, and works for orchestra. Early in the seventeenth century, the sonata was adapted especially for string playing, one of the chief Italian attainments. Until about 1600, the viol was the favorite string instrument; in Shakespeare's time, dance music for several viols was popular in England. But viol music went out of fashion when the smaller and higher-pitched violin came to be cultivated in Italy. In brilliant sonority, flexibility, and variety of expression, the violin far surpassed the softer and rather nasal-sounding viol. At the time that Louis XIV established his famous court orchestra of twenty-four violins, under Lully's leadership, the violin was the prime favorite among string instruments.

For nearly two hundred years Italy maintained undisputed leadership in playing and manufacturing the violin. She sent a legion of brilliant performers and teachers to other lands, and her craftsmen made violins of superlative quality. In composition for the violin and in virtuosity of performance, France became a dangerous rival in the eighteenth century; in the second half of the nineteenth century Germany surpassed both Italy and France as the country of virtuoso violinists. Still, in the art of making violins, Italy remained unchallenged. The instruments created by Stradivarius, Amati, and Guarneri exercise their magic power even after two hundred years. Their violins are of incomparable visual beauty; they are masterpieces of the woodcarver's art, a joy to the eye, with their varnish of glowing color, their depth of hues, and a play of light and shade that defies all attempts at imitation. In beauty and brillance, the Italian string instruments approach the human voice, nature's noblest creation in the domain of sound.

The flourishing state of Italian violin-making produced a generation of virtuosos and composers. The earliest string compositions that still survive as a vital art are the violin sonatas and *concerti grossi* of Arcangelo Corelli (1653–1713). The excellence of Corelli's works does not consist of novel treatment or daring virtuosity; it resides in the harmonious blending of all factors, in their finely proportioned form and their melodic beauty. Handel, as a young man, had made Corelli's acquaintance in Rome, and how much the Roman master's art impressed him can be clearly perceived in Handel's own violin sonatas and *concerti grossi*, which are in the Corelli tradition but which exceed Corelli's music in creative power.

Several of Corelli's contemporaries are known to violinists

through a few works of special merit. The chamber sonatas of Antonio Veracini (*c.* 1650–*c.* 1710) contain largos of exquisite beauty. Tommaso Vitali (1665–*c.* 1720) is still remembered through his famous *Ciacona*, often played in modern arrangements. The Bolognese master Giuseppe Torelli (1658–1709) claims our attention mainly by his violin concertos with orchestra, the earliest known representatives of this species.

The Venetian master Antonio Vivaldi (1675–1741) influenced Bach as much as Corelli influenced Handel. Bach transcribed for organ a number of Vivaldi's violin concertos. Vivaldi's original works are now available in the scholarly edition of Francesco Malipiero.

Corelli's pupil Pietro Antonio Locatelli (1695–1764) bequeathed to us twelve concertos and twenty-four capriccios. Another pupil of Corelli, Francesco Geminiani (1687–1762) was, like Locatelli, a great representative of progressive Italian violin-playing in foreign countries. Locatelli made Amsterdam his permanent home, while Geminiani settled in London, where he was much admired as a virtuoso, composer, conductor, and teacher. His manual *The Art of Playing on the Violin* holds a prominent place in the didactic literature of music. In his numerous concertos and sonatas for the violin, he anticipated the fugal writing of Bach's famous fugues for solo violin.

Francesco Maria Veracini (1690–1750), nephew of Antonio Veracini, acquired fame in London, Dresden, and Prague. His twelve *Sonate accademiche* contain some of the finest music written for the violin in the eighteenth century.

Guiseppe Tartini (1692–1770) was one of the greatest virtuosos of his time, as well as being a composer, teacher, and theorist. His numerous and fine compositions, comprising some hundred and forty concertos and as many sonatas, have not yet been sufficiently studied and appraised; but his virtuoso piece *Trillo del diavolo* (The Devil's Trill) has endured for two centuries as one of the greatest favorites in the violin repertoire.

As head of the famous Padua school, Tartini had many talented pupils, among whom Pugnani and Nardini were the most eminent. Gateano Pugnani (1731–1798) was highly esteemed in London and Paris, but he was mainly active in Italy. Pietro Nardini (1722–1793) was one of Europe's most outstanding virtuosos. The German poet Christian Schubart describes his art in the following enthusiastic words: "Nardini was raised in the lap of the Graces. The tenderness of his playing cannot possibly be described: every grace note seems to be a declaration of love. He possessed an extraordinary power to awaken the emotions of his listeners." About twenty of Nardini's sonatas exist in print or in manuscript. They contain some of the best music for the violin.

The two most eminent representatives of the French school of violin-playing, Leclair and Viotti, were both disciples of the Italian school. In the chapter on French music it will be shown what a great role Italian instrumental art played in advancing French music for string instruments to the high level attained by Leclair.

The name of Giovanni Battista Viotti (1755–1824) is generally associated with French music, but he was an Italian by birth and education. His great achievement was incorporating all the various trends of violin-playing in Italy and France into a comprehensive modern style, which became the basis of virtuoso playing in the nineteenth century. Though master of all technical resources, he subordinated virtuosity to true expressiveness. The best known of Viotti's compositions is his Concerto No. 22, which ranks with the greatest works in the literature for the instrument.

This rapid survey of Italian achievements in the field of violin-playing and violin composition finds its natural climax in Niccolò Paganini (1782–1840). This phenomenal artist cannot be classified as a follower of any particular school: he was his own model. Strangely enough, he left no disciples of the virtuoso technique for which he was famous. Some of his sensational feats in harmonics and pizzicato have been imitated by such virtuosos as Sarasate, but they have not become legitimate features in the serious literature of the violin. Looking over the violin concertos of Spohr, Beethoven, Mendelssohn, Vieuxtemps, Joachim, Brahms, Bruch, Tchaikovsky, and Saint-Saëns, we find few traces of the influence of Paganini's technical devices. Yet his role is not to be underestimated, for he set a high mark for violin performers of later generations and showed them how to conquer the greatest technical difficulties of the instrument.

Paradoxically, piano technique profited more immediately from Paganini's dazzling virtuosity than did that of the violin. His performances in the capitals of Europe excited musicians to fever pitch. Violinists may have felt unable to compete with him, but pianists and composers, among them Schumann and Liszt, were inspired by his virtuosity and attempted to duplicate his technical feats on the keyboard. Liszt wrote *Paganini Etudes*; Schumann, *Studien nach Capricen von Paganini*; and Brahms, *Paganini Variations*. Among Paganini's own compositions, the twenty-four *Caprices* are the most enduring, and, apart from their virtuosity, their polished form and fine melodic and harmonic qualities give them genuine value.

The Italian contribution to organ technique and composition in the eighteenth century was not as great as it had been a century before. And in the literature for harpsichord, Italy could not match such masters as Couperin and Rameau, Handel and Bach. Two Italian masters, however, considerably advanced the art of clavier playing: Scarlatti and Clementi. Domenico Scarlatti (1685–1757), son of the great Neapolitan master Alessandro Scarlatti (1660–1725), was not his father's equal in universality of production, but in one field he left a rich legacy, for he was the founder of the modern keyboard technique, using such novel devices as crossing of the hands and rapid passage work in sparkling staccato. Muzio Clementi (1752–1832) spent the greater part of his long career in London. One of the most brilliant piano virtuosos of his time, he was a rival of Mozart, and the Emperor Joseph II once arranged a contest between the two in Vienna. Clementi's fame is founded upon his book of piano studies *Gradus ad Parnassum*, a collection of a hundred pieces which have been highly useful to generations of professional pianists.

Another Italian musician, Luigi Cherubini (1760–1842), enjoyed a great reputation in all Europe as a master of the art of composition. It seems more fitting, however, to discuss him in connection with French music, since he spent the most productive years of his life in France.

Among Italian creations in music, oratorio occupies a place of great importance. It originated about 1600 as allegorical opera, adapted to the social conditions of papal Rome. As time went by, oratorio developed its own style, distinct from that of opera. It retained its dramatic character, but the action on stage was left to the listener's imagination. The abandonment of scenery was fortunate in that it encouraged oratorio to become a form of concert music, thus providing more opportunities for choral and instrumental writing. The greatest master of early Italian oratorio was Giacomo Carissimi (1605–1674), who excelled in dramatic effects, ranging from tender melancholy to outbursts of religious fervor.

For a long time the Italian oratorio, using Latin words, was a powerful agency in the struggle of the Catholic church against the rising tide of Protestantism. Composers of the Protestant faith eventually, however, adopted the oratorio themselves and modeled it musically after the Italian prototype. Handel began to write such Italian-type oratorios during his early travels in Italy. Later, the Protestant oratorio chose a new path; it developed in Germany and England into a form of spiritual concert piece. But the creative impulse issuing from Italy was still felt strongly in all these dissident forms.

In the field of opera, the Italian hegemony was absolute for at least two centuries. Originating in Florence about 1600 as a would-be revival of ancient Greek drama, Italian opera soon bewitched the world of music. During the early stages of its development, it was the plaything of the nobility, whose wealth allowed them to maintain the lavish and costly apparatus necessary for operatic productions. No other theatrical art commanded such an extraordinary variety of services: poetry, musical composition, singing, instrumental playing, mimicry, dancing, painting, decorative arts, stage machinery, costumes, and finally plastic arts and architecture. No wonder that such an opulent combination of arts and skills should have produced a luxurious and tremendously impressive spectacle!

Throughout the three and a half centuries of operatic history, the essential features of opera have undergone surprisingly little change. The earliest Florentine operas and those by Monteverdi and his Venetian followers, Francesco Cavalli (1602–1676) and Pietro Antonio Cesti (1623–1669), established the framework of operatic construction that is largely retained today. Now as then, the standard opera has its overture, sinfonia, or prologue, its recitatives and arias, its duets and trios, its ensemble and choral pieces, its ballet music. The libretto usually follows a legend from Greek mythology, Roman antiquity, or the Orient, an episode from the Bible, a fairy tale, or an event in national or local history.

The spectacular success of Italian opera gave rise to a peculiar profession, that of the *castrati* singers in the seventeenth and eighteenth centuries. It was discovered that castration in youth imparted to the male voice a flexibility, charm, and attractive coloring that excelled the natural voices of women. Composers, princely patrons, and the general public all over Europe were fascinated by the beauty of these perversely produced voices, and the best artists among the *castrati* earned fabulous sums of money.

The most famous *castrato* of the seventeenth century was Baldassare Ferri of Perugia (1610–1680). He was in the service of three Polish kings and two German emperors; the art-loving queen of Sweden, Christina, called him to Stockholm, and in Venice he was made a "cavaliere di San Marco."

The fame of the great vocal school of Bologna rests on three singers of the very first rank: Francesco Antonio Pistocchi (1659–1726), Pier Francesco Tosi (1646–1732), and Antonio Bernacchi (1685–1756). Pistocchi, a *castrato* singer of great artistry, gained in his later years even a greater renown as a teacher. Indeed, he is acknowledged to be one of the founders of the *bel canto* method. Tosi, born and educated in Bologna, spent the greater part of his later career in London as an opera singer. For several years he was also active as court composer in Vienna. In the history of vocal art, Tosi is notable as the author of an important treatise on the art of singing entitled *Opinioni de' cantori antichi e moderni* (Bologna, 1723). The book is dedicated to Lord Peterborough, Tosi's devoted friend and benefactor.

Pistocchi's pupil Antonio Bernacchi was a *castrato* singer of wide fame. When Handel in 1729 reorganized the Italian Opera House in London, he engaged Bernacchi as a chief attraction. Among Bernacchi's pupils, Giovanni Carestini (c. 1705–1759) and Francesco Senesino (c. 1680–c. 1750) were the most famous. Carestini was eagerly sought by the great opera houses. The Imperial Opera in Vienna, Handel's London Opera, the Dresden Opera, and the Imperial Opera of St. Petersburg were the principal scenes of Carestini's triumphs. Even more successful was Senesino, who scored one success after another in Handel's Italian Opera House in London, until Handel had to dismiss him for insubordination.

Perhaps the greatest *castrato* singer of all time was Carlo Broschi Farinelli (1705–1782). Phenomenally gifted, he received rigorous training from two great teachers, Bernacchi and Nicola Antonio Porpora. He thus combined in his art the excellencies of the Neapolitan and the Bolognese schools. The Queen of Spain heard him and decided to try a daring experiment with his help. Relying on the irresistible charm of Farinelli's singing, she made him appear before King Philip V, who suffered from melancholy and who refused to attend to his state duties. Farinelli's voice impressed the ailing monarch so much that he regained his zest for life. Farinelli's duty consisted in singing for the King the same four arias every night, from 1737 to 1746, the year of Philip's death. As the new king, Ferdinand VI, had inherited his father's melancholy temperament, Farinelli retained his position as his chief entertainer and counsellor. The Madrid Royal Library possesses a detailed catalogue and description of all the festivities, operas, dances, concerts, and perform- ances of church music arranged by Farinelli at the royal resi- dences. Supported by the resources of the Spanish Court, Fari- nelli assembled brilliant singers of Bernacchi's and Porpora's school, among them, Caffarelli and a galaxy of women singers, including the famous contralto Vittoria Tesi. The Spanish his- torian Arteaga, in his book *Le rivoluzioni del teatro musicale italiano*, writes that Farinelli "brought back all the splendor and magnificence of ancient Greece and revived all the good taste of Athens." After the death of Ferdinand VI in 1759, Farinelli re- tired to Bologna, where he remained until his death in 1782.

Majorano Caffarelli (1703–1783), the only singer who might be regarded as a rival of Farinelli, was likewise a pupil of Por- pora. The story of his life reads like a romance. Rome, Venice, Milan, Naples, Vienna, Paris, London, Lisbon, and Spain were the scenes of his triumphant career. His enormous wealth enabled him to purchase a duchy and thus acquire the title of Duke of Santo Dorato.

The last of the famous group of *castrati* in Bologna was Giro- lamo Crescentini (1762-1846), who evoked the enthusiasm of all Europe for many decades, well into the nineteenth century. Napoleon heard him in Vienna and was so enchanted with his singing that he invited him to Paris, where Crescentini held a privileged position from 1806 to 1812.

A vivid contemporary account of opera in Italy in the eighteenth century is found in the writings of that cultivated English gentleman, Dr. Charles Burney. He knew personally many great masters of opera, composers as well as performers, and his reports of these meetings are fascinating. In 1722 he visited two celebrated Italian operatic stars living in retirement in Vienna: Faustina Bordoni and Vittoria Tesi, and recorded his conversations with them.

Faustina Bordoni was born in 1693 and grew up in Venice, at that time the world's operatic capital. Realizing that in order to compete successfully with the *castrati*, her partners on the stage, a woman had to do more than display her feminine charm, Faustina diligently applied herself to vocal study, and in time became one of the greatest favorites of the opera audiences. In 1724 the Imperial Opera of Vienna paid her a salary of 15,000 florins. Two years later Handel engaged her for London at the still higher salary of two thousand pounds. In London, under Handel's direction, she reached the culminating point of her triumphant career, though it was marred by a scandalous quarrel on the public stage with her chief rival, Francesca Cuzzoni. Back in Venice in 1730, she married Johann Adolf Hasse (1699–1783), a German composer who became an expert in the use of the Italian vocal style and a formidable competitor of the Italians themselves in producing successful Italian operas. Hasse and Faustina settled in Dresden, at the sumptuous court of Augustus II, and for more than thirty years helped maintain the city's reputation as the most brilliant musical center of Germany. After Hasse's retirement the couple resided in Vienna and finally in Venice, where Faustina died in 1781 and Hasse two years later.

Faustina's rival, Francesca Cuzzoni (1700–1770), was small, ugly, and of a disagreeable disposition, a sad contrast to the beautiful and enticing Faustina. But when "the golden lyre" (as the Italians called her) began to sing, her bodily imperfections were quickly forgotten, and warm applause rewarded her art. Her singing was soulful and lyrical, despite her debatable private life. She lost her voice, spent some time in a debtor's prison, and in the last years of her life earned a meager subsistence by selling buttons.

The gallery of bizarre, capricious, adventurous, and immensely gifted prima donnas of eighteenth-century Italian opera would be incomplete without including Vittoria Tesi (1700–1775). When Burney paid a visit to her in 1772 in Vienna, she told the inquisitive English historian some stirring stories from her eventful life, beginning with her marriage to a barber. A great actress on the stage of life as well as the theater, Vittoria Tesi was a dominating personality. It is characteristic that she excelled in the roles of male characters; one of her greatest triumphs was achieved in the part of Achilles.

Very different from Vittoria Tesi was Catterina Gabrielli (1730–1796), daughter of a Roman cook in the service of Prince Gabrielli, who discovered her phenomenal voice, paid for her education, and gave her his name. The great Porpora was one of her teachers; in 1747, at the age of seventeen, she made her successful debut at Lucca. Called to Vienna, she fascinated the Emperor Francis I. The court poet Metastasio gave her instruction in dramatic declamation and fell in love with her, without getting much response. Her amorous adventures were notorious, but Burney called her "the most intelligent and best-bred virtuosa" whom he had ever encountered.

After the decline of Venetian and Roman opera, the leadership in Italian operatic art shifted to Naples. The great Neapolitan school numbers among its representatives such resplendent names as Alessandro Scarlatti, Leonardo Leo, Porpora, Stradella, Durante, Traetta, Piccini, Jommelli, Sacchini, Pergolesi, Paesiello, Cimarosa. A number of German composers adopted in part the precepts of the Neapolitan school of opera: Reinhard Keiser, Handel, Gluck (at least in his earlier works), Hasse, Graun, even Mozart. To say that at least a thousand Neapolitan operas were heard all over Europe, from Naples to Stockholm, from Paris and London to St. Petersburg, would be no exaggeration.

In the field of Italian musical scholarship, the name of Padre Martini (1706–1784) stands high. Students from all parts of Europe flocked to Bologna in order to benefit from his teaching. His historical and theoretical works have left a profound imprint on musicology.

Neapolitan opera could not have achieved its spectacular triumphs without the collaboration of the master librettist, Pietro Antonio Metastasio (1698–1782). His numerous dramatic poems and texts for cantatas and oratorios were so effective that eighteenth-century opera composers preferred his librettos to any others. Metastasio had a profound understanding of operatic music and the cantabile style. He was familiar with the demands not only of the public but also of the composers and the singers, and he gave due consideration to all of them. For the public, he invented stirring stories full of alluring intrigue. For the composers, he wrote lyric poetry of great beauty, redolent of fine imagery; his recitative sections are couched in an easily flowing narrative style, dramatically leading to a climax. His melodious verses, his meters and rhythms, were carefully chosen so as to be suitable for singing. Modern critics regret the lack in Metastasio's librettos of psychological analysis of the dramatic characters. It must be remembered, however, that Neapolitan opera never pretended to be more than playful entertainment, even when the librettos were tragic, and never aimed at realism in the modern sense. Neapolitan opera portrays conflicts not between individuals but between various *affetti* (sentiments), expressed by the voices of the participating characters.

The music of Neapolitan opera revolved around the recitative and the aria, particularly the so-called *da capo* aria. The recitative was often treated in a conventional manner; only very great masters like Handel or Gluck and "reformers" like Jommelli and Traetta elevated the recitative to an expressive and constructive factor of dramatic import. While a growth in expressiveness is noted in the evolution of operatic recitative from 1700 to the time of Mozart, no similar progress is to be found in the aria.

Within its narrow esthetic confines, and with its reliance on the art of *bel canto*, the form of the Neapolitan aria became stabilized as a worthy successor to the Italian madrigal of the preceding century.

The outward form of the *da capo* aria survives in the ternary song form of the nineteenth century. Its formula, *a-b-a*, denotes a first section, followed by an intermediate section having a new theme, after which *a* is repeated. We find the formula applied in countless works by nineteenth-century masters, in Chopin's nocturnes and impromptus, in Schubert's *Moments musicaux*, in the intermezzi of Brahms. But the spirit of the Italian aria eludes instrumental music. Closely tied to *bel canto* virtuosity, to the *concertante* style, and to the *basso continuo* system, it evolved its own peculiar type of melody and accompaniment. The sublime grace and elegance of which this style is capable can be observed in the matchless arias from Handel's operas.

Operatic arias, as they were sung then, cannot be adequately reproduced in modern editions, because much of the music, especially in the *da capo* sections, was improvised by the singer. Italian singers excelled in the art of improvising ornamental passages and brilliant cadenzas. Such practices are, of course, quite unacceptable in more recent vocal music, which does not admit the slightest deviation from the written notes.

Italian operatic art entered a new phase in the second half of the eighteenth century with the so-called "reform" of Neapolitan opera, when new aims and methods were sought by imitating the French operatic art. In their disparate ways, Tommaso Traetta (1727–1779), Niccolò Jommelli (1714–1774), Nicola Piccini (1728–1800), and Gluck were the principal representatives of this reform movement.

The dominance of Italian opera in the eighteenth century was manifested in two ways. Italian opera composers and singers were exported to foreign countries, where they established permanent Italian colonies; and foreign musicians were sent to Italy to study opera. These two processes of interpenetration required a century for their fruition. The first offspring of Italian opera was French opera, set up in Paris by the Italian-born musician Lully. The French offspring was the most independent of all; it soon broke away from motherly supervision and established a national style. It was not until the middle of the eighteenth century that Italian opera had regained lost ground in France and succeeded in reaching a compromise with its rebellious Parisian progeny. In the works of Gluck and Piccini, assimilating both Italian and French operatic styles, we find such a compromise.

In Germany, Italian opera was established throughout the seventeenth and eighteenth centuries at the numerous royal and princely courts, and it flourished there as late as 1830. Vienna, Dresden, Berlin, Munich, and Stuttgart were the principal strongholds of Italian tradition and taste. Isolated attempts at creating a national German opera were made in Hamburg. But in spite of the labors of Reinhard Keiser (1674–1739), a prodigiously gifted Hamburg composer, the attractions of Italian opera proved too strong, and it soon became sovereign there. To gain a hearing, German dramatic composers accepted the artistic tutelage of Italian masters and wrote operas in the Italian language and style. Among composers of German culture who wrote Italian operas were Hasse in Dresden, Graun in Berlin, Handel in London, Gluck in Vienna and Paris, and Mozart. Such was the triumphant power of Italian opera!

Yet this conquest of Germanic nations by the Italians carried in itself the seed of dissolution. Artistic proximity to the Italian masters enabled German musicians to learn their secrets and enhance their art. After 1775, German oratorios, chamber music, and symphonies completely eclipsed Italian works in these genres. In the nineteenth century German composers challenged the Italians even in opera.

The opera stage of the first half of the nineteenth century was dominated by Rossini, Donizetti, and Bellini. These three masters acquired their international fame when they took up residence in Paris and were given a national colony in the Théâtre des Italiens. This turn of events was all the more remarkable in that elsewhere in Europe Italian opera was declining. By 1806 the Berlin Italian Opera had disbanded; Munich followed in 1826, Vienna in 1828, and Dresden — the strongest outpost of Italian opera in Germany — terminated its Italian opera company in 1832.

Gioacchino Rossini (1792–1868) wrote more than fifty operas, but among them only *The Barber of Seville* has survived every change in taste and is acknowledged all over the musical world as an unsurpassed masterpiece. One may safely predict that the future will not alter this verdict. After a period of astonishing creativity, Rossini finished his career as a dramatic composer with *William Tell*, heard for the first time at the Paris Opera in 1829, when Rossini was only thirty-seven years old. He was to live another forty years, but during this long period he produced nothing but a few works of sacred music and some minor instrumental pieces.

Rossini prided himself on having regained for vocal art its legitimate place on the stage. Yet even in this special field, his influence on later music was slight. He formed no school. His masterpiece, *The Barber of Seville*, was the last and most brilliant flower of the old Italian *opera buffa*, based on the still older *commedia dell'arte*. Only in the twentieth century did the Italian-German composer Ermanno Wolf-Ferrari (1876–1948) succeed in rejuvenating the Rossinian *buffo* style in his charming operas *Le donne curiose* and *Il segreto di Susanna*.

Gaetano Donizetti (1797–1848) can be compared to Rossini in prodigious facility of composition. In his short life he wrote more music than Rossini. Of his many operas, *Lucia di Lammermoor* is the most popular; its famous sextet is universally admired as a model of effective vocal writing. Another opera by Donizetti, *L'Elisir d'amore*, is frequently performed. His comic opera *La Fille du régiment* was brought out in Paris with great success. Its principal part has provided the most famous singers of the operatic stage—from Jenny Lind, Sontag, and Patti to Lily Pons—with an especially grateful opportunity to display their vocal agility, charm of appearance, and vivacity of mimic action.

Like Mozart, Schubert, Chopin, and Mendelssohn, Vincenzo Bellini (1801–1835) was a composer of precocious talent, whose life was cut short before he was forty years of age. Of his operas at least three became great favorites: *La Sonnambula* (Milan, 1831), *Norma* (Milan, 1831); and *I Puritani* (Paris, 1835). The philosopher of pessimism, Schopenhauer, held a high opinion of Bellini. He described *Norma* as "a true model of tragic order of the motives, tragic progress of the action, and tragic development."

As we consider the vast accomplishment of Italian musicians, beginning with the seventeenth century and extending over a period of three hundred years, we find no sign of the exhaustion of their creative energy. The Italian achievements are not, however, made perceptible to us by any homogeneous mass of immortal works universally cherished and continually performed, like, for instance, the music of Bach; their value consists rather in their spirit of innovation and their vitality.

It is worthy of notice that Italian music has been less affected by foreign influences than has the music of other countries. Indeed, there is only one period in its history when Italian music was dominated by alien forces: the supremacy of Netherlandish music (1450–1550). Since then, Italy has been free from outside domination. All through the seventeenth and eighteenth centuries she was little affected by musical developments in France, Germany, England, or Spain. Not even such universal geniuses as Rameau, Gluck, Handel, Bach, Haydn, Mozart, and Beethoven could swerve the Italian masters from their clearly marked paths; nor did nineteenth-century romanticism have any repercussions in Italy.

Rossini, Bellini, and Donizetti dominated Italian operatic art in the first half of the nineteenth century; Giuseppe Verdi, almost entirely by himself, the second half; and at the threshold of the twentieth century, Puccini, Mascagni, and Leoncavallo brought a new idea into Italian opera by creating the school of *verismo*, the Italian counterpart of operatic realism. Giacomo Puccini (1858–1924) contributed to the Italian stage several masterpieces that occupy an honored place next to the creations of Verdi. Indeed, Puccini's *Tosca*, with its dramatic story from the Napoleonic period, is a worthy successor to Verdi's *Aïda*, with its legendary Egyptian setting; while Puccini's *Madama Butterfly*, bringing to the stage an exotic story from far-away Japan, is in its theme of betrayal in love close to Verdi's sentimental classic *La Traviata*.

Pietro Mascagni (1863–1945) became famous overnight when his opera *Cavalleria Rusticana* won the prize in a publisher's competition; its success was instantaneous and the little opera has maintained its place in the repertoire. Mascagni never succeeded in duplicating his initial success; his subsequent operas were, relatively speaking, failures.

Ruggiero Leoncavallo (1858–1919) was, like Mascagni, destined to be known as the composer of only one successful opera, *Pagliacci*, which is often given with *Cavalleria Rusticana* in a single performance. Both operas treat the subject of tragic love in humble surroundings. These operas established the school of *verismo*.

The instinctive Italian flair for opera is demonstrated once more in the extraordinary success of the modernistic operas by Gian-Carlo Menotti (born in 1911). Menotti, however, has done his mature work in America and is therefore to be regarded as an American composer.

Early in the twentieth century, Italian composers began to pay more attention to symphonic music, and their art gradually assumed a cosmopolitan character. Among the masters of this new Italian music the most significant are Alfredo Casella (1883–1947) and Ottorino Respighi (1879–1936). Casella revived the spirit of Italian art in a modern guise in such works as *Paganiniana* and *Scarlattiana*. But he was also one of the early modernists in Italian music. During his many years of residence in Paris, he experienced the influence of impressionism; at the same time he introduced into his works the most advanced techniques of polytonality and atonality. As a musical scholar and a pedagogue, Casella exercised profound influence on the younger generation of Italian composers.

Ottorino Respighi studied with Rimsky-Korsakov in Russia and became entranced with the possibilities of coloristic orchestral effects. His symphonic tetralogy *Pines of Rome* presents a magnificent panorama of the Roman countryside. A companion piece, *Fountains of Rome* gives an equally colorful tone picture of the capital city.

Francesco Malipiero (born in 1882) and Ildebrando Pizzetti (born in 1880) represent the modern school of composition in Italy but utilize a less agressive idiom than that of Alfredo Casella. Malipiero is the author of symphonies, operas, and chamber music in which classical forms are clearly delineated. Besides his own works, Malipiero has earned the respect of music scholars everywhere for his fine editions of Italian musical classics. Pizzetti is animated by the spirit of lyric poetry. His operas and mystery plays establish a certain kinship with the Florentine beginnings of the art of opera. He has written a great deal of sacred music as well as numerous vocal and instrumental compositions in a modernistic manner.

Among the younger Italian composers of the twentieth century, Goffredo Petrassi and Luigi Dallapiccola (both born in 1904) have acquired considerable renown through frequent performances at international music festivals. Petrassi is a student of Casella, and in his music preserves classical ideas within a framework of modern technique. Dallapiccola has followed a path thus far untrodden by other Italian musicians. He is fascinated by the expressionist school, particularly Schönberg, and has adopted the twelve-tone system of composition. His opera *The Prisoner*, full of anguished chromaticism, has had numerous successful performances in Italy and elsewhere.

Shortly before World War I, Italy became the playground of a movement known as *futurismo*, of which Marinetti was the ideological spokesman and Luigi Russolo (1885–1947) the leading composer. In his "orchestra of noises" Russolo attempted to represent the modern age in sounds. This movement, however, proved infertile and quite alien to the Italian spirit of practical innovation.

6

Germany, Austria, and Switzerland

Germany and Austria

The contribution of Germany to music is immense. Indeed, most instrumental compositions performed anywhere in the world today are of German origin. The works of Handel, Bach, Haydn, Mozart, Beethoven, Schubert, Mendelssohn, Schumann, Wagner, Brahms, and Richard Strauss, even quantitatively speaking, occupy an area in the empire of music far greater than that taken by composers from the rest of the world. It is surprising, therefore, that of all musical nations Germany was the last to develop polyphonic art.

At a time when the Paris school of composition enjoyed international renown, when England had reached mastery in canon, when Italy created the highly advanced and ingenious *ars nova*, Germany had nothing of importance to contribute to polyphonic music; only in the field of unaccompanied melodic music had Germany been proficient in earlier times, from the tenth to the thirteenth century. The quasi-ecclesiastical form, the sequence, was the pride of German music in those times; the famous monk Notker of the Monastery of St. Gall in Switzerland was the greatest exponent, if not the originator, of the sequence. In the twelfth and thirteenth centuries, the German minnesingers produced remarkable specimens of amorous poetry that might well stand comparison with the graceful and lovely songs of the French and Provençal troubadours. The emotional German folk songs of the fourteenth century, full of genuine sentiment, are quite distinct from the French and Italian tunes and also from the English and Dutch popular melodies of the same period. In the classic book of Rochus von Liliencron, *Deutsches Leben im Volkslied um 1530*, and in the collection of tunes edited by Franz Magnus Böhme in his *Altdeutsches Liederbuch*, many of these fine melodies are faithfully notated.

In the sixteenth century, this valuable raw material of folk song assumed great significance. By then German musicians, at first slow in picking up the subtleties of contrapuntal complexity, had finally succeeded in learning the art of polyphony from the great Dutch masters. Heinrich Isaak, Ludwig Senfl, Heinrich Finck, and many other German masters made use of the magnificent melodic material of German folk song in their polyphonic arrangements of the tunes. These pioneer works were also to serve as models for the revival of German folk song and part song during the romantic period.

Heinrich Finck (1445–1527), one of the leading German masters of his time, was for many years director of the Royal Polish Chapel in Cracow and was later in the service of the German emperors Maximilian and Ferdinand. Among his part songs (printed in 1536 by Hieronymus Formschneyder in Nuremberg under the title *Schöne auserlesene Lieder des hochberühmten Heinrich Finckens*), the four-part "Wach auf, mein höchster Hort" is a particularly fine example of the passionate German style. The tenor melody was originally a folk song, which has been considerably modified and made more expressive. Evidently the plain tune was not emotional enough to satisfy the composer. German depth of feeling, especially when expressing the pangs of love, is here revealed in a striking manner. The lover not only sings of his love, he cries it out. His agitation is suggested by the rhythmic and melodic unrest of the tenor part, by the continual change of meter: 4/4, 3/4, 3/2, 6/4, 5/4, and by intentional deviation from a balanced melodic outline. The collective mood of folk song has been turned into a personal utterance. The singer is not a representative of "the lover" as a class; he is a particular person (perhaps the composer himself) passionately voicing his anguish. The coloratura passages overflow with feeling; the high tones are hurled out with explosive force. The other three parts imitate the tenor; they display the same tendency toward high-pitched agitation and rhythmic variety. At the same time, a complicated contrapuntal texture imparts dramatic intensity to this dialogue, which is exciting in its variety of vocal enunciation but which preserves true unity of sentiment. The art of contrapuntal imitation is mastered here in a supreme degree: every part is saturated with emotional expressiveness and at the same time linked thematically with all the other parts. In this ingenious and animated tonal organism, each particle fits perfectly into the general pattern.

The greatest of the old German song composers was Ludwig Senfl (1490–1543), a Swiss musician from Zurich. He was a pupil of Heinrich Isaak, from whom he learned the art of combining simple folk songs contrapuntally so as to obtain perfect harmony without altering the authentic character of the melody. This skill is demonstrated in Senfl's simultaneous setting of two different folk songs: "O Elslein, liebes Elslein" in the soprano; "Es taget vor dem Walde," in the tenor. The two other parts fill in the harmony, not with homophonic chords but with specially written countermelodies. Four different melodies are thus heard together. The song differs from typical Netherlandish polyphonic writing in that imitation is not used.

Folk music suitable for ecclesiastical purposes was used by Martin Luther, who was intent on giving his newly founded church appropriate music of its own, different in form and spirit from the Gregorian chant of the Catholic church. The German chorale, as shaped by Luther, became the cornerstone of Protestant church music. The magnificent German chorale tunes are still generally performed in many Protestant churches, arranged in countless motets and cantatas as well as in chorale preludes for the organ. An immense German literature of these compositions has been accumulated in the great European libraries; the many volumes of the monumental *Denkmäler deutscher Tonkunst* contain numerous examples of such works.

Among the illustrious masters of the Lutheran chorale, organ music, and German popular song in the first half of the seventeenth century, Michael Praetorius, Johann Hermann Schein, and Samuel Scheidt are in the forefront.

Michael Praetorius (1571–1621) was eminent both as a composer and a theorist. Using Latin and German texts, he wrote thousands of sacred songs, remarkable for the variety of harmonic accompaniment. They are now available in a twenty-volume edition of his works; this edition also contains a reprint of his encyclopedic work *Syntagma musicum,* which gives a compendious account of the state of music in his time.

Johann Hermann Schein (1586–1630) enjoyed great fame as a composer of German songs corresponding in their spirit to the Italian madrigal. His bold polyphonic and harmonic writing marked a transition to the Bach era.

Samuel Scheidt (1587–1654) was the originator of the German chorale prelude for the organ, with ornate variations, as presented in his three-volume collection entitled *Tabulatura nova.* Schein and Scheidt paved the way for the advent of the great Heinrich Schütz; together, they are often referred to as the "three S's" of German church music before Bach.

From the very inception of national art in Germany, one peculiarity of the German musical genius was manifest: the distinctive ability to absorb the best from other countries, to assimilate foreign products and combine them with the native product so intimately that the result has thoroughly German qualities but at the same time appeals to other nations. German music at its best is both national and cosmopolitan, an apparent paradox that can be historically substantiated. The term "eclectic," often used in a derogatory sense, does not apply to this peculiar method of assimilation. It manifests artistic activity on a much higher plane. The world of music sent into Germany many rivers from various directions; these tributaries were there collected into one vast stream of music, which poured out of Germany and traversed many countries — even whole continents — carrying to foreign shores a new wealth of music, German to the core, and yet cosmopolitan in spirit. Neither French nor Italian music possesses assimilative power comparable to this German art of absorption and integration.

In the last decades of the sixteenth century, young German musicians habitually made a pilgrimage to Italy, a journey that was the crowning event of their youth. Among the earliest German students to go to "the blessed land beyond the Alps" was Hans Leo Hassler from Nuremberg (1564–1612). He became a pupil of Andrea Gabrieli in Venice and a friend of Andrea's nephew, Giovanni Gabrieli. Upon his return home, Hassler brought the art of the Gabrielis to Germany, where it throve and produced a whole literature of German music of a similar type. Hassler's great accomplishment is an extensive collection of part songs entitled *Lustgart neuer teutscher Gesäng.* This "pleasure garden of new German songs" possesses a genuine national flavor. Yet its ingredients are for the most part Italian, taken over from the Italian madrigal and other forms of vocal music.

Hassler's songs, though derived from Italian sources, are a revival of the old German minnesongs of the thirteenth century, in modernized form. To the old melodic substance he applied the new Italian formal elegance. The results are a quickened melodic pace, a vivacity and expressiveness of declamation hitherto foreign to German music, an ease and grace of motion that are very different from the old characteristically German qualities of rigidity, earnestness, and ponderous humor. For all its acquired Italian traits, Hassler's music has no trace of affectation. It is thoroughly German in sentiment, but its appeal is cosmopolitan. Though Hassler also wrote excellent motets and madrigals, the most enduring and valuable part of his work are his many German part songs, easily accessible in numerous modern editions.

A striking feature of Hassler's melody is his admirable declamation of the text, which reminds us of the best masters of dramatic music. Observe, for instance, in the four-part "Ach, Fräulein zart," the leading melody in the soprano — no longer a folk song but a new melody, expressly invented for its text. Note how admirably its accents and inflections express the emotional state of a youthful, affectionate, but modest lover. What charming amiability in the opening, with its light eighth-notes in 3/4 time! Then the tone changes; the honest youth reproaches his fickle girl, who, it seems, played with him for a while and then turned her attention elsewhere. The clouds gather in this agitated section, which changes from the principal key of A major to the paler E minor. Then the sky brightens, A major and E major return radiantly, and the hope rises in the heart of our lover that he may yet regain the favor of his lady.

While Hassler, back in his native land, was busily utilizing what he had learned in Venice, another young German musician of superlative talents was spending several years in Venice as a pupil of Giovanni Gabrieli — Heinrich Schütz (1585–1672). He, too, became enraptured with Italian dramatic music. While under its powerful spell, he wrote the first German opera, *Dafne* (the music of which is unfortunately lost), and then he devoted himself exclusively to vocal composition.

Despite his basic Italian technique, Schütz's music remains profoundly German. The complete edition of his works compiled by Philipp Spitta, the famous Bach biographer, makes the study of his compositions comparatively convenient. The Spitta edition contains hundreds of motet-like pieces in the *Cantiones sacrae* and the *Geistliche Chormusik*. The three volumes of *Symphoniae sacrae* and the nearly five hundred pages of the

Psalmen Davids constitute some of the loftiest attainments in religious music.

Schütz's dramatic tendency is often revealed in his music. One of the most striking pieces of his *Symphoniae sacrae*, "Saul, Saul, was verfolgst du mich?" is a dramatice scene of great power. The brief text tells of the conversion of Saul. He hears a mysterious voice from heaven: "Saul, Saul, why persecutest thou Me?" The echo device is here used with great art. The simple triad motive starts very softly in the basses and rises higher at every repetition until it is heard resounding from all sides with tremendous power. Just as quickly, however, the question vanishes in a double echo. For this imaginative piece Schütz uses a six-part main chorus, two four-part supplementary choruses, an organ, and two trumpets. Between the choral sections are interpolated shorter episodes to the words: "It is hard for thee to kick against the pricks." The culmination is reached toward the close, and then the tenor voice, in a series of trumpet-like calls, forces itself through the mass of other voices that again fade away in a double echo.

In the *Psalms of David*, Schütz writes with a sublimity and solemnity worthy of the prophets of the Old Testament. Of all Christian composers, Schütz by intuition comes closest to the old Hebrew spirit, notwithstanding the thoroughly German character of his music. In this power of recreating pre-Christian religious expression, Schütz surpasses even Bach.

His psalm "Wie lieblich sind deine Wohnungen" is one of the most enchanting choral works extant. After an idyllic, lyric opening in madrigal style, the music becomes exalted as the text speaks of the glory of God. Still more elevated is the section "Herr Gott Zebaoth, höre mein Gebet." In psalmodic fauxbourdon recitation the music rises, as it were, in three terraces, from C minor to D major to E flat major. One thinks of a multitude of humble people, worshipping the majesty of God — an overpowering impression!

When we come to the eighteenth century, the German power

of assimilation is evident in the music of the great master Handel. Germany, Italy, England, and France contributed largely to his art; he was cosmopolitan to a degree that had not been equaled since Orlando di Lasso. His music was rooted in German soil, but it was warmed by an Italian sun and nourished by English culture. All three countries influenced Handel's art; it is scarcely possible to find out by analysis where its exact center of gravity is situated. Though his personality reveals mainly German traits, his music is thoroughly cosmopolitan, able to claim citizenship equally in Germany, Italy, and England. Its chief geographic connection, however, is with London, and more detailed remarks on him will therefore be found in the chapter on English music.

The art of Johann Sebastian Bach, on the other hand, was a compound of German, French, and Italian features, in a sort of chemical solution whose ingredients can be separated and identified to some extent by a thorough analysis. Bach's keyboard suites were the German counterpart of the brilliant and highly artistic French suites of Couperin and Rameau. Bach's sonatas and concertos were set in Italian forms. He affixed the title *Italienisches Konzert* to one of his most inspired works, and he did not disdain to call one of his finest keyboard collections of music *French Suites*.

Bach's cantatas stemmed from the Italian form, but they transformed its elegance and lightness into religious profundity. The transparent clearness and graceful motion inherited from Italy counteracted in Bach's music the Germanic tendency toward prolixity.

In his organ compositions especially, Bach shows a universality without parallel. He unites the principles of the Roman school, of the French organ school, and also of the Venetian school. All these varied and specialized principles were integrated and enhanced by Bach.

The *Well-tempered Clavichord*, the *St. John* and *St. Matthew* Passions, the Grand Mass in B minor, the Brandenburg Concertos, and *The Art of Fugue* all testify to Bach's amazing capacity of absorbing the best from the national schools of European music.

In spite of the universality of his music, Bach's fame during his lifetime was only local, confined mainly to Leipzig and to Protestant northern Germany. Only half a dozen of his works appeared in print while he was still living; he never wrote any operas that might have carried his name to distant places; he never traveled abroad or maintained close personal relations with important men in other countries. Moreover, a revolutionary change of taste in European music occurred just at the time of his death, in 1750. The practice of *basso continuo* was abandoned; the fugal style and polyphonic music went out of fashion. The new homophonic style cultivated popular melodies based on dances and folk song; step by step, the sonata was evolving, with its two contrasting themes and with its dramatic features in the so-called development section. All this was diametrically opposed to Bach's practice.

Bach's son Karl Philipp Emanuel (1714–1788), a significant composer in his own right, played the role of connecting link between the polyphonic style of his father and the new sonata style. He also edited a large collection of his father's four-part chorale settings, gathered from some two hundred cantatas and the great Passions. The *Well-tempered Clavichord*, not yet published, circulated in manuscript copies among a small group of the initiated. Beethoven, as a boy, made a sensation by his playing of J. S. Bach's preludes and fugues.

About 1800 Karl Friedrich Zelter (1758–1832) became the dominating musical personality in Berlin. He had inherited the Bach tradition from his teacher J. F. Fasch, and, as conductor of the Berlin Singakademie, he began performing Bach cantatas from manuscript. In the meantime, an invaluable collection of Bach's autograph scores, which had been in the possession of Karl Philipp Emanuel Bach in Hamburg, were acquired by the Berlin Royal Library. There, young Mendelssohn came across the autograph score of the *St. Matthew Passion*. His enthusiasm for this magnificent music was great; he conducted the *St.*

Matthew Passion in 1829, exactly one hundred years after Bach had written it.

The sensation caused by Mendelssohn's discovery led to a Bach revival and to the founding of the Bach Society, for the purpose of collecting and publishing all of Bach's works. As volume after volume of this monumental edition appeared, Bach's genius was finally recognized by all. The German-speaking countries, Holland, Scandinavia, and England, became the Bach countries par excellence; but in France, Italy, and Russia, the master has never acquired the popularity of Mozart or Beethoven.

A generation after Bach we find a similar cosmopolitan spirit in Gluck's operas, which integrate the Italian, French, and German styles in dramatic music. With Gluck, German music acquired for the first time the international reputation that had been denied to it for so long. After having for two centuries nurtured itself on the best products of foreign countries, German music in turn became the preceptor of Europe. The symphonies of Franz Josef Haydn began to be played and admired not only in Vienna and Berlin but also in Paris and Amsterdam; and finally England called that modest composer from his Hungarian retreat to London and honored him as a great teacher and interpreter of continental music. Haydn attained this celebrity by virtue of the international character of his music, which ingeniously utilized the latest aspects of the Italian and French styles.

The music of Haydn marks a turning point. Behind him lay the limitless expanse of the baroque and rococo styles and the majestic landscape of Bach's great art. Before him was a narrow path leading through an agreeable but unexceptional scene of meadows, little streams, and peaceful villages and towns. Talented composers like Johann Stamitz, Anton Filtz, and Franz Xaver Richter had been the first to follow the new path, which around 1770 led to its first flowering meadow. The city of Mannheim in the Rhenish Palatinate (then a part of Bavaria) became the seat of a new school of symphonic composition, radically different from the compositions of Bach.

Haydn did not choose, as Bach and Handel had chosen, to

accept contemporary forms and to continue and perfect them. He was interested in the novel experiments in orchestral dynamics made by the famous Mannheim Orchestra. The Mannheim procedures appealed to Haydn all the more because he was a professional *Kapellmeister*, having led Prince Esterhazy's orchestra for thirty years. Thanks to this experience, he became the greatest orchestral composer of his time, surpassing all others in variety, wealth, novelty, and brilliance. To Haydn even more than to Gluck, we owe the modern method of idiomatic writing for string, wood-wind, and brass instruments. To Bach, instruments had been little different from the members of a polyphonic choral group, with the soprano, alto, tenor, and bass registers. A flute, a violin, and a trumpet were to Bach virtually undifferentiated members of the soprano section. To Haydn, these three instruments possessed distinct sonorities, highly individual in effect and in technical treatment. The older polyphonic style tended to equalize the amount of melodic material given to each instrumental section. The Mannheim school rejected equal treatment and divided the orchestra into principal parts, which carried the dominating melody (preferably a solo part), and subordinate accompanying parts.

Such homophonic simplicity threatened to degenerate into tedious uniformity. This danger could be avoided only by increasing the melodic variety and by utilizing the differing sonorities that had been revealed through differential treatment of instruments. Haydn excelled in both respects. His melodies were popular but at the same time novel in rhythm and sentiment. The main feature of the Mannheim style consisted in sudden changes of melodic expression — pouring into a single phrase a variety of sentiments. Haydn took over from the Mannheim school this new manner of melodic treatment, although his superiority to the Mannheim musicians is evidenced by his interpolation of highly developed polyphonic episodes into the homophonic simplicity of the music. Mozart in turn learned this style from Haydn, and Beethoven from both Haydn and Mozart, dramatizing it still further by sudden accents, contrasts, and powerful climaxes.

Haydn's second great achievement is the creation of the classic style of string quartet, which became the cornerstone of chamber music until the time of Brahms and even later. The freshness, animation, and melodic charm of Haydn's eighty-four quartets, plus his peculiar quaintness and humor, all contributed to the formation of a musical style never surpassed in attractiveness and expressiveness.

Soon the fame of Haydn spread abroad. In the 1770's some of his symphonies, and others of the Mannheim school, were applauded in the Paris Concerts Spirituels, one of the most important institutions in the international exchange of outstanding musical compositions. A good many of Haydn's works were printed in Germany, France, Holland, and England. Some symphonies came out in Paris as early as 1766 and 1771. Thus one may readily understand why the London music lovers were eager to invite so famous a musician. Until his sixtieth year Haydn had never left his native district, which included lower Austria and Hungary. The two trips to London (1791 and 1794) are as important for the progress of music in England as for Haydn's own art. With his twelve new "London" symphonies arose the most advanced and brilliant orchestral art of the eighteenth century, thus setting a new standard for English taste and production. Haydn also profited immensely from the best that England had to offer: the choral art of Purcell and the magnificent Handel oratorios.

In his two oratorios *The Creation* and *The Seasons*, Haydn showed superlatively well what he had learned in England about choral treatment, and he combined with that knowledge his matchless orchestral mastery. These oratorios became models for German choral works of the nineteenth century. The immediate international success of *The Creation* is without parallel in the annals of music; not even the most celebrated Italian operas had so speedy an acclamation. The score was hardly finished when ten Viennese noblemen paid Haydn the sum of seven hundred ducats for the music. They also paid the expenses of the *première* in March 1799, at the Vienna National Theater. The first English performances took place in London and Dublin in 1800. Of the numerous other performances, the one at the Paris Opera by two hundred and fifty players and singers on December 24, 1800 is worthy of special notice, on account of the unique honors bestowed on Haydn. The participants ordered a golden medal bearing his portrait sent to him, with a long letter signed by all two hundred and fifty. A few lines from this letter may be quoted here in translation: "The artists of the Paris Opera, assembled to perform the immortal work, *The Creation*, by the celebrated Haydn, and moved by great admiration for his genius, beg him to accept as a token of their respect and enthusiasm this medal, which has been struck in his honor."

What was said above about Haydn's use of cosmopolitan, Italian and French, elements is true also of Wolfgang Amadeus Mozart. Though Mozart was nurtured in a Germanic tradition, he must be regarded as a great exponent of Italian music, excelling the Italians themselves in Italian opera and instrumental music. In fact, the outstanding feature of his art is the blending of the essential ingredients of both German and Italian music, not in a pale hybrid product, but in an enchanting and durable form. Mozart's German-Italian style is agreeably seasoned with an occasional dash of French spice.

The most penetrating appreciation of Mozart's genius was offered by that great musician Ferruccio Busoni. In 1906, the hundred and fiftieth anniversary of Mozart's birth, Busoni published in the Berlin newspaper *Lokal Anzeiger* a series of thirty-five aphorisms on Mozart, which throw light on the many facets of his sparkling art. Here are some of Busoni's illuminating aphorisms, with commentary.

1. "Mozart is the most perfect specimen of musical genius ever known."

This is indeed the first point that strikes anyone familiar with music history. Has there ever lived a musician who equaled Mozart in wealth of ideas, in melodic invention, in emotional appeal, and dramatic genius? Mozart wrote music of every category, and whatever he touched became in his hands a finished achievement of the first rank, unsurpassable in its genre. In his operas, symphonies, chamber music, and concertos, he enriched the world with more works of permanent value than any other composer, not even excepting Bach and Beethoven. Casting a rapid glance at the illustrious names of the universally recognized geniuses — Josquin de Près, Palestrina, Orlando di Lasso, Monteverdi, Heinrich Schütz, Purcell, Handel, Bach, Haydn, Beethoven, Schubert, Mendelssohn, Schumann, Chopin, Berlioz, Wagner, Liszt, and Verdi — we are bound to conclude that not one of these venerable masters can claim for himself a rank equal to that of Mozart, who is all the more remarkable because his phenomenal musical treasures were produced in the brief lifetime of thirty-five years (1756–1791).

2. "To him a pure musician looks up enraptured and disarmed."

A pure musician is the one for whom music means more than anything else, who lives in and for music. Such a man looks up to Mozart enraptured because in this music he perceives the feeling of happiness, a celestial bliss and untarnished purity. The enraptured musician is disarmed because, in the face of genius, by the grace of God, he feels no shame in acknowledging Mozart's superiority, so that any possible feeling of professional jealousy is smothered at once. Mozart stands alone, in a class all by himself. The greater the musician contemplating Mozart's art, the more he feels himself disinclined to enter into combat with so elemental a musical power. All musicians possessing true insight agree in exalting Mozart, and not even the greatest among them ever uttered an irreverent sentiment against him. To do so would not only show a lamentable lack of judgment but would constitute musical sacrilege. Musicians have criticized

Beethoven, Schumann, Wagner, and Liszt, but no one ever lifted a finger against Mozart.

3. "He finds without seeking, and does not seek that which cannot be found."

A distinction is often drawn between music that sounds natural and music that sounds labored; the former description is commonly applied to folk music, the latter to pretentious art music. Mozart's music sounds natural to popular masses ignorant of artistic problems, and may be erroneously regarded as having no other aim than to satisfy the unexacting demands of an unpretentious listener. For the connoisseur, however, it is full of challenge. It is not problematic music; it solves all its problems with apparent ease and elegance. Mozart always "finds" the effect he needs, but his scores never reveal the effort of "seeking," for that was done before the composition was started. The total absence of a sense of effort imparts to Mozart's music an aura of classical perfection.

It has been said that Mozart as an opera composer belongs to the Neapolitan school, whose outstanding masters were Traetta, Piccini, Jommelli, Paesiello, Cimarosa, and others. The family likeness of Mozart's arias to theirs is evident to every student of the Neapolitan opera. In fact, if we heard one of these Italian arias separately, we might mistake it for Mozart's. But what a difference, when we place a whole act of such an Italian opera beside an act of *Le nozze di Figaro* or *Don Giovanni!* Mozart's genius becomes manifest in the distinctiveness of his melodies: they are not types, but sound as though created by the character who sings the aria rather than by the composer.

Amorous developments, central in all dramatic works, are treated by Mozart with a clairvoyance and psychological soundness never duplicated in the history of opera. How sharply differentiated are the characters in *Le nozze di Figaro!* The fickle Count, who discovers his real self only when he finds himself the dupe of his own schemes; the shrewd and alert Figaro; the amiable and amorous youth Cherubino; the Countess, a gentlewoman sincerely devoted to the Count, yet not averse to a little flirtation with Cherubino; Susanna, a young woman with decent and healthy instincts, yet clever and daring in her intrigue! What dramatic impact in the ensemble scenes, the duets, trios, and quartets, in which each participant retains his or her own characteristic accent, rhythm, and sentiment! What climactic power in those animated, broadly expanded symphonic finales! And all this is done with a simplicity that seems calculated to hide the master's art rather than to display it.

From a purely musical point of view, Mozart exhibits an amazing wealth of technical resources. The modern art of modulation was for the first time fully exploited in its extended ramifications in the development sections of Mozart's symphonies, quartets, and sonatas. An equally important innovation was the extensive coda in his piano concertos. After the brilliant cadenza, the culmination of the entire movement, the coda opens a whole panorama of changing sights: the ascent, a moment of rest, recreation, satisfaction, and delight, all in one, as the traveler looks back on the path he has traversed. Such contemplative, retrospective codas were something new, not found in the music of Bach, Handel, or any other composer before Mozart. Beethoven in his piano concertos and his violin concerto and Brahms in his violin concerto well understood the secret of Mozart's art of effective endings, and emulated this art in his own manner.

The apparent ease with which Mozart solved the most complex technical problems is illustrated by the famous finale of the "Jupiter" symphony. Here is found a unique organic combination of sonata form and fugue, embodying the most ingenious devices of contrapuntal workmanship: inversions in double and triple counterpoint, and canonic imitation in augmentation and diminution. The culmination is reached in the longest and most elaborate coda ever written by Mozart, when all five motives flash by in a kaleidoscopic ensemble. Yet this exciting and brilliant exhibition of technical prowess is presented effortlessly, with a smile, as it were, its intricacy being apparent only to initiated listeners.

4. "He can say very much, but he never says too much."

5. "He can drink from any glass, because he never empties a glass."

6. "He is passionate, but always observes the forms of chivalry."

These three statements of Busoni are variations of the basic theme. The difference between the classical and romantic attitudes, between a restrained and an unbounded art, is here expressed in three different ways. Mozart can say very much, but he never spends more music than absolutely necessary on a specific idea. There is no overabundance of contrapuntal complexity, no "heavenly length" of melody (as sometimes in Schubert), no needless complication of harmony. Mozart can drink from any glass; he has many types of music at his disposal. Yet he never empties a glass; he always leaves some reserve power. Wagner and Tchaikovsky come dangerously close to abusing the expressive power of music by driving it to utter exhaustion. Stravinsky in *Le Sacre du Printemps*, and Ravel in the famous *Bolero*, are as un-Mozartean as could be imagined; they empty their glasses to the last drop. The consequence is that after the first strong impact, the listener's senses are dulled, and repeated climaxes leave him unmoved.

This Mozart impromptu may best be brought to a close with Busoni's last aphorism:

7. "He is as unaffected as a youth and as wise as an old man, never antiquated and never modern, laid in his tomb, and yet living. His smile, so human even in transfiguration, radiates happiness."

With Beethoven, for the first time in history the realm of music is dominated by a new force: the moral power of a great individual. We see religious fervor as an active ingredient in the music of Palestrina and Bach; we see in Mozart's music eternal humanity emotionally reflected. But with Beethoven, the case is different. As soon as he reached maturity, his music became identified with his own personality. It is animated by his own energetic will. Here, German idealism is revealed in its most concentrated and purest form, in terms of musical sounds that voice faith in the dignity of man.

Beethoven's cosmopolitan attitude was strengthened by his study of great works of literature, philosophy, and the pantheistic religions. Their wisdom was eagerly consumed by Beethoven; this intercourse with creative spirits took the place of the formal education that he had never had. The Bible, Homer, Plutarch, Dante, Shakespeare, Goethe, and Schiller were his spiritual companions. His knowledge of philosophy and poetry gave his music an impetus of unequaled power. The dramatic and the tragic elements in literature were balanced in Beethoven by gaiety and by jubilant outbursts of joy. Between these two extremes, his music reveals the breadth and majesty of calm contemplation. Beethoven's outlook on the world is that of the superman, whose aspirations and capacities exceed even those of exceptionally gifted men. Yet this superman always retains warm human feelings; what he expresses is the emotional experience of the ordinary person, intensified, purified, and ennobled. Here lies the secret of Beethoven's universal appeal. Throbbing life, not mere intellectual art, is the essence of Beethoven's music. Beethoven's hero is Man — not the nationally specified human being, but every man within the entire compass of Western civilization.

No creative artist has ever exercised a more profound influence on art than Beethoven. No other musician, not even Bach or Mozart, no poet, be it Dante, Shakespeare, or Goethe, could speak the language of universal brotherhood with the power of Beethoven. Spiritually an offspring of the French Revolution, Beethoven proclaimed the new freedom from tradition and conventions. His appeal is cosmopolitan, but his art is animated by his individual artistic beliefs.

In Beethoven's monumental symphonies, his majestic sonatas, his extraordinary string quartets, every trace of regionalism is erased. Regionalism possesses a certain quaint charm in much of Haydn's and some of Mozart's music, but it appears in very few of Beethoven's works. True, some of the early productions that he brought with him to Vienna from his native Bonn breathe a certain conventional German amiability; we sense this in the two little piano sonatinas, the early serenades, the wind-instrument ensemble music, and the septet. But, starting with his third symphony, the "Eroica," Beethoven gave himself to that glorious German idealism which illuminated all Europe and which united him with his great contemporaries Goethe and Schiller, Kant and Fichte. Their humanism was stronger than their nationalism, and their culture had a mental horizon extending in time back to classical antiquity and in space to all the nations of Europe, even to the Orient. Not in vain did Beethoven's Germany earn the honorable title "Das Volk der Dichter und Denker" — the nation of poets and thinkers. Up to the time of the French Revolution, French was the international language of all educated Europeans and Paris was regarded as the center of culture. After the revolution, France become the dominant political power on the continent, but around 1800 the cultural leadership passed to Germany, then a politically insignificant and divided nation. To French materialism was opposed German idealism, which led to the burgeoning of German poetry, philosophy, music, and science.

The democratic idea was deeply implanted in Beethoven; he expressed it in German music for the first time. In his symphonies and overtures Beethoven spoke to everyone. The popular appeal of his symphonic music differs from the popularity of Haydn's music. The rustic freshness and quaintness of Haydn's melody and rhythm reflect the folk music of the Austrian countryside, full of spirit and amiability. But Haydn also observed the social and cultural conventions of the eighteenth century in many of his formal minuets, lively rondos, and lyrical slow movements.

Beethoven's music is rustic only occasionally, in short episodes; and it possesses little that would be congenial to the prosperous middle class. Its passionate vehemence, dramatic power, and grandiose sweep seemed barbaric to the aristocratic music-lovers of his day. The rising generation, on the other hand, understood the democratic message of Beethoven's symphonic music; the romantic youth heard in it the outcry of the masses, the march of the people's army, the fight for freedom. Yet Beethoven was not partisan in his art. For him, "the people" meant not only peasants and workers but the whole population, including scholars and artists; nor did he exclude the members of aristocracy, with some of whom he maintained personal (though not always agreeable) relations. In his later sonatas and his last quartets he speaks to the intellectual elite capable of following his innermost thought. In these works we hear the soliloquy of a lofty mind, soaring to heights accessible only to the great of spirit.

The classical works of Haydn, Mozart, and Beethoven vastly enriched the treasure of orchestral and chamber music, oratorio, opera, and to a lesser extent, church music. Early in the nineteenth century, a new art form was introduced into German and Austrian music: the accompanied song, or lied, the lovely creation of Franz Schubert, which was adopted and varied by Schumann, Mendelssohn, Robert Franz, Brahms, Richard Strauss, and Hugo Wolf.

Before the advent of lieder, solo songs had been restricted to folk tunes and to a few conventional species of lyric poetry, never venturing into the more complex and profound regions of emotional experience. The emergence of great German poetry, beginning with Goethe's work, coincided with the rise of German music. Together they possessed the ingredients necessary for the creation of the new form of art song: refinement ,variety, flexibility, and expressive power.

The creation of lieder alone — leaving out of consideration his symphonies, chamber music, and piano compositions — would have sufficed to give Franz Schubert (1797–1828) a place among the greatest geniuses of all time. What enabled Schubert to utilize his lyric talent for the creation of lieder was, paradoxically, the excellence of German instrumental music, the sonatas and the symphonies of Haydn, Mozart, and Beethoven. By using elements of this instrumental style in piano accompaniment, which before him had been hardly more than a succession of simple arpeggios and chords, Schubert gained for his melody new dimensions, width and depth. Tone painting, dramatic scenes, and emotional conflicts became legitimate forms of vocal art, made possible by the development of the florid style of piano accompaniment. Moreover, the enlarged function of the accompaniment directed Schubert's imagination toward new types of vocal melody, and the interaction of new instrumental and vocal methods enriched the romantic expessiveness of the finished product.

Robert Schumann (1810–1856) introduced a new treatment of lieder accompaniment; Friedrich Silcher (1789–1860) and Robert Franz (1815-1892) cultivated the *volkstümliches Lied* — song in the folk manner. In his great song cycles, Brahms added a touch of intimacy, the typical German *Gemütlichkeit*; Richard Strauss applied modern devices to the art of the song. The culmination of the century-long evolution of lieder was reached in the songs of that supersensitive Viennese musician, Hugo Wolf, who introduced Wagnerian harmony and color into the piano accompaniment.

Nineteenth-century German music was influenced by the romantic movement, a spiritual phenomenon manifested in the lyric poetry and novels of the German writers Uhland, Eichendorff, Brentano, Rückert, Heine, Mörike, E. T. A. Hoffmann, Tieck, Schlegel, Novalis, and of course, Goethe. It was this abundant literature that inspired the great nineteenth-century musicians of Germany. Beethoven, though not a full-fledged romanticist, has very distinct romantic traits; Schubert is closer to the romantic ideal; in Schumann we see the central luminary of romantic music, while Spohr and Marschner serve as respectable satellites. Brahms carried the romantic spirit to the end of the century. Wagner's gigantic music dramas used the romantic imagination to revive ancient Greek ideas about dramatic art in a setting from Nordic mythology.

In this general survey only the towering peaks of romanticism will be observed, from a distance in time that gives perspective. For Schubert, Chopin, Weber, and Mendelssohn — four great figures of romantic music — life was finished before the completion of the fortieth year. Their creative ecstasy, a distinctive romantic trait, was so fierce and all-consuming that their physical resistance was weakened and they were quickly exhausted.

In musical landscape painting, Carl Maria von Weber (1786–1826) and Felix Mendelssohn (1809–1847) are particularly notable. Weber's last opera, *Oberon* (written for presentation in London), contains a tonal painting of the ocean as masterly as his musical picture of the forest in *Der Freischütz*, a model that Wagner reproduced on a still larger canvas in the finest scene of the opera *Siegfried*. Mendelssohn was accorded the title of a great landscape painter even by his detractor, Richard Wagner. Mendelssohn's attainments in this field still appear fresh and youthful, a hundred years after his death. His enormous vogue in England was due not only to his mastery of all branches of his art, but also to the homage he paid to England in some of his best works. His musical illustration of the realm of the elves and fairies for Shakespeare's *A Midsummer Night's Dream* is enchanting. *Fingal's Cave* overture, the melancholy northern scenery of the Hebrides, Scotland's lonely outpost in the ocean, comes vividly alive; while in the "Scotch" Symphony, Mendelssohn caught the mood and the characteristic rhythms and melodies of Scotland. A southern counterpart of this music is his "Italian" Symphony.

Though folk song in itself can hardly be called a romantic art, it often served the ends of romantic composers. This was true of Chopin, the Russian composers, of the Scandinavians Grieg and Sibelius, and of the Bohemians Smetana and Dvořák.

It is worth noting that we often speak of romantic melody, harmony, and orchestral color, but not of romantic rhythm. Rhythm was the weakest factor in romantic music. It is, of course, impossible to eliminate it from any musical work, but in comparison with the harmonic and coloristic effects in romantic music, its rhythms were bloodless. Perhaps coloristic effect can be achieved only at the expense of rhythmic energy. Furthermore, vigorous and complex rhythm produces a formal structure and a precise melodic outline, attributes not in keeping with romanticism. Compared to the intensely differentiated rhythms in the music of Bach, Haydn, Mozart, and Beethoven, the rhythm of Schumann's music lacks variety. The device of syncopation, inherent in romantic rhythms, weakens the main pulse. Wagner's rhythms depend mainly on two devices: gentle syncopation and violent dotted-note figures, often associated with melodic leaps. The rhythmic life that animates a Bach fugue was largely lost in romantic music, and all but vanished in the French offspring of romantic art, impressionism. The accolade for restoring differentiated rhythm to romantic music goes to Brahms, who returned to the classical principles of clarity and directness.

It was natural that the antiromantic twentieth century stressed the rhythmic factor above all others. The rhythmic ingenuity of the music of Stravinsky, Hindemith, Milhaud, and other leaders of modernism is amazing, but this rhythmic energy has been introduced at the expense of melody. The most common reproach brought against radically modernistic music is that it has lost, voluntarily or involuntarily, all the melodic charm of romantic music. The future great man of music ought to be able to restore melodic beauty, while retaining the rhythmic innovations of the twentieth century.

The romantic melody is ineffective unless accompanied by opulent harmony, chromatically embellished and freely changing from one coloristic pattern to another. Romantic counterpoint is a texture of undulating lines of different colored sounds. In such a setting, the principal melody often ceases to be predominant, being obscured by the iridescent fluctuation of harmonic modulations. Schumann's little piano piece *Träumerei* may serve to typify the romantic melody. Its structural content is slight: a four-bar phrase is repeated six times, with some melodic variations. Yet the ever changing harmony, with modulations leading to a different key at every cadence, is sufficient to insure variety of expression.

The romantic melody appears in many national guises. German, French, Italian, and Russian melodies, though musically similar, are distinct from each other in their characteristic esthetic premises. The German melody of the Schumann type can be described only by the evocative German words *innerlich* (intimate) and *sehnsuchtsvoll* (full of yearning). Its lyric exuberance, its poetic character, and its purity of emotion are eminently German traits, rarely found in the music of other nations.

In the works of the French composers Gounod, Massenet, Franck, and Fauré, we observe reflections of German romanticism. Around 1875, Wagner's flaming and exciting music became the model for French artists. Bizet, Saint-Saëns, Chabrier, Chausson, d'Indy, Lalo, and Debussy were all ensnared by Wagner's siren sounds, and the later hostility of Saint-Saëns and Debussy toward Wagner demonstrates how much they secretly feared his power.

Here it is proper to comment on Richard Wagner (1813–1883) as a figure in German and international art. His early works — *Rienzi* and *Der fliegende Holländer* — show few national characteristics; they follow the typical operatic pattern of their day, as it had been shaped by the joint efforts of German, Italian, and French composers — Weber, Marschner, Meyerbeer, Auber, Cherubini, and Rossini. Beginning with *Tannhäuser*, however, Wagner's nationalistic tendency becomes more outspoken. The works of his middle period draw their dramatic themes from medieval German epics. It should be said, however, that this Germanic spirit is revealed more in Wagner's texts than in his music. Wagner did not confine himself musically: he freely borrowed foreign material useful for his purpose. His point of departure was Beethoven's symphonic art, but he was also influenced by Liszt's chromatic harmony and by the colorful orchestral display of Berlioz. He even profited by Meyerbeer's theatrical skill and ingenuity. The universal success obtained by Wagner's music dramas may be explained not so much by their national German character as by their passionate and glowingly sensuous music, supranational in origin and in appeal. Only in *Die Meistersinger von Nürnberg* did Wagner accentuate the German tone, sentiment, and character to the exclusion of all elements of supranational art.

The position of Johannes Brahms (1833–1897) in German and international music was not established until the close of his career. The partisan Wagnerites considered it an article of faith to oppose Brahms. Wagner spoke of him in slighting terms; when Brahms died, Cosima Wagner admitted that she had never heard any of his music. Hans von Bülow, the champion of Wagner's music, became an admirer of Brahms only after Wagner's act of treachery in accepting, apparently without scruple, the surrender to him of Bülow's wife Cosima, Liszt's daughter.

The artistic enmity between Wagner and Brahms was exacerbated by a public declaration made by young Brahms condemning the esthetic tenets of Wagner and Liszt. This sensational document, signed also by Joseph Joachim and others, broke German music into two hostile camps: the Wagnerites and the Brahmsians. Advocates of Wagner's music drama usually opposed Brahms; admirers of Brahms were compelled to reject

Wagner. Thus in Vienna Wagner's most persistent opponent, the influential critic of the *Neue freie Presse,* Eduard Hanslick, became an ardent Brahms advocate. Hugo Wolf, an ardent Wagnerian, wrote violent articles against Brahms.

Hence it is not surprising to find that Brahms was very late in winning full recognition in other countries. In Paris his music was persistently given the scornful label "lourdeur teutonique" (Germanic heaviness). In Boston, the respected critic and famous program annotator for the Boston Symphony Orchestra, Philip Hale, for years after the master's death frankly admitted his dislike of Brahms. Tchaikovsky, the most famous contemporary of Brahms, found the latter's music devoid of soul. In Italy, Brahms has never been popular. It is only in the twentieth century that he has finally been acknowledged as a true German classic, the legitimate heir of Beethoven, Schubert, and Schumann. His four symphonies, his concertos, his chamber music, and the major part of his piano music have acquired international validity. A symphony concert season without a Brahms work would be inconceivable today.

What made Brahms a classic after his death? To answer this question we must consider the esthetic theories of his time. The movement launched by Wagner as *Zukunftmusic* (the music of the future) was predicated upon the belief that Beethoven had exhausted the possibilities of the sonata form and of "absolute music" in general, and that it was imperative to discover new musical forms. The proffered solution to the problem was Wagnerian music drama and the program music of Liszt. As time passed, however, it became evident that the idea behind music drama had rendered German opera sterile, and that the cult of program music had led to the decline of symphonic forms. It was the great merit of Brahms to revive faith in absolute forms and to check the spread of Wagnerism. In the sixteenth century the epithet "Savior of Church Music" was given to Palestrina. With even greater propriety Brahms deserves the title "Savior of Absolute Music," for he demonstrated in his instrumental works (he never wrote an opera) that programmatic concepts were not essential to musical art. Thus, Brahms became the curator and the conservator of classical ideals: distinct and expressive melody, logical structure and development, perfection of form, and economy of means. It is true that these qualities are also the attributes of academic music, but the music of Brahms was not academic. Its conservative air was a reflection of the master's personality — tranquil, dispassionate, considerate, and friendly. An artist of his frame of mind, of his great expressive power, was in need of disciplined craftsmanship, a chiseled melodic curve, a harmony that never lost sight of a central tonality, and an orchestration that preserved the clarity of the melodic design without extravagant display of tonal color. Thus his own nature led him to the classical models. But, growing up in the romantic age, Brahms could not help absorbing its rich nourishment. At the start of his career he was hailed by Schumann and Liszt as a rising star in the romantic firmament. His problem was to reconcile the romantic aspirations of his soul with the classical framework of his intellect, and he solved it by creating a new classical art of romantic inspiration.

Anton Bruckner (1824–1896) and Gustav Mahler (1860–1911) are two great Austrian masters whose art was not accepted wholeheartedly while they were living. Their remarkable symphonic works were misunderstood, and the artistic value of their music was depreciated by those arbiters of public taste, the music critics. The critics failed to understand the spiritual message of these works of art. In his symphonies, Bruckner ignored the petty sentimentalities of daily life and contemplated space and time beyond them. The cosmic aspect of his symphonic music challenges the receptive capacity of the average listener. Yet Bruckner's music is also very human, and lies close to the soil. In the scherzos of his symphonies one hears the heavy stamp of peasant boots; at other moments there is a loveliness, suggesting fresh wild flowers on dewy meadows. Austrian in sentiment to the core, Bruckner's rustic tunes have great appeal for the listener familiar with the Austrian tone, accent, and rhythm.

Gustav Mahler, an Austrian Jew by birth and, in a sense, a disciple and successor of Bruckner, adopted in his nine symphonies a pantheistic attitude. In contrast to Bruckner's stubborn concentration on a limited number of ideas, Mahler's multitude of themes suggests the musical spendthrift. In his music we hear tunes invented by him in the spirit of authentic melodies of the German people. March rhythms mark the steps of the youth of the Austrian countryside: the Alpine mountain climbers; the *fahrende Schüler*, roving medieval students; the *Wanderburschen*, young artisans traveling on foot with knapsacks on their backs from one city to another in quest of work; and those typical German figures, the pleasure hikers. But there are also elements of universal appeal. Mahler expands his adoration of nature into pantheistic contemplation; he was deeply concerned with the enigmas of life and death, of time and eternity, of despair and hope, of man and God. With passionate vehemence he expressed in his symphonies contradictory states of mind; hence his triumphant climaxes, when confidence and hope emerge victorious.

The great length and complexity of Mahler's symphonies is lightened by the incidence of popular refrains. He was criticized for these lapses into simplicity as much as for his flights into esoteric regions, and was accused of lack of consistency in relating artless episodes to more turbulent and dramatic sections. This apparent incongruity is explained by the presence of both national (simple) and supranational (complex) elements in Mahler's music.

In contradistinction to Bruckner and Mahler, Richard Strauss (1864–1949) was recognized as a composer of international stature early in his spectacular career. Indeed, his fame rests almost entirely on the symphonic poems composed before 1900: *Don Juan, Till Eulenspiegel,* and *Tod und Verklärung.* Nothing that he wrote in the twentieth century has attained comparable popularity.

Strauss was fittingly nicknamed by Hans von Bülow "Richard the Second." In his tone poems and sensational operas *Salome* and *Elektra,* Strauss expanded to the point of *ne plus ultra* the Wagnerian system of leitmotifs, or leading motifs (musical identification themes that signalize the appearances of each personage on the stage). A special guide published for the first performance of his *Ein Heldenleben* lists no fewer than seventy leitmotifs, the most important of which represents the hero, Strauss himself. In his philosophical tone poem *Also sprach Zarathustra,* Strauss introduces thematic motifs of yearning, joy, and science. The use of identification motifs is particularly abundant in his extraordinary set of variations for violoncello and orchestra, *Don Quixote,* in which the famous incidents of the Cervantes classic are realistically illustrated, down to the bleating of sheep. In his *Sinfonia domestica,* which is a sort of musical autobiography, introduces special motifs for the parents, the baby, and the paternal and maternal relatives.

Hans Pfitzner (1869–1949) combined in his operas and chamber music the Germanic interest in strict polyphony with a romantic exuberance of color. But he never achieved success equal to that of his brilliant contemporary, Strauss. Pfitzner's best known work is the opera *Palestrina,* in which he pays homage to the great master of the Italian Renaissance.

Among Austrian contemporaries of Strauss and Pfitzner, Franz Schreker (1878–1934) acquired considerable renown with his opera *Der ferne Klang,* which reflects the sensuous and morbid atmosphere in central Europe immediately preceding World War I. Schreker's music, though dazzling and brilliant, is weak in expressive melody. This deficiency is compensated by an extravagant display of orchestral color, an agglomeration of external effect. Schreker exercised his technical skill at the expense of the spiritual content.

Two composers stood aloof from the popular modernist movement in Germany: Max Reger (1873–1916) and Ferruccio Busoni (1866–1924). It may be difficult to give an idea of the sincere enthusiasm that Reger's music evoked during his lifetime. Yet Reger fully justified this acclaim. He was a master of polyphony, a virtuoso of contrapuntal writing rivaling Bach, while in structural solidity, melodic expressiveness, and lyric sentiment he approaches Brahms. In violent outbursts of emotion he outdoes both Wagner and Strauss, reveling in an excess of chromatic harmony. This romantic eclecticism had a peculiar appeal to the German public; but Reger's music failed to traverse national frontiers and is not sufficiently known and appreciated outside Germany. His prodigious productivity was demonstrated by the fact that during his brief life he wrote no fewer than one hundred and forty large works. Recently a complete edition of his works, in many volumes, was begun in Germany; this fact testifies to Reger's enduring place in music, at least in his native country.

Ferruccio Busoni was, unlike Reger, a cosmopolitan musician. Born in Italy and educated in Austria, he became a world-famous pianist. He was as much at home in Paris and London as in Moscow; he taught at the Conservatory of Helsingfors in Finland and at the New England Conservatory in Boston. Later he took up permanent residence in Berlin.

In Busoni's art, Italy and Germany enter into a close union. In his playing, as well as in his compositions, the Italian heritage was expressed in the qualities of grace, vivacity, and brilliance. Germany gave him his great contrapuntal mastery, his sense of logical and organic form, and his philosophical bent of mind, reflected in a passionate search for the ultimate truths of life and art. No other Italian-born musician possessed so profound an understanding of German music as did Busoni. To Bach he devoted a lifetime of study, whose mature fruits are the seven volumes of his monumental Bach edition. Busoni's ambition was to translate Bach's keyboard music into the idiom of the modern grand piano. This he achieved with superior skill and with reverence for Bach's spirit. His magnificent piano transcription of Bach's *Chaconne* transformed the music into a grandiose structure, far more impressive than Bach's original version for violin solo, limited as it inevitably was in its polyphonic possibilities.

The culmination of Busoni's lifelong study of Bach was his great work for piano entitled *Fantasia Contrappuntistica*. Around three fugues from *The Art of Fugue*, and the torso of the triple fugue left unfinished at Bach's death, Busoni built a grandiloquent tonal edifice and added to it his own prelude, variations, and cadenza, which completes the triple fugue and adds a new quadruple fugue and a coda. Busoni's own performances of this long and difficult work produced a powerful impression; but nowadays pianists are afraid to tackle it.

Beethoven's art, imbued with the spirit of the French Revolution, has been characterized here as democratic; the romantic art of Weber, Schubert, Schumann, Mendelssohn, and Brahms was the fruit of the vast cultural and economic advance of the German middle class during the nineteenth century. In the productions of Richard Strauss we stand face to face with the outspoken imperialistic spirit of the newly founded German *Reich*.

World War I put an end to German imperialism, not only politically but also spiritually. After that war, the short-lived Weimar Republic left its imprint on German music in the revolt against the exalted aspirations of romanticism and against middle-class mentality. This was the age of *Gebrauchsmusik* (utility music), *Gemeinschaftsmusik* (community music), *Schulmusik* (school music), and of so-called "objective" music. In these pursuits, two German composers, Paul Hindemith (born in 1895) and Kurt Weill (1900–1950), and one Austrian, Ernst Krenek (born in 1900) were particularly active. All three were later expelled from Germany by the fury of the Nazis, and settled in America. In the turbulent 1920's Hindemith's esthetic creed was not yet crystallized; he took special delight in extravagant procedures that were offensive to the old-fashioned music lover. The perverted esthetic view of the young German radical movement was boldly formulated in the program booklet for the *première* of Hindemith's opera *Neues vom Tage* (The News of the Day), presented by the Berlin State Opera in 1929. The booklet informed the public that "at present a great number of advanced musicians indignantly protest against having their works regarded as art," that music should be treated like any marketable merchandise; and Hindemith himself was quoted as saying of one of his works: "It should not be individually interpreted, but simply 'swept down' (*einfach heruntergerasselt*) vigorously." All this, however, was in Hindemith's rebellious youth. In his mature years, he has produced enduring musical masterpieces, among which his opera and symphonic suite *Mathis der Maler* has become a modern classic.

A sensational success was achieved in the 1920's by Krenek's opera *Jonny spielt auf*, in which American jazz, then new in Germany, was introduced on the stage. Some fifty opera houses, including the Metropolitan Opera House in New York, presented Krenek's opera at the time — but it soon went out of fashion. Four or five other operas by Krenek were heard, passionately discussed, and as quickly forgotten. His adoption of Schönberg's twelve-tone technique has not, since then, made his music more palatable; yet it cannot be denied that he played a historic role in modern music for the theater.

Kurt Weill, a capable and talented German Jew, was a pupil of the great Busoni in composition. He began his career by writing concert music in a fairly modern style. Recognizing after a few years that stage music was his proper field, he turned decisively to light opera. His first outstanding success was a modernized version of *The Beggar's Opera*, in ballad style. During his American period he produced several successful musical comedies.

Following World War I, Vienna lost its great musical prestige, owing to the political chaos that reigned in Austrian commerce, industry, and finance. Berlin took over the uncontested leadership in musical matters during the five fairly prosperous years from 1925 to 1930. Franz Schreker, who had been a teacher of composition at the Vienna Conservatory, became director of the reorganized Berlin State High School of Music. He brought with him to Berlin a group of highly gifted young pupils, among them Krenek, Alois Hába from Prague (later known as the champion of quarter-tone music), Karol Rathaus (1895–1955), and others. A few years later, Arnold Schönberg (1874–1951) left his native city of Vienna for Berlin and was appointed professor of composition at the Prussian State Academy of Arts. Thanks to the initiative of progressive conductors like Fritz Stiedry, Otto Klemperer, Erich Kleiber, Wilhelm Furtwängler, Hermann Scherchen, and others, Berlin became the only city in the world where Schönberg's enigmatic and immensely difficult works were publicly performed almost in their entirety, including his curious Five Orchestral Pieces, the gigantic score of the *Gurre-Lieder*, and the monodramas *Erwartung* and *Die glückliche Hand*. Schönberg lived the last seventeen years of his life in the United States; yet America has heard little of his music of the later period; his only work that is frequently performed is *Verklärte Nacht*, a youthful composition written when he was in his twenties!

Many other German composers found a refuge in America. Among them should be named Ernst Toch, a versatile and highly gifted artist, and Erich Korngold, once a child prodigy in composition, who became a composer for Hollywood films.

The best-known and certainly the most brilliant exponent of the Schönberg school of composition was his pupil Alban Berg of Vienna (1885–1935). His opera *Wozzeck*, performed for the first time at the Berlin State Opera in 1925, produced a sensation. This immensely stimulating music, however, appeals only to a small number of highly trained listeners interested in experimental methods. The general public in 1925 could hear nothing but musical chaos in *Wozzeck*. It was, however, revived after World War II in several European countries, and in America, with considerable success. Alban Berg's last work, a violin concerto written in the twelve-tone technique, has become known to the public through increasingly frequent performances.

Anton von Webern (1883–1945), also a Viennese disciple of Schönberg, wrote chamber music for small ensembles. Most of his works are very short, but their lack of essence is compensated by an abundance of subtle coloring.

Among the later representatives of German music in the twentieth century the following are to be mentioned: Carl Orff (born in 1895), whose choral work, *Carmina Burana*, to the text of medieval songs, has become extremely popular; Werner Egk (born in 1901), who wrote a setting of *Peer Gynt* in a style quite different from Grieg's familiar music; and the modernistic composer Boris Blacher (born in 1903) who enjoys considerable success not only in Germany but also abroad. The name of Gottfried von Einem (born in 1918) is known through his bold psychological operas.

As far as general musical culture is concerned, until lately Germany stood foremost in the world. With a territory that before World War II was hardly larger than the state of Texas, she maintained at least one hundred and thirty good opera houses and numerous orchestras and chamber music groups, active even in the smallest communities. Germany was also the greatest music publishing center. One has only to name the houses of Breitkopf & Härtel, C. F. Peters, Schott, Eulenburg, and many others to give a measure of the German contribution in this field. In Austria, Universal Edition has done a great deal to make known the works of the modern school. In the field of musicology, Germany has for over a century been distinguished by industrious scholarship.

During the period of Nazi domination, many of Germany's best composers and scholars were forced to leave the country, and, as a result, mediocrity reigned in music. Since the end of World War II, however, German scholarship has steadily regained lost ground, and many splendid publications have been initiated, among them the largest musical encyclopedia yet undertaken in any language, *Die Musik in Geschichte und Gegenwart.* In the field of composition, there are also signs that German inventiveness has overcome the disastrous spiritual and material destruction of the Nazi period, and has returned to the path of artistic prosperity.

Switzerland

Switzerland, with its compound of German, French, and Italian populations and languages, has long had political unity, but its national music has been sharply divided along racial lines. Of the three national groups, the German section was the first to attain musical importance. In medieval times, the Swiss monasteries were seats of musical learning. Notker, known also as Balbulus (840–912), a monk at the Monastery of St. Gall, won lasting recognition by his work on ecclesiastical sequences; his contemporary Tutilo, also a monk at St. Gall, made an important contribution to the art of tropes. Hermannus Contractus (1013–1054), who studied at St. Gall and later entered the monastery at Reichenau, was the author of historically important music.

In the sixteenth century Swiss musicians participated in the glorious rise of German polyphonic art. Ludwig Senfl of Zurich (c. 1490–c. 1555) was a leading master of German polyphonic song. Henricus Glareanus (1488–1563), active at Basel, was the author of the famous theoretical treatise, the *Dodecachordon.* Never again in music history, however, were Swiss musicians to attain such international eminence. In the seventeenth century, the contribution of Swiss music was negligible; in the eighteenth and nineteenth centuries it was reduced to the status of an annex to German music. It was not until the twentieth century that Swiss music again asserted its independence.

Toward the beginning of the nineteenth century, vocal and instrumental organizations known under the generic name

Collegium Musicum became a Swiss specialty. In these efforts at democratic organization, Hans Georg Nägeli (1773–1836) of Zurich played a conspicuous part. He founded the Schweizerische Musikgesellschaft (Swiss Music Society). It became the driving force in a flourishing musical movement that attracted to Switzerland a number of famous musicians, who either sought refuge there or were frequent guests and sincere friends of the little republic. Among the refugees was no less a personage than Richard Wagner, while the list of temporary residents included Johannes Brahms and Richard Strauss.

A number of outstanding Swiss composers were well known throughout Germany, though hardly elsewhere. Friedrich Hegar (1841–1927) of Zurich was considered the greatest master of the German choral ballad; Hans Huber (1852–1921), director of the Basel Conservatory, was a highly esteemed and prolific composer of symphonic and chamber music; Hermann Suter (1870–1926) of Basel enjoyed a considerable reputation as a conductor and composer of choral, orchestral, and chamber works. Othmar Schoeck (born in 1886) is regarded by many as one of the most significant composers of lieder; indeed, his are perhaps the most remarkable songs to German words since those of Hugo Wolf.

Among composers of the French cantons of Switzerland, the greatest is Ernest Bloch of Geneva, who wrote racially Jewish music and settled in America. In recent years, Frank Martin (born in 1890), also of Geneva, has become widely known through his ingenious instrumental works in a highly advanced harmonic idiom. The Swiss musician of modern times who has made the greatest impact on musical education in the twentieth century is Emile Jaques-Dalcroze (1865–1950). He was the creator of eurhythmics, a system of rhythmic gymnastics equally useful for the art of dancing and for developing a sense of rhythm. Schools of eurhythmics now exist in all parts of the world.

Arthur Honegger is sometimes placed among Swiss composers

because his parents were from Switzerland, a classification that is hardly justified, since Honegger was born in France and all his musical activities were carried on in Paris.

In the field of performance, the Swiss conductor Ernest Ansermet (born in 1883) has done a great deal for Swiss musical culture, as the leader of the celebrated Orchestre de la Suisse-Romande in Geneva.

Among Swiss composers born in the twentieth century, the names of Willy Burkhard (1900–1955) of Berne and of Conrad Beck (born in 1901) of Schaffhausen have frequently appeared in the programs of international festivals. They are both middle-of-the-road composers, excelling in choral and instrumental music. Rolf Liebermann (born in 1910) of Zurich has attracted attention by his modernistic stage works. The younger generation of Swiss composers, however, tends to steer clear of the extremes, maintaining an artistic neutrality that conforms spiritually with the political neutrality that Switzerland has succeeded in preserving through centuries of peaceful progress.

7

France and Belgium

France

The earliest evidence of music in France appears in the time
of Charlemagne, during the ninth century. But since Charlemagne's empire comprised Germany as well as France, it is not
always possible to draw a clear line of demarcation between
French and German contributions to music during that period.
Monasteries were then the principal seats of musical scholarship.
Many of them were situated on the present border between
German and French territory, in western Germany, in Switzerland, and in eastern France. Musical studies were pursued by
monks in Cologne, Mainz, and St. Gall on the German side, and
at Metz, Tours, Soissons, and Paris on the French side. Gregorian
chant was the unifying factor among these ecclesiastical scholars,
transcending regional divisions.

It was St. Ambrose who said that Gregorian chant was a bless-
ing for music. Wherever it was accepted, music found a home,
and thus a proper foundation was laid for the future; whereas
the nations that long resisted the spread of Gregorian chant
were ineluctably held back from the great cosmopolitan stream
of European music. Italy, France, England, Germany, and the
Netherlands — all Gregorian nations — developed a high musical
culture. Only Spain stood aloof; Gregorian chant was introduced
there relatively late. At the other end of the continent the

separation of the Orthodox churches from the Roman Catholic church precluded the use of Gregorian chant in Byzantium and in Russia.

In the twelfth century, a fundamental change was brought about in European culture by the founding of great universities, which gradually replaced the monasteries as seats of musical learning. The new curriculum, expressed by the term *universitas septem artium liberalium* (universality of the seven liberal arts), included music, which was taught as a part of the medieval *quadrivium* (music, arithmetic, geometry, and astronomy) on an equal basis with exact sciences. Of these new schools, the University of Paris was the most renowned; its curriculum gave the impetus for the development of the so-called Notre Dame school, represented by two musicians who flourished in the late twelfth and early thirteenth centuries, Leoninus, the *maître de chapelle* at the Cathedral of Notre Dame, and his successor Perotinus. They developed a new and free art of writing music for several voices, culminating in the French motet. This period also marked the transition from the rather austere *ars antiqua* to the more mundane *ars nova*.

The medieval French motet grew out of free counterpoint of sacred and secular elements; in it, an ecclesiastical melody of Gregorian chant was combined with a countermelody of popular origin, often taken from the songs of the troubadours. The musical structure of the French motet may be described as a terzetto, a composition for three voices; more accurately, it is a duet for two high voices above a *basso continuo*. If regarded in this light, as a duet with bass accompaniment, the old French motet appears to be an early precursor of the trio sonatas of the seventeenth century, with their two closely intertwined melodic parts and a governing line in the bass establishing the harmonic foundation.

The counterpoint of the early French motet, still rooted in the *ars antiqua*, included an astonishing amount of dissonance. This style, with its clashing seconds, sevenths, and fourths was a glimpse into the future. Modern music has revived many devices of dissonant counterpoint of the French motet.

The technical plan for the old French motet was as follows: to a strictly measured, symmetrically built piece of Gregorian chant in the tenor, with Latin words, a higher countermelody was written in the alto. This countermelody was usually a lyric tune in French with rhythms widely differing from the Gregorian theme of the tenor. The soprano would then come in with a gay drinking song or a love song, such as were sung by the troubadours. The superposition of frivolous lines in the vernacular over the austere line of Gregorian chant presented an extremely difficult contrapuntal problem. The creation and propagation of the French motet, combining these disparate elements, is an achievement that is beginning to be appreciated only now, when modern counterpoint has revived these medieval practices.

If the French motet was prophetic in its boldness of harmony and counterpoint, the monumental organa of Leoninus and Perotinus — with their elaborate coloratura passages above sustained notes in the tenor — were even more remarkable. Yet this art bore no seed of further development; the works of Leoninus and Perotinus, the great masters of the *ars antiqua,* possess little more than archeological interest.

After the great creative impulse given by the Paris masters in the thirteenth century, French leadership was increasingly challenged by other nations: England, the Netherlands, Italy, and Germany. The sixteenth century may be called the Netherlandish era in music; the seventeenth and eighteenth centuries, the Italian era; and the later eighteenth and the nineteenth centuries, the German era. Yet the French never ceased to contribute to the music of other European nations. One of the most potent musical forms of the sixteenth century was the *canzon francese*; The French ballet captured the imagination of the seventeenth century; the clavecin suites of Couperin and Rameau created a fashion in the eighteenth; in the nineteenth, the orchestral virtuosity of Berlioz, the skillful and polished formal-ism of Saint-Saëns, the operas of Auber, Gounod, and Bizet, and the austere art of César Franck, all in their different ways impressed Europe; finally, in the twentieth century, the impressionism of Debussy and Ravel determined the early developments of modern music.

It was from the troubadour songs that French popular music received its first national impulse. These songs were the product of the chivalrous spirit of the Crusades, and of the splendid lyric poetry which arose at that time. Provence, in southern France, was the cradle of the troubadour songs in the Provençal language. They are of different genres without a set form: *pastourelles* (pastoral songs), *aubades* and *serenades* (morning and evening songs), *ballades* (dance songs), and *plancs* (plaintive songs). The composers of these songs were often highborn aristocrats; there was among them even a royal prince, later King of Navarre, Thibaut IV (1201–1253).

The French *ars nova* pursued a trend quite different from the popular music of the troubadours. It was an intellectual art reveling in complex contrapuntal forms. Its principal representative was Guillaume de Machaut (1300–1377), whose complicated *chansons balladées*, isorhythmic motets, *virelais*, and *rondeaux* foreshadowed some of the procedures of modern music. However, these products of the French *ars nova* exercised little influence on European music of the period.

During the sixteenth century French music followed the lead of the Netherlandish school. The main French (or Belgian-Flemish) representatives of the various phases of this great Netherlandish movement were Okeghem, Josquin, Brumel, Mouton, Pierre de la Rue, and Compère. Only in the second half of the sixteenth century did typical national traits — grace, vivacity, and lucidity — make their appearance, in the songs of Pierre Certon (d. 1572), Claudin de Sermisy (1490–1562), Clément Jannequin (c. 1475–c. 1560), and Claude Le Jeune (1528–1600).

Throughout the sixteenth century the Italian term *canzon*

francese was familiar to European musicians. It referred to a certain type of French chanson, a part song with a vivid text in the vernacular, an agreeable tune, and an energetic, rhythmic lilt. The most notable composer of these chansons was Clément Jannequin, whose melodies are marked by urbanity and grace. Such French songs were arranged for lute by Italian musicians, and a new instrumental form, the *canzona*, was the result. The most famous of the instrumental *canzone* were by the Venetian masters Andrea and Giovanni Gabrieli. The Venetian *canzona* later branched out into the forms of the sonata, the orchestral overture, and the *concerto grosso,* thus determining the formal evolution of classical music.

Parallel to the development of the popular French chanson, important changes were taking place in French church music. During the second half of the sixteenth century, France was internally rent by the struggle between the Catholics and the Protestant Huguenots. Some of the most prominent French musicians were of Huguenot faith, and in 1572 the greatest of them all, Claude Goudimel, lost his life in the massacre of St. Bartholomew, when great numbers of the Huguenots were put to death.

At this time, the religious reforms of Calvin began to affect French church music. In keeping with the austere character of that faith, all music with a secular tinge was excluded from Calvinist services; only plain hymn tunes and homophonic settings of the psalms were admitted. The Latin masses and motets based on Gregorian chant were eliminated, and metrical psalmody in the French language became the cornerstone of Calvinist church music in France.

Calvin's first psalter (1539) was based mainly on Clément Marot's metrical translation of the psalms into French verse, set to beautiful, strong, and dignified original tunes, without harmonic accompaniment or contrapuntal elaboration. Among eminent composers who contributed to the compilation of successive editions of the French psalms were Pierre Certon, Clément Jannequin, Claude Goudimel, Orlando di Lasso, Sweelinck, and Claude Le Jeune.

The French *ouverture*, an instrumental introduction to an opera or oratorio, is an offspring of the *canzon francese*. In the second half of the seventeenth century two types of orchestral overture evolved: the so-called "Italian" overture of Alessandro Scarlatti, and the French overture created by Jean-Baptiste Lully (1632–1687), court conductor to Louis XIV. An Italian by birth, Lully was thoroughly acclimatized to France, and his music acquired a national French character. The theater was his special domain, and early French opera owes much to him. The French overture, as treated by Lully, was of a simple, cyclic form: andante-allegro-andante. The opening was usually of a stately, slow nature, generally in dotted rhythms. It was followed by a brisk allegro, often written in fugato style; the overture concluded with another slow movement.

Another French specialty that developed during the sixteenth, seventeenth, and eighteenth centuries was the art of ballet. Though during the Renaissance the Italians were the leaders of stage dance combined with scenic action and music, it was French talent and taste for choreographic performance that gave ballet its artistic basis. One of the earliest choreographic spectacles in France was *Ballet comique de la reine*, presented in 1581 at the wedding of the Duc de Joyeux. The performance lasted from ten o'clock at night until four o'clock in the morning, and its lavish splendor became legendary. Ballet spectacles were a favorite form of entertainment at the courts of Henri IV, Louis XIII, and Louis XIV. Cardinal Richelieu patronized dancing, and not infrequently Louis XIV himself took part in court ballets. Lully included ballet in his operas, thus influencing the formation of instrumental dance suites.

The classical perfection of French dancing and dance music was reached in the eighteenth century, at the height of the rococo period of European taste. The French dancers Milles, Sallé, and Camargo enchanted the populace; Rameau's ballet music, in its refinement, grace, beauty, and nobility of style, set a new standard of excellence, and ballet remained a peculiarly French art until about 1900, when the Russian style of scenic dancing superseded it.

As we consider the clavecin, or harpsichord, music of Couperin and Rameau, we find that in its special field it is not inferior to that of Bach. The popular ballet suite was taken over from the operatic art of Lully by two generations of French clavecinists, and many masterpieces of refinement, cultured taste, and finished style were developed.

Jacques Champion Chambonnières (1602–1672), court clavecinist to Louis XIV, founded a school of great keyboard performers. Among his numerous pupils were several members of the Couperin family who won fame as organists and clavecin virtuosos. One of them, François Couperin (1668–1733), became known as Couperin le Grand, and the quality of his music fully justified this lofty sobriquet.

In his suites, Couperin adopted the external structure of the dance suite as it was evolved in Italy and France, with the *allemande, courante, sarabande,* and *gigue* as four main pillars, and other dances — *minuet, rigaudon, loure, gavotte, musette, bourrée, chaconne,* and *passepied* — as additional architectural supports. In their contents, however, these suites can no longer be regarded as dance music; they are, rather, fantasies in dance, anticipating in form Chopin's valses, polonaises, and mazurkas. Their fanciful titles suggest personal musical portraits or picturesque descriptions of actual scenes; the music is alternately graceful and delicate, pompous and festive, or even comical in the spirit of burlesque; but it is always in excellent taste, full of exquisite sound effects, and adorned with elegant and delicate ornamentation. The rococo mentality in its diverse aspects was never more faithfully expressed than in Couperin's clavecin music.

Jean Philippe Rameau (1683–1764) continued the tradition

of Couperin. However, he did not confine himself to writing for the clavecin; he was also a composer of great dramatic music. His operas combine the grandiose, baroque style with the exquisite refinement of rococo music. Rameau was a true successor of Lully, as a master of French opera; in regard to the future, Rameau was the forerunner of Gluck, the reformer of opera. As a pure musician, Rameau stands far above Lully, and he surpasses Gluck in the refinement and skill of his technical devices.

In the twentieth century, appreciation of Rameau's music has greatly increased. Claude Debussy spoke of Rameau as the incarnation of national French genius. The slogan "Back to Rameau" resounded from the Debussy camp at the time when the Wagnerian tide was stirring up higher waves than the guardians of French national ideals could bear. In the science of musical theory, too, Rameau was an epoch-making figure. In his *Traité de l'harmonie*, the theory of chords and their functions was presented for the first time. Rameau was thus the father of modern harmony and legislator of the modern regulations of harmonic usage.

The French clavecin suite, as perfected by Couperin and Rameau, became a model for the composers of keyboard music in all European countries. Bach gave the title of *French Suites* to some of his greatest keyboard works. Handel's splendid clavecin suites also pay homage to the French genius.

Yet in France itself, the tradition of Rameau and Couperin suffered a decline late in the eighteenth century. It was an era of light operatic music written by amateurs; the social philosopher Jean-Jacques Rousseau acquired musical fame by his comic operetta *Le Devin du village*, and incidentally contributed to this change of taste toward light music. Rousseau also cultivated the melodrama or opera without singing, the words being merely recited to music. The celebrated chess player François André Philidor (1726–1795), too, wrote pretty operettas.

During this period of stagnation, French art was helped by the influx of Italian music through the youthful genius of Giovanni Battista Pergolesi (1710–1736), whose career was cut off by premature death at the age of twenty-six. His small stage work *La Serva padrona* was presented with tremendous success in Paris in 1752; this occasion served to implement the rise of the French comic opera. The Italian musician Egidio Duni (1709–1775), who lived in France, created a new genre of French comic opera in a style well calculated to please Parisian taste. There was also the great Belgian composer Grétry, who became a classic master of the Parisian sentimental opera.

The greatest figure in French musical life during the eighteenth century was Christoph Willibald Gluck, a German-Austrian, who introduced the most far-reaching reform in French opera and in whose works music and poetry became a single, unified art. A generation later, the Italian master Luigi Cherubini achieved fame in Paris as a composer of operas and sacred music. The cosmopolitan charm of Paris attracted foreigners and stimulated them to their mightiest efforts. Of all world capitals, Paris alone seems able to combine an outspoken national character with international values of the broadest type, allowing these seemingly antagonistic tendencies to live side by side.

Some words of Voltaire's, from Chapter XXXIII of *Le Siècle de Louis XIV*, may give a perspective on French music as seen by the intellectuals of his time: "The music was in its cradle; a few nostalgic songs, some airs for the violin, the guitar and the lute, most of them not even French but composed in Spain, were all that was available. Lully astonished the public by his taste and by his science. He was the first in France to organize the basses, the middle voices, the fugal passages. Musicians had some trouble at first in performing Lully's works, which seem so simple and so easy now. For each person who knew something about music at the time of Louis XIII, there are now a thousand who have this knowledge, and the art of music has progressed at a similar ratio. There is hardly a single large town in France that does not have public concerts, while in those times even Paris did not have them; the twenty-four 'Violons du Roi' constituted all of French music."

Voltaire was not too well informed about musical history; he evidently knew nothing about the composers of the sixteenth-century French Renaissance, and his high opinion of Lully is justified only because, in the musical desert that Paris had become in the middle of the seventeenth century, Lully's compositions must certainly have impressed the ignorant public as being full of "learning." Voltaire says that Lully was the "first in France to write basses, milieux, and fugues." The basses must refer to the Italian *basso continuo*; the mysterious term "milieux" probably meant middle voices. As for Lully's fugues, they were not real fugues at all. Voltaire says that Lully's compositions were regarded by his contemporaries as difficult to understand, but were found simple a century later. Voltaire also says that in his own time public concerts were given in many towns, whereas in the seventeenth century there had been none even in Paris; the King's famous "twenty-four violins" had provided the only musical entertainment of artistic quality. We know that this report is superficial, but at least it throws a gleam of light onto the musical thinking of the eighteenth century.

French clavecin music attained maturity early in the eighteenth century. The development of French violin music was the next important phase. Lully prepared this development in his capacity as conductor of the "violons du roi," but it took another century for the French masters of violin music to challenge the supremacy of Italian virtuosos and instrumental composers.

Among these masters of violin music, the name of Jean-Marie Leclair (1697–1764) stands high. He studied in Italy; when he arrived in Paris, he found the city full of Italian violinists. In composition, Italian masters dominated the field and were eagerly imitated by the French musicians. Presently, however, opposition began to assert itself. Jacques Aubert (1689–1753), composer of instrumental suites, declared in the preface to his

Concerts de symphonies that the genre of Italian sonata was repugnant to French music lovers and should be replaced by specifically French music, marked by "the gracefulness, brilliance, and beautiful simplicity that are characteristically French," and that this change was demanded by the ladies of France "whose judgment has always determined the pleasures of the nation."

This appeal to national pride was a challenge to French composers, who had to compete with foreign masters of the caliber of Corelli and Tartini. Jean-Marie Leclair fully met this challenge, and his music — forty-eight violin sonatas, twelve concertos, and a number of violin duos — is in quality comparable with the best Italian productions. Leclair had a remarkable pupil, Chevalier de Saint-Georges, a mulatto from Guadeloupe, who made a sensation in Paris as a brilliant virtuoso; he also composed violin sonatas of a considerably advanced nature.

Jean-Joseph Mondonville (1711–1772), intendant of the Royal Chapel at Versailles, was a highly esteemed violin virtuoso and composer. His set of sonatas *Les Sons harmoniques* is of historic importance, owing to the systematic use of harmonics in the violin part. Mondonville enjoyed the special protection of Mme. de Pompadour, the mistress of Louis XV. When the Italians scored their triumph in Paris with Pergolesi's *La Serva padrona* in 1752, Mondonville led the opposing French national movement in opera; he also wrote a charming pastoral play, in which he introduced genuine Provençal tunes, thus stressing the French element of the music.

Every violin student is familiar with the 24 *Exercices pour le violon* by Pierre Gaviniés (1728–1800). The composer of this famous compendium of virtuosity was, at the height of the revolution, appointed first professor of violin at the newly founded Paris Conservatoire.

The revolution, which brought about so many fundamental changes in France, marked a change in French musical style and expression, evident in the violin literature. The leader in this movement was Giovanni Battista Viotti (1755–1824), who, although he was Italian by birth and by training, is rightfully identified with the French school. He lived for many years in Paris, and was one of the favorite musicians of Marie Antoinette.

Kreutzer, Rode, Baillot, and Cartier continued the Viotti tradition. The name of Rodolphe Kreutzer (1766–1831) has become immortal because of Beethoven's dedication to him of the violin sonata that bears his name. The son of a German military bandmaster in the French service, Kreutzer was born at Versailles and educated in Paris. He was a member of the Royal Chapel, then a violinist at the Théâtre des Italiens. After the revolution he taught at the Paris Conservatoire and later became chief violinist at Napoleon's court. He made Beethoven's acquaintance in Vienna in 1798. He must have produced a lasting impression on the master, who dedicated to him his greatest violin sonata. Among professional violinists, Kreutzer is known by his 40 *Etudes ou Caprices pour un violon seul.* This classical work is indispensable for the training of a violinist, owing to its systematic treatment of the fundamental factors of bowing, fingering, change of positions, double stops, chords, and trills; and all this within the framework of tasteful musical forms.

Viotti's pupil Pierre Rode (1774–1830) retained a great reputation for more than a century, thanks to his 24 *Caprices en forme d'études pour le violon seul dans les 24 tons de la gamme.* These extremely useful pieces supplemented the Kreutzer *Etudes.* Some of Rode's violin concertos are still played; they are fine specimens of the brilliant postrevolutionary type, with its martial, heroic features and dramatic agitation. Rode was an eminently successful virtuoso, greatly admired not only in Paris but all over Europe. He was equally at home in Berlin, where King Frederick William II tried to secure his services, in Madrid, where he became Boccherini's close friend, and in St. Petersburg, where for five years he was violinist to the Tsar Alexander I.

Another Viotti pupil, Jean-Baptiste Cartier (1765–1841), is remembered for his *L'Art du violon*, a valuable collection of violin compositions of the best Italian, French, and German composers.

In the nineteenth century, the French tradition of violin playing was maintained by a long line of professors at the Paris Conservatoire; these included great teachers as well as great performers. Among them was Pierre-François Baillot (1771–1842), a virtuoso of European celebrity and founder of the first permanent string quartet in Paris.

Baillot's pupil François-Antoine Habeneck (1781–1849) was not only an eminent teacher but also an outstanding orchestral conductor in Paris and a compelling force in the musical life of the capital. Under his leadership, the orchestra of the Paris Conservatoire achieved a new standard of performance. Mendelssohn, in a letter to Zelter from Paris, gives his old teacher a long, enthusiastic report on the excellence of Habeneck's orchestra. In his autobiography, Wagner speaks of the overwhelming impression he received on hearing Habeneck's performance of Beethoven's Ninth Symphony. Even the quarrelsome Berlioz, who found fault with everybody in Paris, had to acknowledge Habeneck's great musicianship in spite of his personal animosity toward him.

Jacques-Féréol Mazas (1782–1849), Baillot's pupil, is remembered for his *Etudes*, well known to advanced players. Jean-Baptiste Charles Dancla (1817–1907), likewise a pupil of Baillot, enriched the literature by his 20 *Etudes brillantes et caractéristiques*. Jean-Delphin Alard (1815–1888), a pupil of Habeneck and his successor at the Conservatoire, is now best known for his *École de violon*, one of the outstanding works of its type, and for his fine collection of eighteenth-century violin music, *Les maîtres classiques du violon*. Among Alard's celebrated pupils was Pablo Sarasate.

The question now arises: did French composers contribute adequate violin music for these master performers? A survey reveals a lamentable paucity of creative achievement. After 1850 a few French concertos took root in the violin repertory. For a long time the unjustly underrated French master Camille Saint-Saëns exercised a monopoly in French violin music. His three violin concertos (especially the one in B minor) have maintained their place in the favor of performers and public alike. In the 1870's the brilliant *Symphone espagnole* by Edouard Lalo (1823–1892) was added to the small number of internationally accepted French violin concertos.

The situation of French chamber music in the nineteenth century was not much better than that of violin music, until César Franck created his great violin sonata at the very close of his career. This composition is unquestionably the most enduring and beautiful French instrumental work of the nineteenth century. For more than fifty years it has found no worthy counterpart in France, in spite of the highly commendable efforts of such remarkable musicians as Vincent d'Indy, Franck's most prominent pupil, and Gabriel Fauré.

French string quartet literature is extremely scanty, consisting of not more than three works that enjoy international acceptance. Franck's masterly quartet in D Major, written the year before he died, is a synthesis of the late Beethoven style with the spirit of romanticism. Debussy's unique quartet has a decided appeal on account of its surprising and insinuating sound effects, gained, it must be said, at the expense of plastic linear polyphony. Ravel's only string quartet is more substantial in melodic material and still more intricate in its rhythmical devices than that of Debussy, to which it bears a certain family likeness, but its coloristic effects are less impressive.

The vitality of French violin culture through its two centuries of development was not matched by corresponding progress in French music for piano. For more than a century Paris was the home of great pianists. But most of them were foreigners — Kalkbrenner, Chopin, Liszt, Thalberg. In the second half of

the nineteenth century, only Saint-Saëns (1835–1921) represented French pianistic art on the international scene. As a
composer for piano, he had no rival in France. At least two of
his five piano concertos — those in G minor (No. 2) and in C
minor (No. 4) — have become part of the international repertory. César Franck (1822–1890) wrote only a few piano works,
but each of them is important musically as well as technically.
His *Prelude, Chorale, and Fugue* shows an affinity to Bach, as
well as its derivation from the organ — for Franck was a great
organist. We find here a successful adaptation of organ polyphony to the piano, with colorful chromatic harmony, reminding
one of Bach and also of Wagner's *Parsifal*. This music, however,
is thoroughly individual, easily recognized as "Franckian," with
its characteristic chords of the ninth that became a stepping-
stone to Debussy's harmony. Franck's popular work, *Variations
symphoniques*, for piano and orchestra, is remarkable for its
finely balanced dialogue between the solo instrument and the
orchestra.

Charles Alkan (1813–1888) is an unjustly forgotten musician.
This Parisian Jew was one of the great pianists of his day and a
remarkable composer of piano music. His professional career
was limited to private recitals; his many published compositions
have become a bibliographical rarity. Yet Hans von Bülow, in
the preface to his edition of the Cramer *Etudes*, lists Alkan's
etudes as even more difficult than those of Liszt and Rubinstein;
and Ferruccio Busoni wrote on New Year's Day, 1900, that he
considered Alkan's *12 Etudes* "the greatest achievement in piano
music after Liszt." Alkan's monumental Opus 29, comprising
two hundred and seventy-six pages and including whole concertos and symphonies for the piano, is a veritable encyclopedia
of pianistic art.

After Franck, piano music in France had three main representatives: Fauré, Debussy, and Ravel. Gabriel Fauré (1845–
1924), a highly accomplished master of instrumental music
and of French song, occupies a unique position in the history

of music. In France his numerous songs are regarded as models of their kind, somewhat like the Schumann songs in Germany. They are so closely tied to French poetry that they lose their flavor by translation into any foreign language. His piano music is a descendant of Chopin's art, with occasional glances over the fence, so to speak, into impressionism. Refinement, rather than vigor, passion, or expressive power, is the signature of this somewhat decadent art, too narrowly conceived to force its way into the broader expanses of international music.

Unlike Fauré, Claude Debussy (1862–1918) enjoyed international success. He was the protagonist of impressionism, a typically French product. The name was originally applied to the group of painters led by Manet, Monet, Sisley, Pissarro, and others. The impressionists painted nature not as an external phenomenon but as a subjective vision, as it appeared to them at the moment; they depicted — to use the language of philosophy — not the thing in itself, but the transitory phenomenon. For the eye this passing vision depends mainly on the play of light; the same object appears different at noon or at twilight, in the sunshine or in the rain, and the task of the impressionistic painter was to record on canvas the fleeting appearance of this changing scene. In poetry, Mallarmé and Verlaine pursued a similarly elusive art. Debussy embodied impressionistic ideas in music: for him, music was an interplay of infinite varieties of sound. Construction, polyphony, and dramatic development receded into the background. He worked with tone colors, using a palette of infinite subtlety, and his musical ideas were products of aural and visual impressions, which he translated into sounds.

A glance at the titles of Debussy's pieces reveals his predilection for subjects infused with subtle coloration. In his piano piece *Jardins sous la pluie*, one hears the drops of rain softly falling on the shrubs and flower beds. His musical picture, *La Cathédrale engloutie* reverberates with the chimes sounding from the tower of an ancient cathedral submerged in the sea; in his symphonic triptych *La Mer*, waves and wind conduct a fascinating play upon the sunlit ocean. As a tonal landscape painter, Debussy has no equal. His horizon may be limited in comparison with the immense vistas of Bach, Mozart, or Beethoven, but within these self-imposed limitations, he created an inimitable art.

Impressionism, however, was not the invention of Debussy alone. The romantic composers of the nineteenth century occasionally produced works that may well be described as impressionistic. Liszt's *Années de pèlerinage*, travel sketches from Switzerland and Italy, are impressionistic in content and in pianistic color; Schumann, Berlioz, and Wagner also had their impressionistic moments. The historical importance of Debussy's music lies in the systematic exploration of impressionistic sound with subtlety and variety never before envisaged. He devised an original kind of colorful harmony, suggesting delicate and subdued sounds; his melodies were set in the unusual progressions of whole tones and pentatonic scales. He used archaic-sounding diatonic church modes in plain chordal harmonies, and also chromatic harmonies that stem from Wagner's *Tristan* but lack Wagner's impassioned power. Indeed, passion is totally absent from Debussy's music. He was little interested in soul-searching, in the joys and sorrows of mankind; he was mainly concerned with surface phenomena, reflected in beautiful sound images.

Debussy's music may be a distilled product, a weakened extract of the warm artistic sentiment, "un petit art." But this small art has become great through its perfection, and has acquired lasting value through the infinite care it bestows on the acoustic portrayal of the musical moment. Impressionism in music, as practiced by Debussy, became a dominant factor in the early decades of the twentieth century. In France it was represented by Debussy, Ravel, and Roussel; in England by Frederick Delius and Cyril Scott. In Russia, Scriabin cultivated an Eastern variety of impressionism. In Poland, impressionistic music is represented by Szymanowski and Rozycki, in Rumania by Georges Enesco;

in Spain by Manuel de Falla; and in Italy by Respighi, Pizzetti, Malipiero, and Casella. Richard Strauss and the leaders of ultramodern music, Schönberg and Stravinsky, also passed through their impressionistic phases; and French impressionism profoundly influenced a whole generation of American musicians, of whom Charles Martin Loeffler is an outstanding example.

On the sidelines, all by himself, stands the tragicomic figure of Erik Satie (1866–1925), an eccentric clown in the musical circus, regarded by some as the creator of the new esthetics of the twentieth century. There seems to be no reason for accepting seriously Satie's little piano pieces, exhibiting a peculiarly mocking contempt for all tradition, without the redeeming grace of worthwhile innovation.

In his piano music, Maurice Ravel (1875–1937) was a strong rival of Debussy. He first attracted attention early in the century with his brilliant and picturesque piano piece *Jeux d'eau*. It is a veritable cascade of tones, remarkable in its novel pianistic style, derived from the juxtaposition of the five black and the seven white keys as harmonic groups. Chronologically, this work precedes Debussy's famous impressionistic pieces. In the genre of "water music" it is a worthy successor to Liszt's admirable *Jeux d'eau à la Villa d'Este*. Another sparkling "water piece" entitled *Ondine* forms part of Ravel's piano cycle *Gaspard de la nuit*. Several other piano works by Ravel have reached a larger audience in their orchestral settings than in their original versions: they include the simple and pleasing children's pieces called *Ma mère l'oye* (Mother Goose), the suite *Valses nobles et sentimentales*, and *Tombeau de Couperin*, written in homage to the old French master, in the form of an eighteenth-century suite.

Among French symphonists, one must single out Hector Berlioz (1803–1869) as the only French musician of the nineteenth century who decisively influenced the national music of other countries, notably Germany and Russia. He was, figuratively speaking, a grandson of Gluck and a son of Beethoven; the influence of Berlioz upon the art of modern orchestration is incalculable. He was the first to systematize, in his famous *Traité de l'instrumentation*, the devices and usages of orchestral writing. Liszt and Wagner, Borodin and Mussorgsky, Rimsky-Korsakov and Stravinsky, Strauss and Mahler, Puccini and Casella, Ravel and Debussy are all pupils of Hector Berlioz in the art of judicious mixing of the colors provided by the many instruments that make up the modern orchestra.

The most striking of Berlioz' scores is undoubtedly his *Symphonie fantastique*. In the finale, representing the Witches' Sabbath, the cult of the grotesque and gruesome reaches its peak of expressive power. Liszt followed Berlioz' method in the finale of his "Faust" Symphony; Wagner, too, was influenced by Berlioz' picturesque colors, but he applied them to evoke the comic rather than the demoniacal quality, as in the part of Beckmesser in *Die Meistersinger*. The music of Richard Strauss reveals the Berlioz influence, especially in the exciting last scene of *Elektra*, where the heroine eagerly awaits the news of the death of her mother at the hand of her brother, and of the slaying of her mother's lover. Like a fury, intoxicated by the flaming spirit of revenge, Elektra celebrates the double murder by a stupendous and terrible dance of victory, which is at the same time her dance of death. This tremendous scene could never have been written without the precedent set by Berlioz in his orgiastic music of despair and violence.

The history of French symphonic music after Berlioz is summarized by the names of Camille Saint-Saëns, César Franck, Vincent d'Indy, Claude Debussy, Maurice Ravel, Paul Dukas, and Albert Roussel. Among the symphonies of Saint-Saëns, only the third, with organ, is still heard occasionally. The symphonies of Vincent d'Indy and his set of orchestral variations, *Istar*, are rare guests on concert programs. Franck's only symphony, the child of his old age, is very popular, but it is played oftener than is good for its reputation. These French symphonies, diverse though they are in style, pursue the romantic pattern established by Beethoven, with certain modifications in treatment that are natural to the French temperament.

Paul Dukas (1865–1935) was one of the most original figures in modern French music. He possessed a strong individual talent, but of his music only one composition has retained its hold on the international repertory—the brilliant symphonic scherzo, *L'Apprenti sorcier*, which illustrates in vivid tone colors and incisive rhythms Goethe's poem about a hapless student of magic, who in the absence of his master invokes the magic powers but has no ability to control them.

Albert Roussel (1869–1937) began his career as a composer of impressionist tone poems. In his mature years he returned to the ancient ideals of classical organization and polyphonic structure. Rather than writing music that appeals to the senses by its picturesque colors, he wrote symphonies without any illustrative program but of considerable musical weight.

The foundations of French opera were laid by foreign masters —Lully, Gluck, Cherubini. It was the German-born Christoph Willibald Gluck (1714–1787) who initiated the famous reform in French opera that led to a reconsideration of all accepted ideas in operatic art. Gluck wrote in the preface to the published score of his opera *Alceste*: "I sought to reduce music to its true function, that of seconding poetry in order to strengthen the emotional expression and the impact of the dramatic situations without interrupting the action and without weakening it by superfluous ornament." Gluck's ideas were ardently supported by the French nationalists and opposed by the adherents of Italian opera. Thus opened the celebrated controversy between the champions of Gluck's reform and the Italian faction of Nicola Piccini.

Gluck's French operas brought him tremendous acclaim. In them, he introduced a true classical spirit, with its noble austerity of style and its plastic beauty, in contrast with the excesses of the sensuous rococo age. The subjects of Gluck's operas were taken mostly from Greek mythology.

A unique position among opera composers in France at the threshold of the nineteenth century was that filled by Luigi Cherubini (1760–1842). He spent nearly fifty years in Paris and was regarded there as a great master. In his operas he combined the Italian tradition of effective vocal treatment with considerable dramatic skill. But while Gluck's operas are still performed, the music of Cherubini survives only through his brilliant and picturesque overtures.

A contemporary of Cherubini who also won fame in Paris was Gasparo Spontini (1774–1851). His opera *La Vestale* obtained an immense success in 1807. This powerful score belongs to the Gluck tradition in its dramatic intensity and theatrical effectiveness. The amalgamation of the Italian *opera seria* with the French *tragédie lyrique* in *La Vestale* was an achievement of prime historical importance. In his exotic opera *Ferdinand Cortez*, Spontini brought pompous, grandiose mass effects to a climax scarcely ever surpassed, and thus inspired the art of such masters of French opera as Auber, Meyerbeer, Halévy, and Berlioz.

French opera in the nineteenth century progressed in two different directions: toward the ambitious form of grand opera, and toward the more popular *opéra comique*. Some French composers have written operas in both genres. One was Daniel François Auber (1782–1871), who during his long life witnessed the decline of the French Revolution, the rise of Napoleon, the Restoration, the Second Empire, and its downfall, and died at the age of nearly ninety. He lived within the lifetimes of Mozart, Haydn, and Beethoven; he was an older contemporary of Rossini; he outlived by many years his younger contemporaries Schumann and Chopin. Auber has been given the historic name of father of the French comic opera; but he was an adroit practitioner of the art of grand opera as well. He opened the era of French tragic opera with his masterpiece *La Muette de*

Portici, produced in Paris in 1828. After more than a century this opera is still a part of the world-wide repertory. The city of Paris acknowledged Auber's achievement by naming the street leading to the Paris Opera, Rue d'Auber.

Chronologically next in the series of French grand operas was Rossini's *William Tell,* first performed at the Paris Opera in 1829. Here the Italian opera style — with its vivacity, merriment, enticing melody, and brilliant coloratura — reached a peak of glory. Its apparatus of scenic pomp, massed finales, grand climaxes, artistically involved ensembles, and picturesque orchestration was exploited by Rossini with the utmost dramatic power.

French romantic grand opera came to its greatest expansion with Giacomo Meyerbeer (1791–1864), a German Jew who settled in Paris in 1830. Meyerbeer's ambition was to combine the artistic effects of the three great national schools of music — the Italian, German, and French. He planned to provide musical settings for dramatic episodes from the past, to create historical offers in a combination of German, French, and Italian styles, which, with the help of his supranational Jewish mentality, he hoped to amalgamate into one broadly European style. However, his musical talent was not sufficient for this formidable task. Certain weaknesses and blemishes marred the stylistic purity of his operas, and Meyerbeer's opponents gleefully pointed out these faults.

Robert le Diable, Meyerbeer's first French opera, met with great success. Translated into a dozen languages, it became a sensation all over Europe. Meyerbeer had found a collaborator of great gifts, Eugène Scribe, the most skillful librettist of his time. Scribe wrote for Meyerbeer the librettos of *Robert le Diable, Les Huguenots, Le Prophète,* and *L'Africaine;* for Auber, *La Muette de Portici, Fra Diavolo,* and many others; and for Halévy, *La Juive,* besides dozens of librettos for less known operas. Even more successful than *Robert le Diable* was Meyerbeer's next opera, *Les Huguenots,* generally acknowledged to be his masterpiece. The theme he chose was the mortal struggle between the French Catholics and the Protestant Huguenots, which led to the Massacre of St. Bartholomew; its dramatic final act is one of the most overwhelming creations of the opera stage.

Another historical episode from the age of the Reformation, the rule of the Anabaptists under the command of their insane "King of Zion" in the German city of Münster, is treated in Meyerbeer's opera *Le Prophète*. This score, which abounds in powerful, brilliant scenes, had wide success in spite of violent opposition. Quite different in character is Meyerbeer's *L'Africaine*; its music exhales exotic charm in illustration of the tropical scene. These and other operas by Meyerbeer dominated the stages of all opera houses in every musical country for half a century, until they were displaced by the works of Wagner and Verdi.

Meyerbeer had to recognize a powerful competitor in the French Jew, Jacques Fromental Halévy (1799–1862), whose opera *La Juive*, produced in Paris in 1835, was as resoundingly successful as Meyerbeer's *Les Huguenots*.

In the middle of the nineteenth century, a French opera was staged that eclipsed all operatic successes achieved by Meyerbeer, Halévy, and even Rossini. It was *Faust* by Charles Gounod (1818–1893). Its production in 1859 aroused spontaneous enthusiasm, and its popularity has never waned since. The exciting dramatic libretto, freely adapted from Goethe's *Faust,* the irresistible melodic charm of the music, and the mastery of theatrical effects explain the extraordinary success of the opera. Yet this French *Faust* is by no means a masterpiece of dramatic art. It degrades Goethe's sublime poem to the level of melodrama, with Faust playing the role of a cunning seducer and Mephistopheles acting like a typical theatrical devil. In Germany, the opera is performed under the title *Margarethe,* to avoid all association with Goethe's great poem. Of Gounod's later operas, only one, *Roméo et Juliette*, has become a favorite. His opera *Mireille*, with its pastoral charm and idyllic Provençal poetry, is much more refined in treatment than *Faust*, but it is hardly ever heard outside France.

Like Gounod, Ambroise Thomas (1811–1896) sought in Goethe the inspiration for his most successful work, the opera *Mignon*, based on Goethe's novel *Wilhelm Meister*. Its melodious music has a popular appeal, even if it lacks originality. Thomas also set to music Shakespeare's greatest play, *Hamlet*, but after an initial success, this opera failed to hold a place in the world's repertory comparable to that of *Mignon*.

Samson et Dalila by Camille Saint-Saëns (1835–1921) stands on a far higher artistic level than the operas of Ambroise Thomas. The Biblical scene is depicted here with superior art in powerful and characteristic choral episodes, free from the clichés of traditional opera. The solo arias, the ensemble pieces, and the orchestral treatment reveal the hand of a sensitive musician. *Samson et Dalila* has deservedly acquired world-wide celebrity and a permanent place in the international repertory.

The most charming and appealing opera written by a Frenchman is undoubtedly *Carmen* by Georges Bizet (1838–1875). First produced in 1875 in Paris, it quickly became popular all over the world. The libretto is a penetrating character study of a profligate woman who has ensnared a soldier, only to cast him aside disdainfully for the favors of a bullfighter, thus driving him to an insane pitch of passion and to murder. From the purely musical point of view, *Carmen* is one of the most effective operas ever written. Its melodic and rhythmical charm is spontaneous and engrossing; the picturesque music depicting a gathering of Spanish gypsy smugglers has an especially authentic flavor, and Bizet's genius for drama is revealed on every page. Some Spanish musicians have pointed out that Bizet's enticing melodies in *Carmen* are not Spanish in character. They forget, however, that in art the authenticity of material is less important than the power of suggesting it to the listener's imagination; and this power Bizet possessed to a very high degree.

Bizet's earlier operas are rarely heard nowadays. Yet his

Djamileh is well worth reviving. It is a veritable gem, sparkling with Oriental colors, a delight for musical gourmets, but too refined, perhaps, to please the general opera-going public. The beautiful incidental music written by Bizet to Alphonse Daudet's play *L'Arlésienne* has survived in the form of two orchestral suites. The fragrant charm of the southern melodies in this music is akin to the Mediterranean color of *Carmen*.

The most popular French opera composer of the late nineteenth century was Jules Massenet (1842–1912). His greatest triumph came in 1884 with *Manon*. He had already had some success with several operas now forgotten, and some choral and symphonic music, of which the orchestral suites entitled *Scènes pittoresques* and *Scènes alsaciennes* are still occasionally heard. But only with *Manon* did he acquire international renown. Along with *Faust, Manon* became the official representative of "national" opera in France, *Faust* dominating the Grand Opéra of Paris, and its younger companion, *Manon*, becoming a perennial entry in the repertory of the Opéra-Comique. The libretto of *Manon* was taken from the Abbé Prévost's famous story *Manon Lescaut*, depicting the lax morals of eighteenth-century French society, in which a pretty young girl is ensnared and carried to the crest of good fortune, only to sink down eventually to the lowest depths of misery. This affecting story is faithfully reflected in Massenet's music. His melodious and thoroughly French tunes, tastefully dressed with pleasing harmonies; his lilting rhythms, effective climaxes, and impressive contrasts in portraying frivolous gaiety followed by inevitable retribution — all this creates an ensemble of harmonious proportions, even though the component structural elements may be of little artistic worth. Verdi treated a similar theme in *La Traviata*, whose heroine seems to be an Italian cousin of the French Manon. Puccini, too, contributed operatic portraits to this gallery of amorous and amiable young women who fall victim to their own simplicity.

Massenet dominated the French opera of the last quarter of

the nineteenth century. His nearest rival for success was Léo Delibes (1836–1891), whose opera *Lakmé* has retained its popularity even in our own time. Its "Bell Song" is one of the most elaborate specimens of coloratura arias, and it is a perennial item in the repertory of every high soprano singer. Delibes also gained international reputation by his charming and effective ballets *Coppélia* and *Sylvia*.

Several estimable French opera composers had considerable success late in the nineteenth and early in the twentieth centuries, but this success was transitory. Ernest Reyer (1823–1909), who hoped to emulate Wagner, had a brief hour of glory with his opera *Sigurd,* and Edouard Lalo (1823–1892) with *Le Roi d'Ys.* Even such an outstanding master of French music as Vincent d'Indy (1851–1931) could not obtain more than a *succès d'estime* with his ambitious operas *Fervaal* and *L'Etranger,* both of which were written in a grandiose Wagnerian vein. For a time great interest was evinced, not only in France but in Germany as well, in the dramatic works of the highly gifted French composer Emmanuel Chabrier (1841–1894), who also began his career as an enthusiastic Wagnerian. His opera *Gwendoline* contains much unusually brilliant and beautiful music, but it is now virtually forgotten. Finally, the name of Ernest Chausson (1855–1899) may be mentioned among French Wagnerians who tried to adapt Wagner's theories to French realities; his opera *Le Roi Arthus* was produced posthumously and never revived. Chausson is known now chiefly by his attractive *Poème* for violin.

More fortunate than Chabrier and Chausson was Gustave Charpentier (1860–1956), who during his long life produced one work that insured him a place of honor in the annals of opera. This was *Louise,* performed in Paris in 1900 with tremendous success. In it he paints, in realistic tones, the life of Paris, and it is the city itself, rather than the personages in the libretto, that is the heroine of Charpentier's opera. *Louise* was not the first realistic opera produced in France. Alfred Bruneau

(1857–1934) found his inspiration in the realistic novels of Emile Zola. His first work, *Le Rêve* (1891), made a stir in Paris comparable to that created by the Italian *verismo* of Mascagni and Leoncavallo. Among other French opera composers, Henri Rabaud (1873–1949) returned to the fantastic Oriental milieu and to the elegance of Delibes in his attractive opera *Marouf*. None of the numerous operas by Gabriel Pierné (1863–1937) have become known outside France, although his children's oratorio *La Croisade des enfants* was widely performed in Europe and America.

The only twentieth-century French opera to cause a real sensation all over the musical world was Claude Debussy's *Pelléas et Mélisande* (1902). This work is unique, because it apparently breaks away from all operatic tradition. In fact, it is not an opera in the generally accepted sense. Nothing is left of the aria, of the Italian coloratura, of the brilliant solo singing with its long sustained tones, its exciting crescendos, its relaxing diminuendos, its emphatic accents, its jubilant and sparkling trills and runs, its continuous and plastic melodic lines. For all this Debussy substitutes a melodious parlando recitative. This recitative resembles somewhat the Gregorian psalmody but is much more supple and varied. Its vocal line is usually maintained *mezza voce,* at times sinking to a mere whisper, then rising to a shout of passion; hardly ever does it evolve into a well-rounded melody.

Novel as is the vocal treatment in *Pelléas et Mélisande,* still more remarkable is the instrumental writing in this score. Debussy's luminous orchestration is the soul of his music. The orchestra is not a mere accompaniment to the vocal parts; it is a complex symphonic poem. In translating Maeterlinck's somber medieval tragedy into music, Debussy treats the vocal parts as a sort of commentary, explaining to the listener the contents and mood of the successive scenes. Yet with all its undeniable innovations, the music of *Pelléas et Mélisande* reveals, to a close observer, visible threads that connect it with certain portions of

Wagner's *Tristan und Isolde,* of which *Pelléas* seems to be an illegitimate child, somewhat bashful about admitting its origin.

No opera comparable to *Pelléas et Mélisande* has since come from France. Maurice Ravel, Debussy's most potent rival as a composer of the impressionist school, wrote the comic opera *L'Heure espagnole,* sparkling with wit and artistry. The score is a treat for connoisseurs; to ordinary music-lovers, however, Ravel's opera offers too little to savor and enjoy.

These operas — from Gluck to Debussy — represent in their varying ways the growth of the species of grand opera in France. A brief survey of French *opéra comique,* a lesser art, must be made here to round out the account of French operatic production. Auber is the acknowledged father of French comic opera. Among other proponents of this genre, the Italian composer who settled in Paris, Niccolò Isouard (1775–1818), charmed the Parisian audiences with his melodious and entertaining confections, such as *Cendrillon, Joconde,* and *Le Billet de loterie.* Much more significant than Isouard was his French-born contemporary François Adrien Boieldieu (1775–1834), a prolific composer who wrote many entertaining but insignificant light operas before producing his masterpiece, *La Dame blanche,* at the age of fifty.

Boieldieu's pupil and friend Adolphe Adam (1803–1856) became known to the musical world through his rollicking comic opera *Le Postillon de Longjumeau.* The libretto deals with the adventures of a mail-coach driver who, with his traditional post-horn, was a familiar figure before the introduction of the railroads in Europe. For three generations Adam's *postillon* blew his horn, cracked his long whip, and sang high notes, bringing delight to audiences not only in France but in the rest of Europe. The town of Longjumeau, immortalized by Adam, expressed the gratitude of its citizens by erecting a monument to him.

Louis-Joseph-Ferdinand Hérold (1791–1833) was the son of a pupil of Philipp Emanuel Bach. He himself had been a pupil of Adolphe Adam's father, who was a professor at the Paris Conservatoire. A brilliantly gifted musician, Hérold wrote an enormous mass of music during his short life. At least one of his numerous light operas, *Zampa*, escaped oblivion. Its brilliant overture is constantly played in popular concerts.

Friedrich von Flotow (1812–1883), a German nobleman educated in Paris, may also be described as a member of the French comic opera school. Of his eighteen operas, one has survived to this day and is still given in many countries: the pleasant and melodious *Martha*, a great favorite in spite of, or perhaps because of, its outspoken sentimentality.

Modern operetta — an illegitimate daughter of *opéra comique* — is a Parisian product that originated about 1850 and reached its culmination during the years of the Second Empire. Offenbach, and on a somewhat lower grade, Lecocq and Hervé, were the leading masters of this new genre. Jacques Offenbach (1819–1880), son of a Jewish synagogue cantor at Cologne, eventually became more Parisian than the Parisians themselves. The unbridled display of licentious sensuality in his operettas, interlarded with breathtaking and insolent galops and cancans, documents the Parisian *joie de vivre* of the time. Next to Offenbach, Florimond Hervé (1825–1892) and Alexandre-Charles Lecocq (1832–1918) were the most famous masters of the Parisian operetta. Hervé's best-known *opera buffa*, applauded all over Europe, was *Mam'zelle Nitouche*; Lecocq's most popular work was *La Fille de Madame Angot*.

A few words should now be said about new developments in French music between the two great wars of the twentieth century. In 1920, a group of young French musicians representing ultramodern French music banded together and became known as "Les Six." Of these composers, four have achieved fame. They are Darius Milhaud, Arthur Honegger, Georges Auric, and Francis Poulenc.

Darius Milhaud (born in 1892) first achieved celebrity as the composer of highly original stage music. His setting of Paul Claudel's dramatic poem *Christophe Colombe* presented in a series of tableaux the life of Christopher Columbus and the discovery of America. The dramatic element was supplied by a chorus, which, in the ancient Greek fashion, participated in the performance by offering comments on the situations involved. *Christophe Colombe* is thus a combination of modern grand opera, oratorio, and medieval mystery play. Furthermore, the use of motion pictures is specified by the composer in the score. Despite its grandiose design, Milhaud's music appears static; it lacks broad melodic lines, lógical structure, and dynamic tension, so that the impression upon a listener is one of sober dryness rather than emotional stimulation. This broad synthesis of ancient and modern elements has remained the chief method of Milhaud's stage works throughout his productive career. He has also written an enormous amount of instrumental works that exhibit a characteristic Gallic facility of composition and elegance of technique.

The name of Arthur Honegger (1892–1955) became widely known when he wrote his symphonic movement entitled *Pacific 231*, which glorified the powerful American-built locomotive. Honegger himself said that he treated this subject with the same degree of emotional involvement that the romantic composers felt toward the image of a beloved woman. Later in life Honegger turned to religious and historic subjects, as exemplified in his mystery play, *Jeanne d'Arc au bûcher*, which has had numerous successful performances in Europe and America.

Francis Poulenc and Georges Auric (both born in 1899) have written music mainly for the ballet and for the motion pictures. Poulenc also wrote many songs in the national French style.

Some years after "Les Six," a new group of French musicians appeared on the Paris scene, and published a manifesto under the collective name of "La Jeune France," expressing the purpose of reviving the national spirit of eternal France. The best-known member of "La Jeune France" is Olivier Messiaen (born in 1908). In his religious works, animated by an ardent Catholic faith, Messiaen has revived the spirit of medieval Gregorian modes. At the same time he shows great interest in Oriental musical systems. In his extraordinary symphony *Turangalila,* scored for the piano, the electronic instrument Ondes Martenot, and orchestra, and subdivided into ten movements, he explores Hindu rhythms and scales in a setting of great complexity.

Thus we find that French music for nearly a millennium has moved in a well-defined cycle, beginning with the great Parisian school of Leoninus and Perotinus — religious in its main function — through the development of the secular French motet, the *canzon francese,* the French *ouverture,* and the French suite; through the age of grand opera and its slighter companion, the French operetta; through the picturesque impressionism of Debussy, to a modern exposition of the religious spirit in the form of the twentieth-century mystery play. Through all these transformations, French music has kept its natural qualities of grace, refinement, good taste, and subtle charm — its unique *esprit* — that will ever remain peculiarly international in its appeal.

The great accomplishments of French musical scholarship should be mentioned. Proud of its musical heritage, France has published complete editions of its masters from the *ars antiqua* to Couperin and Rameau. The great *Encyclopédie de la musique* begun by Albert Lavignac is a monument of research. Among French musicologists, the names of Pierre Aubry (1874–1910), Lionel de La Laurencie (1861–1933), Adolphe Boschot (1871–1955), Henry Prunières (1886–1942), and Paul-Marie Masson (1882–1954) are justly celebrated.

Belgium

The music of Belgium, in its French-speaking part, has been naturally connected with French music. François-Joseph Gossec (1734–1829) was the first composer from the present territory of

Belgium to acquire universal fame. As a young man he went to Paris, where he attracted the attention of Rameau. The historical importance of Gossec lies in the fact that he was one of the earliest composers of symphonies and string quartets, antedating those of Haydn. Later he became a successful composer of operas, which were greatly acclaimed in Paris. During the French Revolution he wrote many songs celebrating the republic. He died at the age of ninety-five.

André-Modeste Grétry (1741–1813), a native of Liège, also made his career in Paris, where he achieved tremendous success with his opera *Richard Cœur-de-Lion* (1784), his most enduring work, which still enjoys numerous revivals. Grétry's music is distinguished by a wealth of graceful melody and fine dramatic effects.

Although both Gossec and Grétry became internationally known, their reputations were not as Belgian composers but as thoroughly acclimatized Parisians. Paris remained the spiritual goal of Belgian composers throughout the nineteenth century; thus Belgian art became in great measure a part of French musical culture.

The great composer and organist César Franck was born in Liège. His family was of German-Dutch descent, but this circumstance did not prevent his becoming one of the greatest exponents of Gallic music. His entire creative period was spent in Paris, and thus his music became a part of the French heritage.

Liège was also the native city of Guillaume Lekeu (1870–1894). This highly gifted Belgian musician is also generally associated with modern French music. As a pupil of Franck and Vincent d'Indy in Paris, he had begun to attract attention; but his premature death at twenty-four cut off a highly promising career. Among his works, the sonata for violin and piano has gained an honored place in the international repertory of chamber music.

One of the most eminent composers of the modern Belgian school was Joseph Jongen (1873–1953). Born in Liège, he remained there for many years as teacher and organist. Later he became director of the Brussels Conservatory. His noble chamber music, in a fairly modern style, has been occasionally heard in Germany and England but is not adequately appreciated by the musical world at large.

In the twentieth century, Belgian composers have become more and more independent of French musical life. Jean Absil (born in 1893), composer of many works for the stage, for orchestra, and for chamber music ensemble, represents modern Belgian music. The names of Francis de Bourguignon (born in 1890), Raymond Chevreuille (born in 1901), and Marcel Poot (born in 1901) are also well known as Belgian modernists.

The Flemish composers of Belgium have for nearly a century maintained their separate culture and language, with Antwerp as the center of Flemish art. An excellent Flemish opera house has provided an opportunity for national composers to present their dramatic works.

The founder of the national Flemish school of composition was Peter Benoit (1834–1901). After studying in Germany and Italy, he tried to gain a foothold in Paris. Following a brief sojourn there, he returned to Antwerp and launched a vigorous campaign for Flemish national music. In 1867 he founded in Antwerp the Flemish Conservatory, which gave instruction in the Flemish language. Benoit wrote Flemish oratorios which glorify the landscape and the history of his country and are remarkable for their national expressiveness. His *Rhine Oratorio*, in particular, is worthy of attention for its melodious freshness, rustic humor, and wealth of picturesque details.

Jan Blockx (1851–1912), Benoit's successor as head of the Flemish Conservatory, continued his teacher's national tradition. He was the leading master of Flemish opera, and a composer of strong theatrical instinct.

Edgar Tinel (1854–1912) was perhaps the greatest composer of modern Flemish choral music. Tinel's music is not Flemish in a restricted, regional sense; it is European in its scope and romantic in its inspiration, and this combination makes it accessible to any listener.

Paul Gilson (1865–1942) acquired a European reputation with one score only, the symphonic poem *La Mer* (1890), which was widely performed at the time. This somewhat massive and overexuberant musical picture of the sea was later eclipsed by Debussy's celebrated tone painting of the same title. Gilson's Flemish opera *Zeevolk* (Sea Folk) was successfully produced in Antwerp but failed to gain international validity.

Lodewijk Mortelmans (1868–1952), a native of Antwerp and a pupil of Benoit, was the composer of a Flemish opera *De Kinderen der Zee* (Children of the Sea) and of a children's cantata in the Flemish language.

Turning from composition to violin playing, we find that in this field the Belgian school has justly acquired international fame. Its founder was Charles de Bériot (1802–1870), whose concertos and violin studies are still much played by students. Bériot's most famous pupil was the great Belgian master Henri Vieuxtemps (1820–1881), who excelled as a virtuoso and as a composer of violin concertos that still retain a position of honor on the concert platform.

From Belgium also came César Thomson (1857–1931), one of the most brilliant technicians of the century, a Paganini redivivus. But after Vieuxtemps, it was Eugene Ysaÿe (1858–1931) who won the greatest fame in the world at large. Many of our older contemporaries still have a vivid recollection of Ysaÿe, his masive figure, his huge head, his fiery countenance, and his mane of unruly gray hair, seconded at the piano by the equally bulky but gentle and placid-looking Raoul Pugno! This unsightly couple formed a perfect team, complementing each other effectively and producing an unforgettable impression. Two of the greatest modern French masterpieces are dedicated to Ysaÿe: César Franck's violin sonata, which received its first and most authoritative rendering from him, and Debussy's string quartet, for which the Ysaÿe Quartet found the appropriate novel colors and accents, setting a model for all subsequent performances.

It only remains to speak of Belgium's achievements in the field of scholarly musical research, which are, internationally speaking, even superior to her creative efforts in composition. The founder of the modern method of musical lexicography and theoretical research, François Joseph Fétis (1784–1871), was a Belgian. His monumental work in eight large volumes, *Biographie universelle des musiciens et bibliographie générale de la musique*, published in Brussels in 1835–1844, is the first encyclopedia of musical biography. In spite of its many errors of fact and mistaken evaluations, the *Biographie universelle* remains the basic source of all subsequent music dictionaries.

Another Belgian scholar of the first rank was François-Auguste Gevaert (1828–1908). His *Histoire et théorie de la musique de l'antiquité* is a compendium of fundamental value. To the public at large, Gevaert is best known for his excellent treatise on orchestration.

In the twentieth century, the task of musical research was continued by the distinguished Belgian scholar Charles van den Borren, who has contributed many valuable essays on various aspects of the Netherlandish school.

The recently formed Belgian Center for Musical Documentation has published a series of catalogues of Belgian composers, with their brief biographical sketches. This collection is of great value to all those interested in the progress of music in twentieth-century Belgium.

8

Spain and Portugal

Spain

In folk song, and especially in dance, Spain is one of the richest countries of the world. This Spanish treasure was, however, hidden away from the musical world at large for a very long time before it was discovered.

The golden age of Spanish music was the sixteenth century, when Spanish ecclesiastical music, as well as organ and lute music, reached its peak, and the names of the great Spanish masters were honored throughout the musical world. From about 1650 to 1900 the musical activities of Spain scarcely reverberated beyond the borders of the Pyrenees, and only in the last fifty years has a modern national school of Spanish composers attracted the attention of other nations.

St. Isidore, Archbishop of Seville, who lived during the seventh century, is the earliest Spanish authority on music. He was the originator of a liturgical code, which differed from Gregorian chant and was perpetuated in the so-called Mozarabic service. The Mozarabic cult of the Spanish Christians under Moorish-Arab rule became so deeply rooted in some parts of Spain that it was retained even after the expulsion of the Moors. Its principal champion was Cardinal Jiménez de Cisneros (1437–1517), who made a determined attempt to revive the Mozarabic ritual within the church, and who collected for this purpose the ancient

Spanish melodies and had them transcribed in magnificent codices.

A great impetus to medieval Spanish music came from the famous Benedictine monastery of Montserrat — the legendary seat of the Holy Grail, glorified by Wagner in *Lohengrin* and *Parsifal*. In form and technique the early polyphonic music from Montserrat is a branch of the French *ars antiqua* and of the Italian *ars nova*, but its melodic substance differs from both, having an accent, sentiment, and melodic line of its own and a distinctive Spanish inflection.

The truly national Spanish type of melody was developed in the *villancico*, the Spanish part song. The greatest composer of *villancicos* was Juan del Encina (1469–1530), who also excelled as a poet. The collective title *villancico* embraces a great variety of melodic and stylistic types, from a plain, note-against-note treatment to contrapuntally involved, motet-like pieces.

In the sixteenth century, Spanish music came under the spell of the Netherlandish system, victorious over all Europe. Spanish disciples of the great Netherlandish and Italian masters, while taking over the forms and technical procedures of their teachers, knew how to impart to their own music an individual color. Those who have made a close study of polyphonic music have little difficulty in distinguishing the Spanish products from those of Josquin, Palestrina, Lasso, and Gabrieli. Spanish church music is imbued with a passionate piety, an ecstatic Catholicism, a mystic intensity, a dark splendor; it is austere, somber, and grandiose, creating an impression quite different from the more orderly and orthodox Italian Masses and motets.

Numerous reprints of old Spanish music are available to us, beginning with the comprehensive collection of 459 songs, *Cancionero musical de los siglos XV y XVI*, published by Barbieri (1890); the ten volumes of Miguel Hilarión Eslava's *Lira sacro-hispana* (1869); Felipe Pedrell's *Hispaniæ schola musica sacra* (1895–1898); and others. In Lavignac's voluminous *Encyclopédie de la musique*, the article "La Musique en Espagne" by Rafaël Mitjana gives a detailed account of the main currents of Spanish music.

In the first half of the sixteenth century, Spain was the center of lute and guitar playing as well as composition. Don Luis Milán (c. 1500–1561) published his *Libro de música de vihuela de mano intitulado el maestro* in 1535. The *vihuela de mano* was a Spanish form of the lute, and two modern editions of this collection, one by Count Morphy and one by Leo Schrade, make this classical lute music easily accessible to the modern student and music-lover. These early Spanish pieces served as models for the later Italian, French, and German compositions for the lute, which was the favorite European instrument in the sixteenth and seventeenth centuries. The delicate, pinched sound of the lute and the peculiar tuning of its strings made it incapable of rendering a sustained melodic line, and to compensate for this deficiency composers of lute music indulged in profuse embellishments, manifold figurations, and ornate flourishes. Luis Milán's collection of lute music is typical in this respect.

In organ playing, Spain was a leading nation in the sixteenth century. The decisive progress in Spanish organ style was due to Antonio de Cabezón (1510–1566), a blind musician (like many other famous organists, among them Paumann of Nuremberg and Landino of Florence) who was court organist to the Emperor Charles V and to King Philip II. His *Obras de música para tecla, arpa y vihuela* (Musical Works for Keyboard Instruments, Harp, and Lute), published in 1578 by his son Hernando de Cabezón, demonstrates that Spanish organ, clavier, harp, and lute music before 1550 was considerably in advance of Italian music of the same time.

The glory of Spanish music in the period of the Renaissance is exemplified by the names of the great masters of the sixteenth century: Bartolomeo Escobedo, a member of the Papal Chapel in Rome; Cristóbal Morales, who also served in the Papal Chapel, and later led the choirs in the cathedrals of Málaga and Toledo; Francisco Guerrero, master of the chapel at the cathedral of Seville; and, above all, Tomás Luis de Victoria (c. 1548–1611), who studied with Escobedo and Morales in Rome but who later eclipsed them with his great hymns and motets. The music of Victoria is regarded by many authorities as not inferior to the best works of his great Italian contemporary, Palestrina.

Spanish musical scholarship was also highly developed during the Renaissance. One of the greatest Spanish music theorists was Francisco Salinas (1513–1590) of Burgos. Blind from childhood, he rose to a professorship at the University of Salamanca and became an authority on musical science. Salinas was the first musical scholar of the Renaissance to become interested in Spanish, Roman, and Neapolitan folk songs; even the modern champion of Spanish folk music, Felipe Pedrell, was able to profit from these early investigations made by Salinas.

Diego Ortiz, of Toledo, was *maestro di cappella* to the Spanish viceroy at Naples, the Duke of Alba, at the time when Salinas was chapel organist there. Oritz' small but important *Tratado de glosas* (Rome, 1553) gives us unique information on instrumental performance and particularly on the improvised dialogue of the accompanying clavier with the solo instrument, as practiced in the sixteenth century.

Pietro Cerone's *El Melopeo y maestro* (Naples, 1613) is the second important theoretical work of the Spanish school. Cerone (1566–1625) was an Italian musician who emigrated to Spain; he was later a member of the Spanish Royal Chapel in Naples. The twenty-two books of the *Melopeo* fill no fewer than 1,160 pages of small print. It is a veritable encyclopedia of music, dealing with theory, vocal instruction, methods of tuning and playing instruments, forms, styles, notation, counterpoint, cadences, ornamentation, improvisation, practice of church music, esthetics, and philosophy.

During the eighteenth century Spanish music lost, for a time, its international validity. Though a considerable amount of ecclesiastical and secular music was produced in Spain at that time, it was of little interest to the musical world at large. An exception was the successful opera *Una cosa rara* by Martín y Soler (1754–1806). Mozart used a melody from this opera in *Don Giovanni*.

Several Italian musicians were active in Spain in the eighteenth century and greatly contributed to the progress of Spanish musical culture. Luigi Boccherini (1743–1805), composer of many melodious trios, quartets, and quintets, spent the greater part of his life in Madrid in the service of the king's brother.

Much more important historically was the sojourn in Spain of Domenico Scarlatti (1685–1757), one of the greatest composers for the harpsichord. He spent the last twenty-five years of his life as chamber virtuoso at the Royal Court of Madrid. Scarlatti's sonatas hold their honored place in the classical literature of piano music and have lost none of their charm after two centuries.

In spite of the dearth of notable Spanish compositions during the late seventeenth, eighteenth, and early nineteenth centuries, Spanish dance rhythms provided attractive material to musicians in all countries for new and striking effects. The *folia,* saraband, fandango, bolero, jota, and other Spanish dances began to enter the musical literature of Europe. "La Folia," an old Spanish or Portuguese tune, became widely known through Corelli's violin variations. In rhythm and structure the *folia* is close to the saraband, a dance of Spanish origin that became an integral part of the classical instrumental suite. In Bach's and Handel's suites, the slow movements are usually entitled "Sarabande," and their noble melody, stately rhythm, and pathetic expression present a curious contrast with the abandoned character of this dance as it was actually performed in Spain.

A Spanish fandango tune with its guitar and castanet accompaniment was used by Gluck in his ballet music for *Don Juan,* to mark the Spanish milieu. Mozart made use of this tune in *Le nozze di Figaro* in a most attractive new setting. A bolero tune was used by Auber in his opera *La Muette de Portici*; Chopin wrote a bolero for piano. The most sensational use of the bolero was made by Ravel in his celebrated symphonic piece of that name.

To German romantic composers of the nineteenth century, Spanish popular music was a source of exotic interest, as can be seen in many songs by Schumann and especially in the *Spanisches Liederbuch* by Hugo Wolf. In this song cycle Wolf did not quote actual Spanish melodies but relied solely on his intuition to express in sound the Spanish mood, color, and atmosphere.

Spanish music in larger forms was transplanted to other countries not by Spanish composers but mainly by Russian and French masters. Glinka, who spent some time in Spain, was the earliest composer of rank to call European attention to Spain, in his brilliant orchestral piece *Jota aragonesa*. About the same time, Liszt made effective use of Spanish themes in his *Rapsodie espagnole* for piano. Rimsky-Korsakov's orchestral *Caprice* on Spanish themes, and Chabrier's rhapsody *España* became popular at a time when hardly a single orchestral piece by a Spanish composer was known anywhere outside Spain. More than any other work, however, Bizet's opera *Carmen* gave the musical world a taste of Spanish popular art.

For a long time Spanish instrumental music was represented solely by a few brilliant solo pieces by the world-famous Spanish violin virtuoso Pablo de Sarasate, in the form of his various *Spanish Dances* and *Gypsy Fantasies*. These effective but rather shallow pieces are greatly surpassed in musical value by Lalo's *Symphonie espagnole,* one of the most successful violin concertos of modern times, which outdid the Spaniards themselves in the artistic treatment of Spanish tunes and dance rhythms. Debussy brought out Spanish color in his evocative piano pieces *La Soirée dans Grenade* and *La Puerta del vino,* and in his exciting symphonic picture *Iberia.* Ravel was also fond of Spanish colors and moods, with which he was familiar from infancy, as a native of the Basque region of the Pyrenees, near the Spanish border. Besides his orchestral tour de force, *Bolero,* Ravel wrote a *Rapsodie espagnole,* one of the most brilliant orchestral pieces in the Spanish vein, and a Spanish-inspired opera, *L'Heure espagnole.*

Spanish national culture owes its greatest advance in modern times to the work of Felipe Pedrell (1841–1922). With his many important publications of sacred music, folk songs, and dance music, he was mainly responsible for reviving the interest of Spanish musicians in their national art.

Three modern Spanish composers succeeded in gaining and holding the attention of the musical world: Isaac Albéniz, Enrique Granados, and Manuel de Falla.

Isaac Albéniz (1860–1909) is best known by his brilliant series of piano pieces entitled *Iberia,* illustrating in a modern idiom the vivid scenes of Spanish life, with ample use of characteristic Spanish dance rhythms. His music has a certain kinship to that of Debussy, but it lacks the French master's exquisite polish and refinement.

Enrique Granados (1867–1916) acquired European fame by a single work, a set of piano pieces called *Goyescas,* inspired by Goya's paintings. Here is virtuoso music imbued with the accent and color of Spain! Granados used the material of *Goyescas* in an opera of the same title, presented in New York by the Metropolitan Opera Company in 1916. It was upon his return to Europe after this occasion that Granados lost his life, when his ship was torpedoed in the English Channel by a German submarine.

The most successful modern Spanish composer was Manuel de Falla (1876–1946). He was influenced by Pedrell, with whom he studied; he also lived for years in Paris and was a friend of Debussy and Ravel. Later, the Spanish Civil War drove Falla to Argentina, where he died. Falla became known to the musical world as a composer of Spanish stage music. His lyric drama *La Vida breve* was his first national, as well as international, success. His three pieces for piano and orchestra, *Nights in the*

Gardens of Spain, are vibrant with Andalusian rhythms, in a refined setting of French impressionism. His piano pieces and his songs represent a colorful mixture of Arabic, Byzantine, Gypsy, Hebrew, and Spanish elements, with their intricate dance rhythms and their passionate, melancholy melodies. In these works Falla achieves a complete authenticity of expression without direct quotation of popular tunes. The exotic local color is balanced by a bold, modern, harmonic treatment. His ballets *El Sombrero de tres picos* (The Three-cornered Hat) and *El Amor brujo* (Love, the Sorcerer) have been widely performed. His opera for marionettes *El Retablo de Maese Pedro* (Master Peter's Puppet Show) marks a change of style, away from the sensuous Andalusian melody. In conformity with his theme from *Don Quixote,* Falla here seeks to regain the classical Spanish tradition of 1600, the limpid clarity of part-writing for small instrumental ensemble.

In his later period, Manuel de Falla adopted a neoclassical mode of expression, particularly in his concerto for harpsichord, flute, oboe, violin, and violoncello. In its delicately traced and graceful melodic lines, this concerto revives the spirit of Domenico Scarlatti, whom the Spaniards have adopted as their own.

The tradition of national Spanish music is maintained in the works of Joaquín Turina (1882–1949) and of Oscar Esplá (born in 1886). Here Spanish rhythms sparkle in energetic outbursts. Turina follows the romantic trend of Albéniz and Granados; Esplá adopts a more modern idiom, close to that of Manuel de Falla.

Spanish music owes its vitality, its fiery animation, to the national dance. It is the music of the body and the senses, savage and enticing, proud and dejected, rigorous and capricious, manly and feminine, raging and of a marble coolness, cruel and compassionate, commanding and yielding, of measured stateliness and filled with nervous unrest; it is European and African, monotonous and dazzlingly colorful, frivolous and pious. At all times, it is sensuous, concerned with the body — its limbs, its muscles, its nerves, its gestures—and its primitive sensations filled with the sexual impulse.

Spanish music is rich and varied, but it lacks the spiritual background, the metaphysical depth, the contemplative repose, the constructive power, the pure idealism of great classical music. The religious fervor that animated the great Spanish composers of the sixteenth century has vanished in the works of Spanish modernists. It would be unjust, however, to demand of this music what, by its nature, it cannot give. Perhaps its very limitations constitute the source of its excellence.

Though Spanish composers have attracted the attention of the musical world only recently, a number of Spanish performers have acquired European celebrity during the last hundred years. The García family, especially, offers astounding evidence of hereditary talent. Manuel del Popolo Vicente García (1775–1832) of Seville was famous as a singer and a composer of operas. His two daughters, Marie Malibran-García and Pauline Viardot-García, were also his pupils. Mme. Malibran became Europe's most celebrated opera singer: as a young woman, she was received in Paris, London, Brussels, and the Italian cities with an enthusiasm bordering on frenzy. Her sensational career was cut short by her sudden death, in 1836, at the age of twenty-eight.

Her sister, the dramatic contralto Pauline Viardot (1821–1910), was one of Europe's most gifted and cultivated women. In her younger years she sang in all the European capitals. When she retired from the stage in 1863, she became a renowned teacher in Baden-Baden, and later in Paris. Berlioz, Liszt, Schumann, and Brahms were among her many distinguished friends. Schumann dedicated his *Liederkreis* to her, and Brahms entrusted to her superb art the first performance of his *Alto Rhapsody*. During her long life of nearly ninety years, Pauline Viardot participated actively in the marvelous growth of music through the entire romantic age.

Her brother, Manuel Patricio Rodriguez García (1805–1906),

lived to be over one hundred years old. A pupil of his father, he entered upon the career of an opera singer, but found more satisfaction in teaching. As professor at the Paris Conservatoire and at the London Royal Academy, he became a famous vocal teacher in Europe. Jenny Lind was one of his celebrated pupils. He was also the inventor of the laryngoscope, an instrument of equal value for the physician and for the teacher of singing.

Among Spanish violinists, Pablo de Sarasate (1844–1908) achieved legendary fame. For nearly half a century his sweet tone, the grace and elegance of his bowing, and the polished virtuosity of his playing brought enchantment to music lovers everywhere.

Enrique Fernández Arbos (1863–1939), another eminent Spanish violinist, was a pupil of Vieuxtemps and Joachim and grew up in the German tradition. He was for some time concertmaster of the Berlin Philharmonic and the Boston Symphony Orchestras; to him in great measure is due the introduction of German symphonic music into Spain and the more thorough education of young Spanish musicians in the German musical idiom.

The guitar is the national Spanish instrument, and the art of playing the guitar (as well as other instruments) has long been cultivated in Spain by both educated musicians and street serenaders. In modern times this art has received a new impetus through the brilliant virtuosity of the famous Spanish guitarist, Andrés Segovia.

The greatest of all Spanish performers, however, is undoubtedly Pablo Casals (born in 1876), an accomplished virtuoso of the violoncello and a musician of the very first rank. He has imparted a new meaning to his instrument. As a symphonic conductor, Casals gave fine concerts in Barcelona. After the Spanish Civil War he withdrew to the little French town of Prades, on the border of Spain, and there he established a series of summer festivals that attract music lovers from all over the world.

Portugal

Portugal was once a leader in travel and discovery; her explorers have remade the map of the globe. But in music Portugal has left little impression. The names of the Portuguese masters of the polyphonic school that flourished in the sixteenth and seventeenth centuries — Manuel Mendes, Duarte Lobo, Manuel Cardoso, and others — are barely known even to scholars; their Masses, motets, hymns, and psalms remain mostly in manuscript. King John IV of Portugal (1604–1656), himself a lover of music, collected a great musical library, which was unfortunately destroyed during the great Lisbon earthquake of 1755. In the eighteenth century, Italian opera flourished at Lisbon, and several Portuguese pupils of famous Italian maestros attracted attention.

The most successful Portuguese opera composer was Marcos Portugal (1762–1830). Dozens of his operas were given all over Europe and Rio de Janeiro, where he spent the last years of his life. Yet his music has remained completely unknown to the world at large. A century later, the operas of Oscar da Silva (born in 1870), a pupil of Clara Schumann, made a stir in his native country, but his music was also confined to Portugal.

A representative Portuguese musician was José Vianna da Motta (1868–1948). A pupil of Liszt, he gained considerable reputation in Europe; he wrote several *Portuguese Rhapsodies* for piano. Of a later generation, Ruy Coelho (born in 1891) has proved to be a prolific composer of Portuguese operas and symphonic works.

9

England

The history of English music goes back to the time of early polyphony. England in the twelfth and thirteenth centuries contributed materially to the rise of early counterpoint by developing the technique of canon, as first revealed in the famous song *Sumer is icumen in,* and in the practice of gymel, the "twin song," with its free and plentiful use of parallel thirds. England was the first nation to sanction parallel thirds, which did so much to soften the austere harmony of the French *ars antiqua,* with its bleak fourths, fifths, and dissonant seconds. Early in the fifteenth century, the English gymel spread to the continent. Netherlandish music owes much of its euphony to the ample use of thirds in parallel motion.

It was during the first half of the fifteenth century that the first great English composer made himself known to the world. He was John Dunstable (1390–1453). In his music he made use of the florid melismas of the *ars antiqua* and also of the ingenious ornamentation peculiar to the practice of the *ars nova,* which he profusely applied with an almost romantic expressiveness and grace. This type of melody is enhanced in Dunstable's music by a rich euphonious harmony. Dunstable's so-called isorhythmic motets, in which the theme retains its rhythm but changes its melodic line, are examples of great ingenuity and skill. Yet Dunstable's music failed to impress itself on the later generations of English composers. The masters of the Tudor period, covering the reigns of Henry VIII and Queen Elizabeth — John Taverner, Christopher Tye, Robert White, Thomas Tallis, and William Byrd — followed the creative ideas of the great representatives of the Netherlandish art, Okeghem and Josquin de Près, rather than those of Dunstable. It was perhaps this dependence on foreign achievements in their method of composition that lessened the significance of Tudor music on the continent. These glorious English motets, psalms, anthems, and sacred services appeared as mere local developments of great Netherlandish art and failed to arouse an interest that they merited.

There were additional reasons why English vocal music of the Tudor period was impeded in its progress in Europe. Sacred choral works by Tudor composers were limited to the liturgy of the new Anglican church, established by Henry VIII, with an English text rather than Latin, rendering it unusable for Roman Catholic services elsewhere. The use of the English language in secular songs created an almost insuperable barrier between English and continental musicians. Furthermore, England was the last of great European nations to start printing music. At a time when both Netherlandish and German settings of folk songs were widely printed and distributed, very few arrangements of English folk songs were available. It may be that this lack of printed English editions discouraged English composers. Church music was performed immediately, whether it was printed or not; secular works, however, were dependent for their promotion on the interests of private patronage. Toward the end of the sixteenth century Tallis and Byrd were granted the privilege of printing music, and English composers received at long last an outlet for their works. By that time, the Italian madrigal had begun its triumphant course across Europe. The English composers of the Elizabethan era were greatly attracted by the charm and poetry of the Italian madrigal and were not slow in producing a similar art of their own. And so the English madrigal, that fairest flower of English secular music, unfolded in all its glory, concomitant with the great dramatic and lyric poetry of Shakespeare, Marlowe, and Spenser.

The flowering of the English madrigal owed as much to the poetry of its texts as to the nobility of its music. But the very excellence of the words precluded its successful transplantation to the continent. For, while English music lovers could relish madrigals in Italian and French (for educated classes in England were familiar with these languages), the English language was entirely incomprehensible to most Frenchmen and Italians.

The language barrier did not, however, interfere with the spread in Europe of instrumental English music, which could be either copied by hand or printed. Among the famous collections of instrumental music by English composers of the sixteenth and seventeenth centuries are the *Fitzwilliam Virginal Book,* which contains no fewer than two hundred and ninety-seven pieces; *My Ladye Nevells Booke,* containing forty-two pieces, mostly by William Byrd; *Will Forster's Virginal Book,* with seventy-eight pieces; and Benjamin Cosyn's *Virginal Book,* with ninety-eight pieces mainly by John Bull and Orlando Gibbons.

Twenty-one compositions by Byrd, Bull, and Gibbons were printed in 1612, in a collection of music for the virginals (the most popular keyboard instrument in English homes at the time) under the quaint title *Parthenia or The Maydenhead of the First Musicke that ever was printed for the Virginals.* This was one of the earliest books printed in England from engraved plates.

The growing literature of instrumental music printed in England contained a number of dances, often arranged into suites: galliards, courantes, pavans, allemandes, passemeasures, gigues, toccatas, preludes, fantasias, and so on. A great many pieces by English composers bore such picturesque titles as *The Carman's Whistle, The Ghost, Sellinger's Round* (all by Byrd) and *The King's Hunt* (by John Bull).

The virtuosity, diversity of form, variety of style, and melodic charm of English keyboard music made a profound impression on composers of other nations. Even greater success was enjoyed by English music for the viol. Early in the seventeenth century, groups of English viol players were invited to the royal courts in Holland, Denmark, Sweden, Germany, and Poland. The viol suites by William Brade (c. 1560–1630), Thomas Simpson, and several others became models of their kind, and were eagerly imitated in other lands.

Toward the middle of the seventeenth century, this flowering of musical culture in England was disrupted by the Cromwellian wars. The severity of Cromwell's government put a stop to England's revelry. Music became suspect as a companion of carnality and was extinguished simultaneously with the deposition and execution of the King.

With the Restoration in 1660, Puritanism lost its political power, and attempts were made to restore the cultivation of English music. However, there were strong countercurrents from foreign lands. King Charles II, who had been educated in France and who had a predilection for French music, sent his court musicians to Paris to study French ways. Soon music at the English court became a pallid copy of the French mannered art. The *ballet de cour* was transplanted from Versailles in the form of spectacular pageants called "masques." They assumed a more or less operatic form, some of them becoming in time true operas. English drama made much use of incidental music: dances, marches, and songs. One of the foremost masters of this new art was Dr. John Blow (1649–1708), who wrote masques for the court and numerous choral works of high quality.

Toward the end of the seventeenth century a genius arose who brought English music to a new glory: Purcell. Henry Purcell (c. 1659–1695) possessed the precious gift of assimilating Italian and French musical elements so thoroughly that they assumed an authentic English appearance. This gift enabled him to enrich English music with new ideas from other cultures, and he accomplished this task without sacrificing the essential

English character of his music. Purcell, who was organist of the Chapel Royal and later of Westminster Abbey, excelled as a composer of masques, dramatic incidental music, and church music. There is a powerful and original personality in his works, a harmonious beauty and perfection of technique that make them unique in the history of English art. A tragic fate cut off Purcell's brilliant career at the age of thirty-six, and he left no successor. With his death, English music became impoverished for a long time. When in 1710 the great Handel was called to London, he found no English musician able to challenge him with any chance of success.

Georg Friedrich Handel (1685–1759) spent nearly fifty years in London; he wrote all his oratorios in the English language; in his choral writing he adopted certain English features, mainly inspired by Purcell. Yet, although he became a British subject, he did not become an English musician. German, Italian, French, and English traditions were intermingled in Handel's music. He was truly a cosmopolitan. His music, however, failed to prosper in France, Italy, and Spain, where performances of his works were few. Handel's lack of appeal to the Latin temperament was again, as with the English madrigalists before him, due to the barrier of language. His great strength lay in his oratorios, written to English texts, and the character of their prosody was too insular to be transplanted to an alien soil.

The following translation from the author's German biography of Handel explains the appeal of the Handel oratorios to the public, at least in English-speaking countries.

"Here, in Handel's oratorios, was art of a monumental character, yet with a popular appeal, understood by everybody. The familiar stories from the Bible are arranged with a view to giving the music the best opportunity to display its charm and power. There is great mastery in these scores, but it is skillfully veiled by pleasing, beautiful melodies, by striking rhythm, and by direct appeal to the listener's sympathy, so as to move and excite the mass of the people, while still containing enough consummate art to hold the interest of the connoisseur. The democratic aspect of Handel's Biblical oratorios secured their success with the people of England. No longer were the myths of classical antiquity the exclusive subject matter of Handel's oratorios; only exceptionally, as in *Semele* or *Hercules*, did he write for classically educated people. In the main he turned to the most popular and yet the most profound of all books, the Bible.

"And Handel preferred the Old Testament, as his aim was to represent the 'common people' in their spiritual and moral life rather than 'the church,' inseparable from the New Testament. In his description of the deeds of the people of Israel he held up to the English masses a mirror in which were reflected the ethical forces, the consequences of good and evil action, the power of divine Providence. He was not a preacher in the theological, dogmatic sense, but an unprejudiced person of independent mind, and of great soul, filled with kindness and love for humanity."

Handel's influence on composers of other lands was strong only in Germany and Austria. Haydn's *Creation*, Mendelssohn's *Elijah*, and the once famous oratorios of Spohr, Löwe, and Max Bruch — all these works are descendants of Handel's oratorio. Beethoven himself professed the greatest veneration for Handel; the lofty spirit of Beethoven's symphonies reflects the art of Handel even though in form these symphonies are derived from Haydn and Mozart.

After Handel's death in 1759, English music suffered a long period of decline as a cosmopolitan force. It was not until the twentieth century that a change of taste and the appearance of talented modernistic composers brought England back into the arena of international art. During this long decline of creativity, musical activities of all sorts flourished in England. London became a clearing house of international music; but the works of England's composers after Handel seemed insufficiently interesting to save them from oblivion.

The English themselves have had little confidence in their

ability to write original music. When the Royal Academy of Music was founded in London in 1719, its aim was to produce Italian operas with Italian singers. Handel and two Italian composers, Giovanni Bononcini (1670–1747) and Attilio Ariosti (1666–c. 1730), were appointed musical directors of the enterprise. The most sensational Italian singers of the time — Signora Cuzzoni, Faustina Bordoni, the *castrato* singer Senesino, and a host of others — descended upon London and captivated London society.

There was a small but influential group of English nationalists who resented this cult of German and Italian music, this invasion of prima donnas and *castrati*. This section of English society came to the conclusion that the most efficient method of driving the foreigners away from England's shores was to ridicule them. Thus the psychological premise was prepared for *The Beggar's Opera*, a devastating parody on Italian operatic art. Its very title implied a protest against the monopoly of opera by the wealthy classes.

The Beggar's Opera put the lowest stratum of the English society on the stage — highway robbers, pickpockets, prostitutes. The music consisted almost entirely of ballads and songs in a popular vein, with the words written by the noted satirist John Gay, who used this medium to attack the profligate court and nobility. An ironic fate decreed that this mockery of foreign musicians could not be launched without the aid of a foreigner, the skillful German immigrant John Christopher Pepusch (1667–1752), who arranged the majority of the ballad music in the score of *The Beggar's Opera* and wrote a clever overture for the production.

It is worth noting that *The Beggar's Opera* outlived the music of all the serious English composers of the eighteenth century. It was first produced in London in 1728. Two centuries later a modernized German version, with lyrics and dialogue by Bert Brecht and new ballad music by Kurt Weill, was presented in Berlin with huge success. In 1948, the most brilliant English opera composer of the twentieth century, Benjamin Britten, be-came fascinated with *The Beggar's Opera*, and adapted and pro-duced it in still another version, with modern orchestration.

Among English composers of Handel's time, only William Boyce (1710–1779) attained success abroad. His brief sym-phonies are often heard in England and America. His collection, *Cathedral Music* (three volumes, 1760–1778), is a monumental publication that brought to public attention many forgotten masterpieces of old English church music.

In the field of musical research in the eighteenth century, two publications by English scholars are fundamental: *A Gen-eral History of Music* by Dr. Charles Burney (four volumes, 1776–1789), and *General History of the Science and Practice of Music* by Sir John Hawkins (five volumes, 1776).

Beginning with Handel, German influence continued to in-crease in England. Eminent German and Austrian musicians were welcomed in London as guests and teachers. Franz Joseph Haydn heads the list of these distinguished guests. Haydn's two visits to England were the culmination of his entire career, ob-taining a success beyond his boldest dreams. Musical culture in England profited immensely from Haydn's visits; but Haydn him-self and the whole musical world profited from his journeys to London in no lesser measure. A dozen of Haydn's symphonies that are universally performed today, his oratorios *The Creation* and *The Seasons* — indeed, the most accomplished and fully mature works of the master — all came into existence as a direct consequence of the London engagements. In England Haydn made his first acquaintance with Handel's oratorios, and what he learned from them is clearly evident in his own vocal music. These magnificent choral scores of Haydn gave in their turn a new impetus to German choral composition.

Next in the line of German celebrities in England was Carl Maria von Weber (1786–1826). In the wake of the tremendous success of his romantic opera *Der Freischütz*, Weber was asked to write a new opera to be given its first performance in London. Though incurably ill, he accepted the offer, and thus *Oberon* came into existence. Written to an English libretto, the opera was enthusiastically received. A few weeks later, while still in London, Weber died.

Louis Spohr (1784–1859), now almost forgotten, enjoyed great fame in Germany and England early in the nineteenth century as a violin virtuoso, composer, and conductor. The London Philharmonic Society, always on the lookout for important artists on the continent, invited Spohr for the first time in 1820. He appeared in four successive concerts, playing and conducting his own works, with excellent success. A novelty for London was his use of the baton while conducting.

England lavished affection on young Felix Mendelssohn. Rarely has a foreign artist been as greatly honored and as much beloved as Mendelssohn was in England. He arrived in London for the first time in 1829 as a youth of twenty, and at once captivated the hearts of musical society. For nearly half a century Mendelssohn's influence was dominant in English music.

William Sterndale Bennett (1816–1875), a personal friend and pupil of Mendelssohn, loomed as a bright star on the London horizon. Yet this talented Englishman never gained international recognition. His music, highly esteemed and still performed in England, is practically unknown elsewhere. Of his many works, the most appealing is the evocative overture *The Naiads*, which exhales a peculiarly British refinement of taste and delicacy of melodic line and color.

During the Victorian era, the spirit of Mendelssohn still reigned in England. Then, at the threshold of the new century, English music regained its national colors. New and rich talents, typically English in culture, appeared on the horizon: the renaissance of British music had finally dawned.

The leaders of the English renaissance, Sir Alexander Mackenzie (1847–1935), Sir Charles Villiers Stanford (1852–1924), Sir Hubert Parry (1848–1918), and Sir Edward Elgar (1857–

1934), strove earnestly to break with the Handel and Mendelssohn tradition, to steer away from the anthems, the church cantatas, and the old oratorio style. They modernized their technique and kept in touch with the neoromantic movement; they produced a large literature of choral, orchestral, and chamber music, embracing many works of real artistic value. But although these masters enjoyed a great reputation at home, only Elgar succeeded in creating music of cosmopolitan interest and attraction. Sarasate occasionally played Mackenzie's Scotch *Pibroch Suite*, which was dedicated to him, and the Joachim Quartet played one of Stanford's chamber compositions in Berlin, but such noble works as Parry's oratorios *Prometheus Unbound* and *Job* have hardly ever been heard outside England.

Sir Edward Elgar was the first English-born composer since Purcell whose music was freely accepted on the continent of Europe. His orchestral works, especially his *Enigma Variations*, are still performed fairly frequently in Germany and in America. His oratorios *The Dream of Gerontius* and *The Apostles* enjoyed considerable success abroad. In Elgar's music the Wagnerian influence superseded the tradition of Handel and Mendelssohn, but this does not affect the powerful individuality of the composer. His command of orchestral color is extraordinary. In his melodies and rhythms there is something characteristically British, subtly joined to a religious mysticism, for Elgar was a devout member of the Roman Catholic church.

While the serious-minded Victorian masters were largely unsuccessful in their attempts to impress their music on the world outside the British Isles, a representative of Albion's lighter muse became famous wherever the English language was spoken. This was Sir Arthur Sullivan (1842–1900), the musical twin of the team of Gilbert and Sullivan, authors of the celebrated comic operas *H. M. S. Pinafore, The Pirates of Penzance,* and *The Mikado.* These witty and melodious productions are the British counterparts of Viennese operettas. In their subject matter, however, and in their music, they are British to the core.

An English composer of cosmopolitan upbringing was Frederick Delius (1862–1934). Born in England, the son of a German father, Delius spent several years in Florida as an amateur orange-grower and musician. He received his professional education in Germany, then took up his residence in France, returning to England only for comparatively short visits. He cannot therefore be regarded as a full-fledged representative of modern British music. Indeed, only rarely did Delius stress his English nationality, as in his orchestral piece *Brigg Fair*, an "English rhapsody" that treats English tunes symphonically. His musical nature was too singular and independent to fit into any category of style. To those who are but superficially acquainted with his music, Delius might pass as an English cousin of Debussy, an impressionist tone painter in the French manner. His enchanting orchestral idyls, *In a Summer Garden*, and *On Hearing the First Cuckoo in Spring*, suggest Debussy's *Jardins sous la pluie*, but it is merely the refinement of sound that is common to them both; the musical substance in the Delius scores is quite different from Debussy's. The tonal landscape *Appalachia* by Delius, with its American background, and his orchestral fantasy *Paris* — a nocturnal improvisation inspired by life in the French metropolis — are often heard; but his powerful choral work *The Mass of Life* is too little known. In his concertos and chamber compositions, the structural demands of "absolute" music seem to be an impediment to Delius, who needed the stimulus of a picturesque scene to set his musical fancy in motion. His opera *A Village Romeo and Juliet* has some beautiful, refined, and penetrating music that has been much admired by sensitive listeners. It has lately had several revivals.

The honor of reviving true national music in the English manner and in a twentieth-century idiom belongs to Ralph Vaughan Williams (born in 1872). His symphonic and choral compositions have been performed frequently on the continent and in the United States; he has been received as a reliable and acceptable representative of modern English music. He is reliable on account of his masterly writing, which always commands respect; he is acceptable, because his music is melodious and euphonious, satisfactory to the majority of listeners, and never experimental or snobbish. These qualities should have made him rather suspect to the radical modernists. Yet the great esteem in which Vaughan Williams is held in England, as a leader of national musical renaissance, has made it impossible to ignore him at international festivals of modern music.

Early in his artistic life Vaughan Williams turned his attention to the musical past of England, to its rich folk songs and its old and masterly art music. He began his career at about the time when the English Folksong Society was founded, and when Cecil Sharp launched his fruitful activities as a collector of English folk tunes. This gave to Vaughan Williams a strong impetus to further study of the natural musical resources of England. The national British tendency of Vaughan Williams was clearly revealed in his *Three Norfolk Rhapsodies* and *Fantasy on Sussex Folktunes*. In his symphonies, the thematic material is not directly taken from folk tunes but is newly invented and assimilated in the folk manner.

The most representative work of Vaughan Williams is probably the *London Symphony* (1914, revised 1920). It ranks with the greatest of contemporary symphonic works. Its masterly structure is enlivened by picturesque touches of local color, so that the spirit of the great metropolis of London comes to life before us. These local allusions speak most strongly, of course, to Londoners: but foreigners, too, are charmed by such episodes as the Westminster chimes, the lavender-seller's cry, and the jingling of cab bells that are heard in the orchestra; beyond these picturesque details there flows through the entire symphony a stream of emotion, artistically expressed. The eminent American critic Philip Hale, in his review of the *London Symphony* when it was played in Boston in 1921, aptly remarked: "The man who has written the mysterious introduction of this symphony, who has expressed loneliness and tragic shabbiness in the second movement, and the cruelty of the great city in the finale, is more than an accomplished musician; he is a rare poet in tones."

The retrospective, historical aspect of the art of Vaughan Williams is exemplified by his *Fantasy on a Theme by Tallis* for string orchestra, inspired by the father of English Cathedral music, Thomas Tallis (1505–1585). It is a beautiful and serene piece, leading us back into the dim interiors of the gothic temples, to the sounds of the little church organ and the double choir of viols and human voices intoning the austere harmony of medieval modes.

Gustav Holst (1874–1934) is internationally known to music lovers principally through his orchestral suite *The Planets*, which represents in a symbolic manner the association of planets with the human temperament. Holst was also the author of many choral works and mystery plays derived from Hindu philosophy; these works are seldom performed outside England.

The name of Frank Bridge (1879–1941), a fine composer and a consummate master of contrapuntal art, is greatly esteemed in England; as a pedagogue, he guided the fruitful development of a whole generation of English composers. Some of his string quartets and songs are well known.

Sir Arnold Bax (1883–1953) was a composer of orchestral music strongly imbued with impressionistic flavor. He was influenced mainly by the new Russian school of composition. He published an autobiography in which he gave an interesting account of British music and British musicians.

Sir Arthur Bliss (born in 1891) began his career as a follower of Debussy and Ravel but soon asserted his birthright as a British composer. His *Color Symphony* (1922) is a study of the heraldic meaning of different colors.

Eugene Goossens (born in 1893) presents a paradox. He was one of the most brilliant of the young modernist composers in London after World War I. He produced excellent chamber music and songs, which enjoyed numerous performances; he also wrote operas and ballets. Then he was engaged as a conductor in America and Australia, and his significance as a composer became obscured by his reputation as an orchestral leader.

Edmund Rubbra (born in 1901), the composer of six symphonies, is very highly regarded in England. For some reason, his interesting orchestral compositions, in a modern contrapuntal manner, are rarely heard on the continent or in America; the same may be said of his choral works, which are, however, given frequent English performances.

William Walton (born in 1902) first claimed attention by his witty modern score *Façade*, combined with amusing verses by Edith Sitwell. This score unites the spirit of true English dance music with the modern technique of accompanied narration. After this youthful but successful musical prank, he turned to the composition of serious works, which have gradually attained international recognition.

Constant Lambert (1905–1951) made his mark as a composer of ballet music. He was the first to use the idiom of American jazz, in his picturesque orchestral work *Rio Grande*.

Michael Tippett (born in 1905) is a composer of choral works of considerable interest. His cantata *A Child of Our Time*, written during World War II, is a moving work of genuine inspiration.

By far the most successful English composer of the twentieth century is Benjamin Britten (born in 1913). His international reputation dates from his opera *Peter Grimes* (1945), frequently heard in Europe and America. It was followed by a series of other operas: *The Rape of Lucretia* (1946), *Albert Herring* (1947), *Billy Budd* (1951), and *Gloriana* (performed before Queen Elizabeth II during the coronation week in 1953). Britten's latest opera, *The Turn of the Screw*, after Henry James, received its first performance at the Venice Festival in 1954.

Britten's music satisfies the requirements set for a deeply national type of music possessing cosmopolitan validity. He employs a free language of modern melody and harmony, but his basic idiom is accessible to traditionalists as well. Besides, he has a remarkable knack of communicating his musical ideas to the masses. An illustration of this facet of his talent is his engaging improvisatory work entitled *Let's Make an Opera* (1949), in which the audience is invited to take part in the singing. Even in the educational field, Britten has been able to introduce an original note: in *The Young Person's Guide to the Orchestra* (1945), he succeeds in demonstrating the capacities of each orchestral instrument by well-chosen solo passages.

Choral music has for centuries been the most outstanding feature of English musical life. The tradition of singing anthems, motets, oratorios, madrigals, and glees has made England the country of organized choral singing and the home of oratorio. The list of programs of the choral festivals in the larger provincial cities — some established two centuries ago — represents a veritable history of choral music, both English and foreign. The Three Choirs Festival (the combined forces of Gloucester, Worcester, and Hereford) and the festivals of Birmingham, Leeds, Norwich, and other cities became, in time, a model for similar organizations in America, and even in Germany.

Opera has never been a readily exportable English product. The world's operatic repertory does not contain a single stage work of English origin, although a good many operas have been written by English composers. The unpretentious and gay opera *The Bohemian Girl* by Michael William Balfe (1808–1870) had a considerable vogue for a time, but eventually vanished from the opera houses. In other countries, English musical theater has largely become identified with the comic operas of Gilbert and Sullivan. Yet London has remained to this day a center of international opera, and the Covent Garden season, ever since the time of Handel, has been the munificent purveyor of operatic spectacles. In the course of time, practically all successful operas have been heard in London, from Meyerbeer to Richard Strauss, with a sprinkling of English operas in between as a matter of patriotic duty.

As regards the presentation of orchestral music, England for a long time gave preference to German conductors, not only as guests but also as educators and repertory builders. What English orchestras owe in these respects to the German musicians Sir Charles Hallé (1819–1895), Sir Georg Henschel (1850–1934), and the great conductor Hans Richter (1843–1916) can hardly be overestimated. Not only London but also Manchester, Liverpool, Edinburgh, and Glasgow were through them made thoroughly familiar with the symphonic literature of the nineteenth century.

As the year 1900 drew closer, however, the supremacy of German conductors became less exclusive, and presently their English pupils began to assert their own powers. Sir Henry Wood (1869–1944), at the head of the Queen's Hall Orchestra in London, was the first English-born conductor of rank. He was followed by Sir Thomas Beecham (born in 1879), who has restored to English performance a magnificence that has something of the eighteenth-century grandeur. Other prominent English conductors who have lately been upholding this new tradition were Sir Hamilton Harty (1879–1941) and Albert Coates (1882–1953). Among English conductors of later generations, Sir Adrian Boult (born in 1889) distinguished himself as the leader of the London Philharmonic Orchestra, and Sir John Barbirolli (born in 1899) as leader of the Hallé Orchestra of Manchester. The London Symphony Orchestra, founded in 1904, has been conducted by many of the world's most eminent orchestral leaders.

In music publishing, Novello & Co. of London has, in its century and a half of fruitful activity, acquired an immense cultural importance throughout the British Empire. Its publications cover practically the entire range of choral music, especially in inexpensive scores. Novello is also the publisher of *The Musical Times*, which during its hundred-odd years of existence has become the leading musical periodical in the English language. Other English music magazines of a scholarly character are *Music & Letters* and *The Music Review*.

Grove's *Dictionary of Music and Musicians*, first issued in four volumes in 1879–1889, is justly famous as a rich source of generally reliable information. Its original editor, Sir George Grove (1820–1900), was an energetic promoter of musical causes and an able writer on music. The fifth edition of Grove's Dictionary, published in 1954 under the editorship of Eric Blom, increased its bulk to nine volumes, purveying an enormous amount of useful information.

Important historical anthologies of English music have been published in voluminous editions. The Purcell Society has issued a complete edition of Purcell's works; the magnificent collection of Tudor church music in ten volumes has made the sacred works by the great English composers of the fifteenth and sixteenth centuries available for performance and study; compositions by Elizabethan madrigalists have been published in thirty-six volumes under the general editorship of the well-known English music scholar Edmund Fellowes (1870–1951); a new edition of *The Oxford History of Music* began publication in 1953. Percy A. Scholes has made musical science accessible to the layman through the publication of his encyclopedic volume *The Oxford Companion to Music*, which in 1955 reached its ninth edition.

The great English universities have for centuries accorded to music a place of honor in their curricula, and are in that respect far in advance of the continental universities. Among professors of music at Oxford University were Sir F. A. G. Ouseley, Sir John Stainer, Sir Hubert H. Parry, Sir Walter Parratt, and Sir Hugh Allen. At Cambridge University, music was taught by Sir William Sterndale Bennett, Sir George Alexander Macfarren, Sir Charles Villiers Stanford, and Edward J. Dent. Sir Donald Francis Tovey (1875–1940), one of England's finest music scholars, was professor at Edinburgh University.

The insularity of English musical life is now a thing of the past. In creative fields, and in musical scholarship, England has reached the position of a major power in the concert of European nations.

1 0

Scandinavia

Denmark

Centuries had to elapse before Scandinavia acquired a distinct musical culture of her own. The famous *Kopenhagener Chansonnier* (brought out in 1927 by Dr. Knud Jeppesen) is a collection of French Burgundian chansons of the fifteenth century, which has nothing to do with Danish music despite the reference to Copenhagen in its title. Shortly after 1600, the names of two Danish composers appear in the historical chronicles: Melchior Borchgrevinck and Mogens Pederson, both pupils of Giovanni Gabrieli in Venice. In the sixteenth and seventeenth centuries the Copenhagen Court Chapel attained considerable artistic reputation, but its leading members were foreigners, mostly from England. King Christian IV had the ambition to make his court chapel the equal of the chapels at other European courts. As his sister, Princess Anne, had married the English King James I, close personal ties existed between the two courts, and English musicians were given preference in Copenhagen. Among them was the famous lute-player and composer John Dowland (1563–1626), who served Christian IV for eight years, drawing an admiral's salary. Dowland wrote some of his most admired works in Denmark, among them *Lachrymae, or Seven Teares, figured in Seven Passionate Pavans* (1604), dedicated to Queen Anne of Denmark.

English viol players were also active at Christian's court.

William Brade, composer of viol suites, was the leader of the Danish Chapel ensemble, which then could boast seventy-seven members: sixteen trumpeters, thirty instrumentalists, and thirty-one singers.

The great German master Heinrich Schütz was for several years conductor of the Royal Chapel at Copenhagen, where he published a part of his *Sinfoniae sacrae*. Dietrich Buxtehude (1637–1707), the greatest organist of the seventeenth century, was a native of Denmark and spent his early youth in that country; but his family was of German origin, and stylistically his music belongs to the German treasury or art.

In the eighteenth century Danish musical culture began to prosper, thanks in a large measure to the artistic work of Johann Ernst Hartmann (1726–1793), the founder of a veritable dynasty of four generations of musicians. He was a German, who settled in Copenhagen as leader of the royal band; in his opera *Fishermen* he included a Danish song, "King Christian," which later became the Danish National Athem. His son August Wilhelm Hartmann (1775–1850) was for half a century an organist in Copenhagen. The most gifted member of the family was Johan Peder Emilius Hartmann (1805–1900), son of August. During his long life, he wrote a number of Danish operas and much concert music in a romantic European style. His son Emil Hartmann (1836–1898) was the composer of several attractive orchestral works; his symphonic fantasy, entitled *Scandinavian Folk Music* was very popular in concert programs for a time.

Among other composers active in Denmark during the romantic musical era, the name of Friedrich Kuhlau (1786–1832) is kept alive thanks to his effective piano music, still played by students. He was a German musician who adopted the national Danish style. His music for the folk tale *Elverhoj* (1828) was extremely successful in Denmark; in this score Kuhlau drew on the wealth of Danish folk songs.

Johann Abraham Peter Schulz (1747–1800), of German birth, was court conductor in Copenhagen for several years and brought out a number of Danish dramatic works; as composer he is distinguished in writing German songs. Friedrich Kunzen (1761–1817) of Lübeck was also a resident of Copenhagen; his Danish opera *Holger Danske* enjoyed a great success. Christoph Ernst Friedrich Weyse (1774–1842) was another German musician who made his career in Denmark; his operas in the Danish style were performed in Copenhagen.

All these German-Danish composers were precursors of the masters of pure Danish national music in the second half of the nineteenth century. Danish dramatic poetry and folk tales supplied literary material for Scandinavian composers. The great dramatic poet Holberg found a congenial composer in Edvard Grieg, whose *Holberg Suite* became very popular. The success of Danish literature on the Continent aroused interest in Danish music as well as Norwegian. Hans Christian Andersen inspired several opera composers, whose libretti were derived from his poetic fairy tales. Jens Peter Jacobsen acquired European celebrity through his excellent novels. His *Gurre-Lieder* served as text for one of Arnold Schönberg's most ambitious choral works.

It was Niels Wilhelm Gade (1817–1890) who brought Danish music out into the world arena. Gade commenced his career as a composer in a sensational manner, with the *Ossian Overture* (1841), his first opus number. It became immensely popular. Mendelssohn conducted it in Leipzig in 1843, when young Gade came there to study with him and Schumann. After Mendelssohn's death Gade succeeded him as conductor of the Gewandhaus Orchestra. During the troublesome period of the 1848 revolutions, Gade returned to his homeland, and he spent the rest of his life in Copenhagen.

In the nineteenth century Gade's eight symphonies, his *Ossian Overture*, the cantata *The Crusaders*, and his violin and piano pieces were much played and well liked. But after Gade's death his popularity declined rapidly, so that now few of his major works are ever heard. This neglect is certainly unjust, and a revival of at least some of Gade's works would be welcome. True, his music is far from novel, but it is poetic and picturesque; it unfolds a vivid panorama of idyllic Denmark, with its contented villages and peaceful towns, its rich pastures, its tidily kept farms, its prodigious herds of cattle, its even-tempered civilized people. Gade's music reflects the pleasantly moist atmosphere in close proximity to the Baltic and the North seas, the fine old Renaissance architecture of the Danish cities, the harmonious character of national life. Denmark lacks mountains and wild uncultivated regions; Gade's music, too, presents a smooth surface devoid of savage upsurges of sound and fantastic scenes of unbridled excitement. Pathos, tragic conflict, dramatic agitation, eccentricity of any sort — these are foreign to Gade's gentle lyric art, a sister of Mendelssohn's and Schumann's; yet Gade's art possesses an affecting, individual character.

August Enna (1860–1939), a disciple of Gade, produced a profound impression with his first opera, *Heksen* (The Witch), which was staged at Copenhagen in 1892 and then in Sweden, Holland, Germany, and Austria. His subsequent operas *Cleopatra* (1894) and *Aucassin and Nicolette* (1896) and his music to Andersen's fairy tales also obtained excellent success. He was hailed as a rising genius of music drama. His later products, however, failed to fulfill the early promise, and his operas gradually sank into oblivion.

Much greater impact on the international scene was made by another disciple of Gade, Carl August Nielsen (1865–1931), a symphonic composer of a progressively modern tendency. He was undoubtedly the most important Danish composer of the twentieth century. His six symphonies, romantic in their inspiration, bear descriptive titles, such as *The Four Temperaments, The Expansive Symphony,* and *The Inextinguishable Symphony.* Nielsen's musical style comes close to Mahler's; there is the same emotional strife, the same yearning for a greater art than is vouchsafed by music alone. In recent years, Nielsen's music has been heard more often, not only in Scandinavia but in all musical countries of the globe.

Nielsen's pupil Jörgen Bentzon (1897–1951) acquired a fine reputation as a worker in the field of musical education of the Danish people, as Director of Copenhagen's first Folk Music School, and as a composer of choral music.

Jörgen Bentzon's younger cousin, Niels Viggo Bentzon (born in 1919), who is also grandson of the romantic Danish composer Emil Hartmann, represents the modernist movement in Denmark. His style owes much to Hindemith's linear writing. He has composed five symphonies and chamber music, some of which have achieved European renown through performances at international festivals of modern music.

Knudage Riisager (born in 1897) is another Danish composer of modernist tendencies. His highly expressive music possesses a distinct national flavor. He wrote much theatrical music, including a ballet based on Eskimo melodies of Greenland, which is Danish territory.

Danish musical scholarship at its best is represented by the achievements of Denmark's leading musicologist, Knud Jeppesen (born in 1892), whose valuable editions of old music and profound studies of contrapuntal methods have earned him an enviable international reputation.

Sweden

In Sweden as in Denmark, the national movement in music was slow to gather strength. For centuries Swedish music was under the direct and strong influence of German music. The Stockholm Royal Chapel, the country's principal center of music, founded in 1526, was for generations dominated by the successive members of the German family of Von Düben, just as Denmark received its musical guidance from the Hartmann family. Andreas von Düben (1590–1662), the first of the German-Swedish dynasty, a pupil of Sweelinck, emigrated to Sweden in 1621 and became court organist and royal court conductor in

Stockholm. His son Gustav von Düben (1624–1690) succeeded him as court organist and conductor. The Uppsala University Library keeps as one of its most precious treasures a large collection of five volumes of manuscript scores, formerly in the possession of Gustav von Düben, embodying an extensive repertory of North German masterpieces of the seventeenth century — source material of prime importance. Gustav's two sons followed the family tradition and occupied in turn the post of court conductor.

The first Swedish-born composer of real distinction was Johan Helmich Roman (1694–1758), called "Svenska Musikens Fader" by Swedish writers. Roman was indeed the father of Swedish music. He paved the way for national musicians of his country and proved that Sweden could achieve musical independence. His enormous heritage of instrumental and choral music is now being brought to light and published in Sweden.

In 1773, the Royal Opera House was founded in Stockholm. Its early organization owes much to the German musician Johann Gottlieb Naumann (1741–1801), who lived by turns in his native city of Dresden, in Italy, in Stockholm, and in Copenhagen. He reorganized the opera houses of the two Scandinavian capitals, performed a number of his Italian operas there, and acted as opera director in Stockholm. His opera *Gustav Vasa*, on a historical Swedish subject, was staged in Stockholm in 1786. Despite its national theme, the music of Naumann's opera was Italian in style and stagecraft.

The greatest classical master of Swedish music in the eighteenth century was the German-born musician Joseph Martin Kraus (1756–1792), an exact contemporary of Mozart. During his brief life of thirty-six years, Kraus produced an enormous quantity of music of all descriptions, marked by elegance and cultivated taste. Influenced mainly by Gluck, he wrote several operas performed in Stockholm. As court conductor, he composed a greatly admired cantata on the death of King Gustavus III, who was assassinated by a party of hostile noblemen. Verdi treated this event in the first version of his opera *Un ballo in maschera*. The works of Kraus, his symphonies, chamber music, and songs, are now beginning to be published.

Another Swedish classical musician of the eighteenth century was Carl Michael Bellman (1740–1795), an accomplished master in a small but unique genre. As poet, singer, lute player, and composer, Bellman depicted in words and in music the realistic scenes of everyday life in Sweden, using suitable melodic material from many sources, including German, French, English, Danish, and Swedish popular melodies — and also tunes of his own invention, which he published in a collection entitled *Fredmans Epistlar*. He sang these native ballads himself with inimitable artistry and simplicity, and enjoyed tremendous success in Sweden.

Only a detailed study of Bellman's music can give an adequate idea of the wealth and variety of his achievement. Here we find a strictly popular national product that rises high above the average songs of this genre and enters the domain of realistic art. The milieu of Bellman's poetry is not attractive: the dingy, narrow, and crooked lanes of picturesque old Stockholm, with their musty taverns filled with tobacco smoke and the stale smell of beer and Swedish punch, and frequented by a noisy, vulgar crowd, gambling, drinking, singing, and dancing. But Bellman was not content with describing these urban scenes of lowly life; he made frequent excursions into the countryside, and here his love of nature and the beauties of the Swedish landscape released in the poet's soul a visionary power enabling him to sketch fantastic pictures of many types — idyllic, intensely lyrical, tragic, humorous, elegiac, and comical.

The national Swedish movement of the nineteenth century was a continued exploration of the national resources first uncovered in Bellman's ballads. Swedish scholars and musicians combined their activities in the collection, publication, and study of the rich Swedish folklore. In 1816 Erik Gustaf Geijer (1783–1847) and Arvid August Afzelius (1785–1871) brought out a large collection in three volumes of *Svenska Folkvisor* (Swedish Folk Tunes). This basic publication, enlarged in later editions, was followed by active research by other scholars.

Erik Gustaf Geijer was one of Sweden's most remarkable personalities. A scholar, philosopher, poet, and musician, he wrote his own music for his beautiful poems, feeling deeply the power of music to strengthen the mood expressed in the words.

An interest in national folklore was also awakened in Denmark and Norway at about this time. This movement marks the beginning of the romantic epoch and is a characteristic feature of the romantic mentality. Andreas Peter Berggreen (1801–1880) in Denmark and Ludvig Mathias Lindeman (1812–1887) in Norway were the pioneers of the folklore movement in their respective countries. The Swedish folk songs stand midway between the more agitated Norwegian songs and the softer, more idyllic Danish muse. Berggreen pointed out this basic difference in a simple diagram: the Norwegian tune, with its frequent leaps and lively motion, he characterized by a jagged line; the Swedish, by an undulating line, and the Danish by a straight line. A peculiarity of Swedish folk music is the so-called *polska*, a dance song in 3/4 time. Taken over from Poland in the seventeenth century, it resembles the mazurka in its rhythm.

The first half of the nineteenth century was marked by a great development of Swedish song-writing. Among the best-known song composers is Adolf Fredrik Lindblad (1801–1878). He owed his European success mainly to his pupil Jenny Lind, the world-famous singer who delighted her audiences in many countries by the simple grace, melodic purity, and beauty of Lindblad's songs. In the world beyond her homeland Jenny Lind represented Sweden more brilliantly than any other Swedish musician. Here is another illustration of the fact that great performing artists spread the musical message of their homelands earlier, and sometimes more successfully, than do national composers. Thus, for example, Hungary as a musical country was revealed to the world at large by Franz Liszt, Russia by Anton Rubinstein, Spain by the García family, and Norway by Ole Bull.

Jenny Lind, born in Stockholm in 1820, began her career as an opera singer at the Stockholm Royal Opera. A few years later she became a pupil of Manuel García in Paris and there made the acquaintance of Meyerbeer, who soon became her most powerful protector. On his urgent recommendation she was engaged by the Berlin Royal Opera in 1844. Her exceptional success in Berlin paved the way to world celebrity, and soon she was in demand all over Germany and in Vienna. Her first appearance in London, in 1847, was a sensational event. After three seasons in England, she was brought to America in 1850 by the impresario P. T. Barnum, and her American concert tour of two seasons was a series of triumphant successes. In 1852 she married Otto Goldschmidt (her German-born accompanist), relinquished her theatrical career, and sang only in oratorios and song recitals. Later she settled in England, and for a long time continued her public appearances. Jenny Lind died in 1887. She belongs to the élite of phenomenal singers of all time.

The rise of Swedish song-writing also included choral composition. Male choirs, made up of Swedish students, became famous at home and abroad. The progress of the finest of these choirs during the nineteenth century was mainly due to the educational work of Gunnar Wennerberg (1817–1901) of Uppsala University. Wennerberg published a series of duets for male voices, to texts treating Swedish student life, and many other choral works. His *Psalms of David*, written in a simple style with instrumental accompaniment, are especially popular in Sweden.

The name of Johan August Söderman (1832–1876) is little known to the musical world at large, but in Sweden he is regarded as a national genius and held in the highest esteem. This important composer of Swedish ballads for chorus or for solo voices was the reformer of Swedish song, in the modern romantic style, in which greater attention is paid to the accompaniment. His Mass for solos, chorus, and orchestra is considered one of the most accomplished works ever created in Scandinavia. His settings of Bellman's rhapsodic poems are much admired.

Ivar Hallström (1826–1901) was the first Swedish composer of vocal music who introduced local color in the melodic substance of his stage works. His opera *Den Bergtagna* (The Mountain King) was performed with great success in Sweden and was also given in Germany.

Among Swedish composers of instrumental music, Franz Berwald (1796–1868) holds an honored place. A follower of the romantic school, he gave curious titles to his compositions: *Symphonie capricieuse, Symphonie sérieuse, Symphonie singulière.* His orchestral piece *Souvenirs of the Norwegian Alps* enjoyed considerable success.

Ludvig Norman (1831–1885) continued Berwald's tradition. A pupil of Moscheles at the Leipzig Conservatory, he imbibed German romanticism at its source. On Schumann's recommendation, Norman's Opus 1 — two piano pieces — was published in Germany. At the age of thirty he was appointed Royal Court Conductor at the Stockholm Opera. He was honored in Sweden for his symphonic and chamber music and for his refined and poetic piano sketches; he was also greatly esteemed as a writer and critic. Norman was the husband of the celebrated violinist Wilma Neruda, who after his death married Sir Charles Hallé. As Mme. Neruda-Norman (and later as Lady Hallé), she was a familiar figure in European concert halls before 1900.

The generation of Swedish composers active at the threshold of the twentieth century comprises a number of outstanding artists. Andreas Hallén (1846–1925) started as an ardent follower of Wagner, but later found his way to the rejuvenation of Swedish national opera. His *Waldemarsskatten* (Stockholm, 1899), treating the conquest of the medieval city of Visby, is his most important operatic work. It was also performed as a festival play in a ruined gothic church at Visby, on the island of Gothland, thus presenting the authentic environment for the subject of the opera. Hallén's other operas contain episodes inspired by Swedish folk song and dance. His symphonic poems and choral works, too, are national in their tendencies. It is unfortunate that Hallén's fine music is virtually unknown to music lovers nowadays.

As far as international recognition is concerned, Emil Sjögren (1853–1918) fared somewhat better than Hallén. He did not write merely national works, of interest mainly to the public of his homeland, but produced internationally valid forms of instrumental music, although the tinge of Scandinavianism is never entirely absent from his music. For some decades his violin sonatas were much played; his piano music also contains pages of singular charm, especially the cycles *Erotikon* and *Auf der Wanderschaft*.

Wilhelm Stenhammar (1871–1927) excited considerable interest with his first opus number, the Piano Concerto in B Flat Minor (1893), which was favorably compared by some critics with the famous piano concerto of Grieg. Stenhammar's romantic music, somewhat influenced by Schumann, Brahms, and Wagner, is colorful, brilliant, and warm in its exuberant melody. For the inauguration of the new Stockholm Opera House in 1898 he wrote the music drama *Tirfing*. His opera *The Banquet at Solhaug*, based on Ibsen's drama, was first performed in Stuttgart (1899) and later at Stockholm. The great reputation earned by Stenhammar did not survive the revolution of musical taste in the early decades of the twentieth century. To the present generation of musicians, the name of Stenhammar means hardly anything at all.

A contemporary of Stenhammar, Wilhelm Peterson-Berger (1867–1942) was a leader of the neoromantic movement in Sweden. He wrote several music dramas in a Wagnerian style. His songs, many of them to German texts, are distinguished by refined lyrical charm; his *Lyric Album* for piano reflects the landscape of some of Sweden's most idyllic regions.

The name of the Swedish violinist Tor Aulin (1866–1914) is widely known in the musical world, thanks to his brilliant Violin Concerto No. 3, which was for many years an international favorite with virtuosos. His smaller pieces for the instrument still survive in concert programs.

The dean of Swedish composers of the first half of the twentieth century is Hugo Alfvén (born in 1872), the prolific composer of several symphonies and symphonic poems, including the fine score *Midsommarvaka* (1904), which has gained international renown. At the age of eighty he was still busily engaged in Stockholm's musical life as composer and conductor of symphonic and choral concerts.

The Swedish composer Kurt Atterberg (born in 1887) attracted attention when he won the $10,000 prize in an international contest in 1928 for the best work to commemorate the centennial of Schubert. The sum offered was many times as much as Schubert himself had ever possessed in his whole life, and it was wasted on a symphony played everywhere for the first time and hardly anywhere for the second time. The futility of prize contests for the promotion of works of art was here demonstrated in a spectacular manner. Atterberg himself declared afterwards that he had deliberately injected into his music imitations of the styles of composers who were members of the jury, Glazunov of Russia, Bruneau of France, and Carl Nielsen of Denmark. The notoriety that Atterberg gained because of this episode did injustice to his standing, for he is an estimable composer, the author of many operas and symphonies, and a fine music critic. Several of his works have been performed in Germany and elsewhere.

Sweden now possesses a number of national composers who write strong and original music in all genres. Natanael Berg (born in 1879) is one of the leaders of Swedish national art, a composer of ballets, operas, and symphonic pieces in a neo-romantic idiom. Oskar Lindberg (born in 1887) has distinguished himself as composer of several orchestral rhapsodies on national Swedish tunes. A very important composer of this group was Ture Rangström (1884–1947), whose passionate music merits recognition abroad as well as in his native country. He was a master of dramatic building of acoustical tension, of contrasts between somber visions and happy moods. He wrote four symphonies and some twenty orchestral suites as well as an opera, *The Crown Bride*. His numerous songs and ballads are excellent examples of Swedish vocal writing.

Gösta Nystroem (born in 1890) and Hilding Rosenberg (born in 1892) are regarded by contemporary Swedish critics as founders of the modern school of national music. Yet there is a great difference between their stylistic backgrounds. Rosenberg studied in Dresden and received the cultural nourishment of German neoromanticism. Nystroem spent most of his youth in France and became fascinated with the achievements of French impressionism. Nystroem's *Sinfonia del Mare* follows Debussy's example in depicting the sea in impressionistic tones, but the waves of his music are roughened by the winds of the North. Nystroem is primarily a symphonic composer; Rosenberg devotes his energies mostly to vocal music. His oratorio *The Revelation of St. John*, which he conducted on his visit in America in 1948, was received by responsible critics as a major achievement in modern religious music.

Dag Wirén (born in 1905) is a Swedish composer of neoclassical tendencies. He described his own musical credo in the following words: "I believe in Bach, Mozart, Carl Nielsen, and absolute music." The formal principle is therefore most important in Wirén's music. His devotion to the Danish master Carl Nielsen is revealed by the passionate outbursts of dynamic force in his symphonies and other works.

Lars-Erik Larsson (born in 1908) represents the neoclassical movement among modern Swedish composers. His works have been performed rather frequently at the international music festivals, and so his name has become known outside Sweden. Gunnar de Frumerie (born in 1908) also follows the neoclassical method of composition, and his works are beginning to spread abroad. The ideal of absolute music is also accepted by Karl Birger Blomdahl (born in 1916), who has written a number of works in a style resembling Hindemith. Among the still younger Swedish composers, Ingvar Lidholm (born in 1921) follows Hindemith's precepts in contrapuntal writing. Thus we find that the modern generation of Swedish musicians has largely abandoned the national tendency, embracing instead the cosmopolitan idea of absolute music.

In a retrospective glance at Swedish music, one finds a great deal of artistic energy and national enthusiasm. Yet not a single work by any Swedish composer has acquired a permanent place in the international repertory. This appears all the more strange since in literature and painting Sweden occupies a high rank. Great Swedish writers, such as Strindberg and Selma Lagerlöf, are well known; their works have been translated into many languages and read by millions in many parts of the globe. The Swedish painters Anders Zorn and Bruno Liljefors are appreciated by connoisseurs of the pictorial arts, and their canvases are found in the world's greatest museums. But Swedish music, even in its most accomplished products, is still largely a terra incognita, even to the best informed of music critics and artists. What is the reason for this obscurity? The only plausible explanation is the circumstance that Swedish music, in its thematic substance and in its treatment, resembles German music too closely, and that the native folk-song material has too little of that specialized quality that is so attractive in Norwegian and Finnish music.

Norway

Before the middle of the nineteenth century, national music in Norway was largely confined to the songs of the people. At the time when artistic life in Denmark and Sweden was well organized, Norway showed no signs of musical activity. This tardiness is traceable to political history. Norway was for five centuries a part of either Denmark or Sweden, governed from either Copenhagen or Stockholm. To be sure, Norwegian musicians did not wait until the formal declaration of independence from Sweden in 1905 to create nationally inspired art. The world beyond Norway's fjords and mountains had become aware of Norway's music long before, when Ole Bull (1810–1880), that eccentric Nordic genius of the violin, exhibited his talents in Europe and America. A brilliant and original virtuoso in the real sense of the term, Ole Bull was not an exponent of classical art. Most of the time he played only his own compositions, in popular style. In America he flattered the audiences by playing such semi-improvised pieces as *Niagara* and *Solitude of the Prairies*. Yet, with all his flair for picturesque display, Ole Bull had an intense love for the simple tunes of his native land; he moved his audiences deeply by playing improvisations upon those fresh and beautiful melodies. Thus he was the first to acquaint the world with this treasure of Nordic folklore. For Norwegian music Ole Bull served as a herald with a marvelous voice. It was he who discovered the talent of young Edvard Grieg and encouraged him. At a meeting with young Grieg, Ole Bull spoke of the music of the Nordic landscape in these words: "Look at the mountains beyond, the lakes and rivers, the valleys and forests, the blue sky above; they all have made my music, not I myself. When I play, I feel that I am only making mechanical motions, that I am a mute listener, while Norway's soul sings within me. When the flower bells on the meadow are swayed by the wind, I hear their sound, and the blades of grass play a faint accompaniment, like a string orchestra."

The first Norwegian composers who recognized the importance of national folk songs were Halfdan Kjerulf (1815–1868) and Ludvig Mathias Lindeman (1812–1887). Kjerulf's domain was that of elegiac expression; passion was foreign to him. He caught the popular tone in a happy vein; but at times he allowed himself to lapse into sentimentality. Lindeman devoted his life to the industrious gathering of Norwegian folk music. His monumental collection of Norwegian mountain melodies, containing six hundred tunes, is an invaluable source of authentic music that was of good service to Grieg and other composers. Lindeman was also the author of a chorale book for the Norwegian church, which has been in constant use in the churches and on concert platforms.

A young Norwegian genius who died at the age of twenty-three was fated by history to exercise the most profound influence on Norwegian music. His name was Richard Nordraak (1842–1866). An enthusiastic patriot and lover of Norway's folk customs, he opened the eyes and ears of Grieg to the power and the beauty of the Nordic folk music. Edvard Grieg (1843–1907) was a year younger than Nordraak. They met in Copenhagen when Grieg was returning home from Germany, disillusioned and dissatisfied with the results of his studies at the Leipzig Conservatory. Nordraak's fiery idealism and passionate nationalism confirmed Grieg in his conviction that his life's task lay in the formation of a Norwegian type of music. Grieg himself acknowledged the debt he owed Nordraak in these words: "I had found myself, and with the greatest ease I conquered difficulties that in Leipzig had appeared insuperable. My imagination was free, and I could write one work after another."

Never during his entire artistic career did Grieg swerve from this national program. Norway's nature, Norway's song and dance, Norway's soul—these remained his only themes; and though his music is subjective in its lyricism, its form of expression and its materials are nationalistic. Grieg seldom made use of actual songs of the people; rather he assimilated national inflections in his original themes, as Chopin did before him. Even in his works of formal structure, such as the violin sonatas, he pursues national expressiveness. However, this national essence, expressed in quaint rhythms and nostalgic melodies, would not have attracted international attention, were it not for the poetic charm of the music and its easily communicated sentiments, so that all Europeans could understand and appreciate Grieg's art without any knowledge of Norwegian folklore.

As a poet of nature, Grieg achieved the greatest expressiveness in his sixty-six piano pieces entitled *Lyrische Stücke*, which he wrote in groups through his entire musical life, from the early opus 12 to opus 71. Here we find the Nordic *Springtänze* — dances of the peasants. One group of pieces deals with the fantastic creatures of the fjord country: the elves, the sylphs, and the gnomes. Other pieces are nature pictures of living things — the *Butterfly*, the *Little Bird*. There is melancholy in *Heimweh*; there is amorous sentiment in *Erotik*. All this is, in a sense, popular music, but it possesses a great refinement of colorful and characteristic harmony and a warmth and sincerity of sentiment appealing directly to the mind and heart of the romantic music-lover, not yet corrupted by the sophisticated modern spirit of caricature and parody. No wonder this unaffected art is now somewhat out of fashion! But a new turn of the wheel of taste may well bring Grieg's music right into vogue again.

Besides these Norwegian miniatures and sketches, Grieg was the composer of one of the most popular piano concertos ever written. It presents a happy combination of native Norwegian melody and virtuoso quality of technique.

Grieg's remarkable music for Ibsen's drama *Peer Gynt* has been demoted to a place on popular concert programs and is no longer admitted at serious symphonic concerts. Few people of the present generation have ever heard *Peer Gynt* as it was originally conceived. To the educated Norwegian, *Peer Gynt* holds a position in literature akin to that of Goethe's *Faust* in Germany, and Grieg's music is congenial to the mood and the philosophy of Ibsen's symbolic play.

Grieg published some hundred and fifty songs with piano accompaniment, many of which were well liked a generation ago. His wife, Nina Hagerup-Grieg, a singer of rank, was their best interpreter.

Grieg's contemporary, the eminent Norwegian composer Johan Severin Svendsen (1840–1911), had an adventurous career as army bandmaster, theater-orchestra player, and roving musician, before a government stipend enabled him to enter the Leipzig Conservatory. Later he lived in Paris, finally settling in Copenhagen as a conductor. Svendsen was not a very prolific composer. His twenty-six works fall into two categories: one, rather international in type; the other, explicitly Scandinavian. Some half-dozen of his compositions had a place in the symphonic concerts of many countries around 1900. From the international group of his works were included his spirited *Carnaval à Paris* and the orchestral legend *Zorahayde*, based upon a tale from Washington Irving's *Alhambra*; and from the Scandinavian group, *Carnaval des artistes norvégiens* and four *Norwegian Rhapsodies*. His last published work, *Romance* for violin and orchestra, is still popular, but otherwise his music has almost entirely disappeared from concert programs.

Next to Grieg, Christian Sinding (1856–1941) was the most popular Norwegian composer. Educated at the Leipzig Conservatory, he lived for many years in Germany and came into close contact with the German neoromantic movement. For some time after World War I, he taught composition at the Eastman School of Music in Rochester, New York. In contrast with Grieg's national lyricism, Sinding's music has something of an epic character, with larger proportions and more structural and symphonic art; but it lacks Grieg's melodic charm. One of Sinding's pieces, *Frühlingsrauschen* (Rustle of Spring) has become a perennial favorite among pianists all over the world.

Sinding's younger compatriot Johan Halvorsen (1864–1935) is remembered only through one early work, *March of the Boyards*, a standard repertory piece at popular summer concerts. His *Norwegian Rhapsodies* are still played in Norway.

Gerhard Schjelderup (1859–1933) was a Norwegian composer who possessed Wagnerian ambitions. His music dramas had successful performances in Germany, but disappeared completely from the European scene after their initial productions.

We now come to Norwegian composers born at the dawn of the new century. Of these, Harold Saeverud (born in 1897) is best known abroad. His charming symphonic dances are full of Norwegian rhythms, and they give a vivid impression of the villages of Norway on a festal day. He also wrote six symphonies and several instrumental concertos. The works of Klaus Egge (born in 1906) have been heard at international music festivals. His symphonies belong to the category of absolute music, but in his vocal works he returns to national sentiments and produces a modern type of Norwegian music that cultivates popular melodic and rhythmic ideas.

Finland

The grand figure of Jean Sibelius (born in 1865) dominates Finnish music. It may even be said that he is symbolic of Finnish culture in general. In his own lifetime he has become a legend. Honors and distinctions have been heaped on him by the government of Finland. Postage stamps with his likeness were issued on his eightieth birthday in 1945. The whole world united in homage to Sibelius on his ninetieth birthday in 1955. There is no precedent of such universal devotion to a living composer.

The name of Jean Sibelius came to the attention of the musical world for the first time when Robert Kajanus took the Helsingfors Philharmonic Orchestra to the Paris Exposition of 1900 and performed there his now famous tone poem *Finlandia*. The majestic chorale-like theme of this work has since become a national song of Finland, inspiring the people to assert their independence. Sibelius expressed in this song the innermost soul of his people.

The music of Sibelius falls into two categories: the first, which includes *Finlandia*, is intensely national in character; the second is more international, and European in essence. A work by Sibelius that has become greatly popular all over the world, *Valse triste*, belongs to the second, cosmopolitan class, for it represents the romantic spirit common to many countries.

Several of Sibelius' tone poems are inspired by the Finnish epic *Kalevala*: they include *The Swan of Tuonela, Lemminkäinen's Homecoming, Pohjola's Daughter,* and *The Origin of Fire*. While these works, which abound in national allusions, can be enjoyed as absolute music, one comes closer to their spirit through a knowledge of their subject matter.

The seven symphonies of Sibelius are also national in sentiment, melodic content, and rhythmic patterns, even though they contain no programmatic allusions. The structure of these symphonies generally follows the development in a highly original form, with a technique as personal as the thematic material itself. Sibelius is here a supreme melodist, assimilating his themes to the Nordic folk music somewhat in the manner of Grieg, but applying to this folk material a symphonic art that has no equal among Scandinavian composers. Sibelius has a peculiar way of building up his main themes like a mosaic, adding one little particle to another, often starting with a seemingly insignificant phrase, dwelling on that phrase, extending it, varying it, hammering it out, until it acquires its proper melodic shape and rhythmic accent. In Beethoven's sketch-books we can observe a similar process in the labor expended in shaping the theme, but a Beethoven score gives us only the result of that labor, whereas Sibelius often makes us watch, and hear, the whole cumulative progress from the germ of his theme through its various transformations to its final form.

The music of Sibelius is strongly suggestive of the Nordic landscape. Finland is a land of immense forests, of a thousand lakes, of rivers and torrents, a land of vast plains and granite rocks, a land of long dark winters, and brief summers with weird displays of northern lights. On the north Finland borders on the Arctic Ocean; on the west and south lies the Baltic Sea. The large cities are mostly seaports; the interior is sparsely populated.

Such a landscape is apt to generate a brooding mentality, a mythology rich in sinister imagery. Somber are some of these moods; but the Finnish people have another side in their temperament. They feel an animal joy of living; they are capable of transports of ecstasy.

These Finnish traits, with their violent contrasts of brooding melancholy and animalistic joy, are reflected in the music of Sibelius, with a power of characterization of which only a very great artist is capable. National consciousness is strong in this music, but it transcends the boundaries of a single nation; its poetry and its grandeur appeal to the souls and minds of the whole world. At its sublime moments, the art of Sibelius touches the frontiers of the cosmic sphere, whence, in a mysterious cycle, the mind is led back to its primitive origin. This conjunction of the transcendental and the realistic aspects makes the art of Sibelius akin to the greatest manifestations of creative power in man.

Like all Scandinavian art, Finnish national music is built upon the rock of folk song. One gets an idea of this wealth of melodic material by looking through the five volumes of *Suomen Kansan Sävelmia* (Melodies of the Finnish People), compiled by the dean of Finnish music scholars, Ilmari Krohn (born in 1867).

The first impetus to Finnish national art was given by a Finnish physician, Elias Lönnrot (1802–1884), who became fascinated with popular song and poetry. He brought out the first edition of the *Kalevala* in 1835, and a few years later published a collection of lyric folk poems, *Kanteletar*. These collections have provided Finnish writers and musicians with a rich treasure of native folklore.

German musicians, who were invited to Finland in the nineteenth century, brought with them the fruits of their romantic imagination. It was a German, Fredrik Pacius (1809–1891), who gave Finland her national anthem. He was also the author of the first native Finnish opera, *The Hunt of King*

Charles (1852). As an educator, Pacius exercised great influence through his teaching at the University of Helsingfors. His successor Richard Faltin (1835–1918) was also a German by birth. He contributed greatly to the development of Finnish musical culture.

Martin Wegelius (1846–1906), a very cultivated musician born in Helsingfors and educated in Vienna and Leipzig, became his country's most eminent music teacher. He was the founder and first director of the Helsingfors Conservatory. Several celebrated Finnish composers were his pupils, among them Sibelius.

Robert Kajanus (1856–1933) did more than any other Finnish musician to bring native music to the attention of Europe. He was the founder of the Philharmonic Society of Helsingfors, and conducted its orchestral concerts. In 1900 Kajanus made a tour with his orchestra through western Europe, and presented Finnish music at the Paris Exposition. As a composer, Kajanus was one of the first to seek inspiration in the *Kalevala*. His orchestral and choral compositions hold an honored place in the Finnish literature of music, though they are seldom heard outside Finland.

The name of Erkki Melartin (1875–1937) is known abroad chiefly through his romantic piano pieces, but he was also the composer of a national opera, *Aino*, of six symphonies, chamber music, and a number of songs. This artistic output entitles him to an eminent position in Finnish national art.

Armas Järnefelt (born in 1869), brother-in-law of Sibelius, follows in the master's footsteps in his national compositions. Among his numerous works, the delicate *Berceuse* is familiar to all music-lovers.

Selim Palmgren (1878–1951) is internationally known for his evocative piano music; his short pieces are touched with impressionistic colors. For some years he taught composition at the Eastman School of Music.

Heikki Klemetti (1876–1953) acquired a great reputation in Finland as a choral composer and conductor. His works are virtually unknown beyond Finland's borders, mainly because of the barrier of language, but they are firmly established in the Finnish repertory.

Among Finnish opera composers, Oskar Merikanto (1868–1924) and Leevi Madetoja (1887–1947) are the most important. Merikanto was the author of the first opera in the Finnish language, *The Maid of the North*, inspired by an episode in the *Kalevala*. His many songs have attained tremendous popularity in Finland. Madetoja's opera *The Bothnians* has had repeated performances at the Helsinki Opera House. His three symphonies suggest a strong influence of Sibelius, but there is enough individual quality to make them worth while.

Finnish composers of the modern school are peculiarly adept in lyric songs similar to the German lieder. The most prominent among these is Yrjö Kilpinen (born in 1892), who has written song cycles in Finnish, Swedish, and German. His masterly fusion of melody with artistic accompaniment elevates him to a place of honor among modern composers of art songs.

The high level of musical culture in Finland is demonstrated by the fact that no fewer than ninety Finnish composers are listed in an extensive volume of 762 pages, *Suomen Säveltäjiä*, published in Helsinki in 1945. With the aid of excellent educational facilities in the Finnish national capital and in other cultural centers of the country, a new generation of talented Finnish composers has appeared on the musical horizon. One of them, Einar Englund (born in 1916) has attracted attention by his effective symphonic works.

Iceland

Iceland belongs geographically to the constellation of Nordic lands. Thanks to the development of aviation, this remote island has established closer cultural communications with the rest of the world. At least one Icelandic composer, Jon Leifs (born in

1899), has achieved an international reputation. Trained in Germany, he has acquired a thorough modern technique of composition. Among his nationally inspired works are the *Icelandic Overture* and several suites of native dances.

11

The Slavic Nations

Poland

In the historical sequence in which the Slavic nations have acquired importance for the musical world, Poland was the first to develop national music, Bohemia second, and Russia third. Serbia, Croatia, Macedonia, and Bulgaria, so rich in folk song and dance, have not yet advanced sufficiently from their national seclusion into the broad plains of European art to secure a place of comparative significance in the Slavic musical brotherhood.

In conformance with its social structure, Poland had two widely different types of music: the music of the rural people who made up five-sixths of the entire population, and the music of the thin upper crust — the luxurious royal court and the wealthy, pleasure-loving aristocracy. Between these two extremes the middle class was too insignificant, too inactive, and too impecunious to evolve its own form and style of art. There was no point of contact between the imported German and Italian art of the court, in the royal residences of Cracow and Warsaw, and the vigorous and colorful songs of the people. In the sixteenth and seventeenth centuries several composers of Polish nationality published church music: Nicolas Gomolka (c. 1535–c. 1585), Thomas Szadek (1550–1611), Gregory Gorczycki (1664–1734); but their psalms and motets, estimable though they were, show no trace of distinctive Polish style.

The seventeenth and eighteenth centuries witnessed a decline of musical art in Poland, parallel to the country's political decline during that time. However, Polish folk music began to interest foreign composers. The German master Heinrich Albert (1604–1651), active in Königsberg near the Polish border, incorporated characteristic Polish dance songs into his collection of arias. The pompous, festive polonaise makes an occasional appearance in German works by J. S. Bach, K. P. E. Bach, Weber, and even Beethoven, though in a rhythmically weakened manner (in his Serenade in D, op. 8).

In the eighteenth and early nineteenth centuries, Polish musicians were active in the fields of opera, orchestral music, cantata, and dance music, but failed to impress their names on the outside world. One of the most gifted of these musicians was Josef Elsner (1769–1854), a German who settled in Warsaw and, in time, thoroughly absorbed Polish culture. For many years he was considered a leading musician of Poland; he was honored as a composer, and became director of the Warsaw Conservatory. To posterity he is known only as the teacher of Chopin, who throughout his life showed affectionate regard for him.

After 1800 Polish musicians began to travel extensively abroad. Maria Szymanowska (1790–1832) was greatly admired in Europe as one of the most accomplished pianists of her time. The great Goethe made her acquaintance at Marienbad and fell passionately in love with her, despite his seventy-three years of age. One of the finest poems in his *Marienbader Elegie* was directly inspired by Maria Szymanowska. The visit she paid him called forth outbursts of delight from the aged poet. Her brilliant career was cut short by her premature death in St. Petersburg.

There were cultivated musicians among the members of the Polish aristocracy. Prince Michael Cleophas Oginski (1765–1833), who wrote polonaises and waltzes, was an ardent Polish patriot who never reconciled himself to the partition of his country. Another titled Polish musician of the time was Prince Anton Radziwill (1775–1833). His incidental music to Goethe's *Faust* was performed in German theaters throughout the nineteenth century. Prince Radziwill was also a friend and patron of the young Chopin.

The soil on which truly great Polish music was to be cultivated was thus well prepared for the appearance of Frédéric Chopin (1810–1849). After his concerts as a youth in Poland, he passed through Austria and Germany like a brilliant meteor, leaving a luminous trail in the hearts of music lovers. Robert Schumann was the first among German musicians to welcome Chopin into their fraternity, by commenting in his review of Chopin's Opus 2: "Hats off — a genius!"

Chopin took up his abode in Paris, at that time the center of the musical world. Within a few years he was firmly established there. His concerts became important social events; his works were printed in three editions, in Leipzig, Paris, and London — and quickly spread throughout Europe.

Chopin wisely limited himself to a single field of art, writing for piano almost exclusively, and thus avoiding the wasteful dispersion of his native genius. His contemporaries attempted to master all genres — opera, symphony, oratorio, concerto, chamber music, song, solo instrumental music — inevitably inviting failure in some of these genres.

Chopin was not the first to devote himself to the cultivation of piano composition. He had able forerunners: Muzio Clementi (1752–1832), Johann Nepomuk Hummel (1778–1837), and particularly the Irish pianist John Field (1782–1837). But these masters could not dissociate themselves from the type of keyboard technique that was inherited from the harpsichord. And their imagination and inventiveness were below the level of their great contemporaries — Haydn, Mozart, and Beethoven.

The phenomenon of Chopin's art could arise only from a synthesis of several spiritual endowments — an exceptional melodic and harmonic gift, the flair of a virtuoso, and the ability to create an entirely new, peculiarly pianistic technique. All these endowments Chopin possessed in the highest degree. Chopin was a Pole, but also a European, and he had the power of transforming national Polish music into cosmopolitan European music without weakening its racial characteristics. This synthesis made him the first great national composer of Poland. His mission was to discover the potentialities of the nostalgic melodies of Polish folk songs and the fiery rhythms of the impassioned Polish dances, and transmit them to the world, in sounds understandable to all. It was Chopin who gave an eloquent and convincing expression to the Slavic musical soul for the first time in history. Following his example, a mighty stream of Slavic music flowed into European art. Moreover, Chopin's national, racial, and at the same time cosmopolitan art encouraged musicians from other musically young nations to enter the arena of world music. He showed the way to national artistic independence to the Russians, to the Czechs, and to the Hungarians. Mussorgsky, Borodin, and Tchaikovsky would never have created their national masterpieces without Chopin's inspiring example. Dvořák and Smetana followed his precepts in effectuating an artistic synthesis of folk material and European art forms. The gypsy strain in Liszt's music emerged so strongly because he had Chopin's successful precedent in mind.

Chopin's amazing penetration of the inner spirit of Polish folk music is demonstrated particularly in his fifty-two mazurkas, in which the rhythms and melodic inflections are the closest of all Chopin's music to the authentic folk dances of Poland. In his youth, Chopin was fond of watching peasant dances in Polish villages. These early impressions retained their freshness in his music. Listening to Chopin's mazurkas, one seems to see joyful groups of Polish peasants making merry. One hears the willow pipe of the shepherd, the fiddle of an itinerant musician. There are felt in Chopin's Polish dances the cool morning breezes, and also the stale air of the roadside inns. Then the strains of an elegant salon mazurka are sounded; there are heard, in Liszt's phrase, "the jingling of sabers, the faint rustling of silk dresses, the tinkling of bracelets and necklaces." Some of these pieces imply philosophical humor; others are sad and melancholy, while still others are feverishly agitated, echoing the noise of a distant battle with faint trumpet sounds and subdued drum rolls. In Chopin's mazurkas, there unfolds a whole panorama of Polish life, from the peasant huts to the aristocratic salons.

The polonaises of Chopin are as thoroughly Polish in sentiment and color as the mazurkas, but they reflect a quite different aspect of the Polish character, aristocratic and haughty. The fine polonaise in A flat major represents the highest achievement of Chopin's aristocratic muse. Its fire and brilliance, its passionate expression, its nobility, its verve, create an irresistible effect. No wonder this polonaise has become one of the most popular compositions in the entire piano repertoire.

It was Chopin who first imparted artistic dignity to the waltz, which had been regarded before him as a popular dance of a rustic character. Beethoven's *Deutsche Tänze* and Schubert's waltzes are of this kind. Carl Maria von Weber was perhaps the first to use a waltz in an elevated concert piece, in his *Invitation to the Dance*. Chopin followed Weber's example; his waltzes are the finest flower of salon music. Elegance, graceful swing, and *esprit* distinguish them; flames of passion flare up but are restrained by the decorum of a man of the world. The sensuous gaiety and swaying charm of the popular Viennese waltz are essentially different from Chopin's worldly music for the aristocratic salon. Such waltzes could only be written by one who, like Chopin, had inherited French blood and who lived in the refined atmosphere of French society. Blended with this French heritage is the Slavic passion for the dance and the delight in it.

Chopin's waltzes had international reverberations. Gounod's waltzes in *Faust*, Liszt's *Mephisto Waltz* — all follow Chopin's model. In his *Rosenkavalier* waltzes, Richard Strauss combines the *esprit* of Chopin's aristocratic salon with the more popular type of Johann Strauss.

Another element in Chopin's music that acquired great meaning for progressive art in all countries was his novel and fascinating chromatic harmony. The romantic craving for picturesque quality in music led to a more refined treatment of harmony, based on the chromatic scale which, with its twelve notes, permits much more varied combinations and much subtler graduations of sound than those afforded by the diatonic scale.

The treatment of chords as elements of musical color was an innovation of romantic music. Weber utilized some effective colorful harmonies. Schubert found many more by a frequent juxtaposition of major and minor tonic chords, by a sudden alternation of distant keys, and by lavish use of harmonic sequences. Chopin proceeds still further down this path, discovering along the way a multitude of new, picturesque, and evocative combinations of harmonic colors. He enhances the concept of tonality by introducing chromatic harmonies. "Dark" and "bright" color effects, with a great many intermediate nuances, are produced by the skillful blending of chromatic and diatonic passages. In this Chopin anticipated some of Wagner's daring harmonic innovations. In *Tristan und Isolde* Wagner applies on a magnified scale what Chopin had already practiced twenty years earlier.

In purely technical matters, Chopin made revolutionary advances in the writing for the piano. He introduced novel color effects, thanks to his imaginative use of the pedal. Yet he was never tempted to imitate the orchestra. He was content with the keyboard sonorities. His twenty-four *Etudes* (app. 10 and 25) give a striking illustration of his new technical methods. Four-part chord writing and organ-like polyphony are here translated into pianistic terms. The massive homophony of piano writing is enlivened by flexible and elegant figurations serving as a colorful background for the chief melodic line. Chopin derives these figurations from scales and arpeggios, but he replaces the traditional octave arpeggios by passages compassing a tenth, with wide intervallic leaps in the left hand. With the help of the pedal, brilliant sonorities are thus obtained, a fullness of power, and a wide gradation of sound that could not be achieved without this unorthodox treatment of the accompaniment.

Strict polyphony, as practiced by Bach, is abandoned by Chopin as unsuitable for the instrument. He rarely uses more than three distinct parts: melody in the upper part, the bass as the foundation of the harmony, and a middle part filling the intermediate space. The functions of these three parts are enhanced in Chopin's music with amazing boldness. The compass of the right-hand melody is extended by gliding over several octaves, and by the insertion of elegant ornamental passages. Similarly, the left-hand part is elevated to a new significance by ingenious and effective variants of the arpeggio, and by chords of a breadth, fullness, and power absent in older piano music. For the intermediate part, the thumbs of the right and of the left hand are brought into service.

Chopin's artistic use of Polish folk music opened the eyes and ears of Polish scholars to the value and beauty of their national musical heritage. The earliest collections of Polish folk songs were brought out between 1833 and 1854. These fragmentary publications were superseded by the monumental collection published by Oskar Kolberg between 1865 and 1889, containing, in twenty-two volumes, more than ten thousand Polish folk songs from regions inhabited by Poles in Russia, Austria, and Germany. Many more collections of Polish folk songs and dances were published in the twentieth century.

Chopin's importance as a Polish composer is so great that his music dwarfs even the most valuable contributions of his compatriots. Yet there were respectable Polish musicians in the nineteenth century whose music merits notice. Among these Polish composers, Stanislaw Moniuszko (1819–1872) became a national figure thanks to his opera *Halka* (1854), which is imbued with the expressive spirit of Polish folk music. This opera is held in reverence by Polish music lovers, but because of its lack of cosmopolitan appeal, it is little known outside Poland except for a few of its dances.

The greatest name in Polish music at the threshold of the twentieth century was that of Jan Paderewski (1860–1941), pianist and statesman. The success of his concert tours in Europe and America was phenomenal. With his lion's mane and flying hands he exercised a hypnotic influence on the public. His playing ranged from the subtlest effects and the most delicate nuances obtainable on the pianoforte to the thundering sonorities of massive chords. Although Paderewski wrote symphonies and operas, only one of his works has survived him — the unpretentious little Minuet in G, which has become a perennial favorite among music-lovers all over the world. After World War I Paderewski was for a brief period of time the premier of the Polish Republic, and in that capacity he was a participant of the Versailles Peace Conference.

Of the more recent Polish composers, only a few have become known to the musical world at large. The most prominent among them was Karol Szymanowski (1882–1937). His picturesque violin pieces entitled *Myths* are often heard on concert programs. Here the poetic spirit of antiquity is revived by means of modern impressionistic harmony, with a Chopinesque feeling for subtlety of rhythm and delicacy of melodic accent. Szymanowski also wrote music in an explicit national manner, derived from the folk songs and dances of the mountaineers of the High Tatra. This music, full of bold and unusual rhythms, constitutes one of the finest artistic transformations of national melodies. Although Szymanowski was one of the most progressive European modernists, and wrote serious operatic, symphonic, and chamber works, very little of this considerable output has so far found its way into the international repertory, one reason being the complexity and difficulty of his scores. Nevertheless, next to Chopin, Szymanowski was the most influential of modern Polish composers, and under his guidance, Polish music of the twentieth century began to play an important part in modern European art.

Miecyslaw Karlowicz (1876–1909) is regarded by Polish scholars as the most important composer of the neoromantic school in Poland. His death in a mountain avalanche at the early age of thirty-two was lamented as a great blow to national art. His symphonic poems received great acclaim in Warsaw and other Polish cities.

Gregor Fitelberg (1879–1953) established himself in Europe as an accomplished symphonic conductor; but he was also a prolific composer, having written many works for orchestra as well as chamber music. His son Jerzy Fitelberg (1903–1950) made a mark at international music festivals as a composer; he eventually settled in America. Attempts have been made since his death to revive his music, which has merit as an example of neoclassical writing in an effective modern manner.

The name of Ludomir Rozycki (1884–1953) is greatly esteemed in Poland but hardly known elsewhere. Rozycki was the composer of operas and instrumental music in a romantic style, tinged with impressionism, often with a Polish background of folklike melodies.

Among Polish composers now living outside Poland, Alexandre Tansman (born in 1897) is the best known. He settled in Paris after World War I but he did not abandon the Polish type of composition. He has written several symphonies and concertos; his Polish dances in modern harmonies for piano are extremely effective.

Twentieth-century Polish composers, Jan Maklakiewicz (1899–1954), Alfred Gradstein (1904–1954), Arthur Malawski (born in 1904), and Roman Palester (born in 1907) have been represented at European concerts. Other Polish composers of importance are Stanislas Wiechowicz (born in 1893), Tadeusz Szeligowski (born in 1896), Boleslaw Woytowicz (born in 1899), and Antoni Szalowski (born in 1907). Poland's foremost woman composer, Grazyna Bacewicz (born in 1913), attracted the attention of the musical world when her string quartet received first prize at the international competition in Liège in 1951.

Andrzej Panufnik (born in 1914) is a Polish composer who began as an extreme modernist, employing dissonant chromatic harmony, even quarter-tones. He was regarded in Poland as one of the most important modern composers after World War II. In 1954 he settled in London.

Of the youngest generation of Polish composers Tadeusz Baird (born in 1928) is the most precocious. He has written two symphonies and many instrumental works of considerable distinction.

Polish musical scholarship is of a very high order. Voluminous publications dealing with Polish folk music and documentary materials on Chopin and other Polish composers have been issued in Poland. Among Polish musicologists, Adolf Chybinski (1880–1952) distinguished himself by valuable contributions to Polish music history.

Bohemia

Bohemia (now a part of Czechoslovakia) has for centuries been a land rich in beautiful folk music. Bohemian musicians were known and esteemed in many countries; but Bohemian folk music stayed at home until the middle of the nineteenth century, when suddenly, like Polish and Russian folk music, it entered the domain of high art and became a prized article of export. During the eighteenth and nineteenth centuries, Bohemian musicians traveled to many countries and were welcomed as fine orchestral players. Handel had a number of Bohemian fiddlers and pipers in his operatic enterprise in London. The great opera composer Gluck started his career as a member of a Bohemian band that was hired for dances, serenades, weddings, and funerals, or for any other occasion at which the music-loving

Bohemian people desired entertainment. For two centuries such Bohemian bands could be heard in many countries in Europe and even in America, striking up their tunes on street corners and collecting a voluntary tribute of copper coins from their not very discriminating listeners.

It should be remembered that for centuries Bohemia had been a bilingual country, both German and Czech being spoken. Gluck was of Bohemian origin, and in his truly cosmopolitan music four different springs poured their waters into one vast central basin: German, French, Italian, and Bohemian. Of all these, the Bohemian rivulet was the smallest; it becomes noticeable only after a minute inspection. In Gluck's century, the value of national folk music as a source of cosmopolitan art had not yet been discovered.

In the eighteenth century, the famous orchestra of Mannheim, the birthplace of the modern symphony, was full of Bohemian musicians, both players and composers. Franz Xaver Richter (1709–1789), Johann Stamitz (1717–1757), his son Karl Stamitz (1745–1801) — the leading composers of the Mannheim school, whose symphonies were played not only in Germany but also in Paris and London — were all natives of Bohemia or Moravia, though it is not easy to discover any Bohemian traits in their music. Other Bohemian masters of rank were Franz Benda (1709–1786), a famous violinist in the service of Frederick the Great, and his brother Georg Benda (1722–1795), who was a successful composer of German comic operas and a much admired master of the melodrama, a form that had gained ground in the eighteenth century. There was also Johann Ladislaus Dussek (1760–1812), a noted piano virtuoso active in Paris, London, Amsterdam, and Berlin, of whose remarkable piano sonatas but few are still played. These composers and many others highly honored in their day were natives of Bohemia, but none of them stressed the national element in their music. The explanation of this neglect is partly racial, for most of them were German Bohemians and, as such, cultivated German music, and partly historical, for folk music had not yet been fully explored by composers.

So great was the abundance of musical talent in Bohemia during the eighteenth century that Prague became an important center of music. The monk Bohuslav Czernohorsky (1684–1742) was greatly respected as a matter of choral music and as an organist. Among his many pupils were Tartini and Gluck. The Prague Opera enjoyed an excellent reputation. Mozart's association with it was of great importance to him. *Don Giovanni* was commissioned by the Prague Opera, partly composed in Prague, and performed there for the first time, in 1787.

Jan Dismas Zelenka (1679–1754), though mainly active in Dresden as court conductor and composer, was one of the earliest pioneers of national Bohemian music; there are elements in his sacred cantatas that possess some native Bohemian inflections.

It was a long time before the Czech ground tone became dominant in Bohemian music. The change came after the Revolution of 1848, when that mighty explosion of national and social aspirations rocked the European continent. Musicians in nationally dormant lands awoke from their slumber and became aware of the racial significance of their art.

The man of genius who understood the national task of the time and possessed the artistic equipment needed for fulfilling it was Bedřich Smetana (1824–1884). He did for Bohemia what Chopin did for Poland. A musician of the first rank, with an intense love of his native land, he was captivated by the melodic beauty and the rhythmic swing of the Bohemian and Moravian folk songs and dances as performed by village musicians who had never learned to handle their fiddles and pipes at a conservatory. With his keen ear and racial sympathy, Smetana realized the tremendous potentialities of this native material, and he devoted his life to creating a deeply authentic national art, which was at the same time elevated to cosmopolitan significance thanks to Smetana's accomplished technique of composition.

As conductor of the Prague Opera, Smetana had the facilities for creating a national opera — national in its use of the Czech language in operas from the history and the life of the people. Smetana's Bohemian opera *The Bartered Bride* (1866) became a favorite all over the world. It owed its success to the abundance of spirited and melodious tunes, happily invented in the style of genuine folk songs and dances. The plot introduced figures characteristic of the life in Bohemian villages: a professional marriage broker, a pretty peasant girl in love with a poor young fellow, a stupid but rich suitor, the parents of the girl, persuaded by the greedy matchmaker to favor the wealthy simpleton. Of course, the evil machinations are eventually foiled, and true love prevails. In combination with a musical score of great melodic charm, this story has a natural appeal. When presented on the opera stage with a colorful display of Bohemian village costumes, *The Bartered Bride* becomes a spectacle of irresistible attraction.

Although Smetana wrote eight national operas, only *The Bartered Bride* has won a place in the international repertory. Yet there are at least two more operas by Smetana, *Libussa* and *Dalibor*, that deserve to be known outside Bohemia.

As a symphonic composer, Smetana is chiefly remembered by one or two movements from his cycle of six orchestral pieces entitled *My Fatherland*; of these the prime favorite is *Vltava* (The Moldau), a masterly tone picture of Bohemia's majestic river, on which Prague is situated. *In Bohemia's Meadows and Forests*, from the same cycle, is a piece of idyllic pastoral music — an inspired tribute to the country and to its people.

Smetana also composed some brilliant and picturesque piano music, now neglected, although some of it might well be revived. Not forgotten, however, is his string quartet *From My Life*, depicting autobiographical episodes and culminating in the tragic onset of deafness. This is marked by an extraordinary coda to the finale, in which a high and protracted E — the tone that sounded endlessly in Smetana's ears after he became totally deaf — cries out despairingly to the accompaniment of sinister tremolo harmonies, in dramatic contrast to the happiness of a rich life told in the first three movements and most of the finale.

The name of Pavel Křižkovský (1820-1885) is almost totally unknown outside his native homeland of Bohemia, although his work was of fundamental importance for national music. He was the first to make a thorough study of Bohemian and Moravian folk songs and to arrange them for male chorus in an artistic manner. Smetana himself acknowledged his debt to Křižkovský as a contemporary master who taught the younger generation the significance and beauty of Bohemian folk music.

Smetana's heir and successor was Antonin Dvořák (1841-1904). From a lowly beginning he rose to the heights of world fame. The decisive role in Dvořák's career was played by Brahms, who recommended him to his own publisher in Berlin and showed him many other signs of friendship. What attracted Brahms to Dvořák's music was its wealth and freshness of melodic invention. In this respect Dvořák's natural talent was greatly aided by the popular music of Bohemia, which had served as an inexhaustible source of supply for Smetana and continued to nourish Dvořák's powerful gifts. In the art of composition, Dvořák learned much from a close study of the scores of his benefactor Brahms, without, however, succumbing to mere imitation of the German master's style. Indeed, Brahms' Germanic melody, tempered and softened by Viennese grace and roundness, has an accent, rhythm, and sentiment quite different from the melody of Dvořák, with its Slavic tunefulness, its spirit of the rustic dance full of fiery rhythms, and its melancholy *dumky* (slow movements), charged with unaffected nostalgic feeling.

Dvořák's ten operas are little known outside Czechoslovakia. In plot as well as in music, they have a strong appeal at home that is not felt by foreigners. Dvořák's choral music is better known. His cantata *The Specter's Bride*, the oratorio *St. Ludmilla*, and the *Requiem* are still a part of the international repertory. But it was his symphonic music, and particularly his symphony *From the New World*, that made Dvořák's name a household word. This symphony eclipsed all his other orchestral works. Inspired by the composer's sojourn in America (1892–1895), the haunting tune of the slow movement is known to multitudes of music lovers. His unpretentious piano piece *Humoresque*, also written in America, has become a perennial favorite. Of his other works, the orchestral suite *Slavonic Dances* and the concerto for cello and orchestra are often performed.

After Dvořák's death there was no Bohemian composer of commensurate stature to take over the reins, as Dvořák himself had done after the death of Smetana. True, there was no lack of excellent musicians in the country. There was Josef Suk (1874–1935), Dvořák's pupil and son-in-law; there were Joseph Foerster (1859–1951) and Vitězslav Novák (1870–1949) — all composers of high aspirations and fine musicianship. But their music was not sufficiently strong to interest many people abroad.

There was one truly great Czech composer, however, whose significance was not fully appreciated until after his death. He was Leoš Janáček (1854–1928), who spent most of his life in the provincial seclusion of the quiet city of Brno. His principal work, the opera *Jenufa*, was performed there in 1904 and in Vienna in 1918. It then made the round of the German opera houses, enjoying increasing success despite the fact that the international musical arena had in the meantime been captured by the modernists. In fact, Janáček, a man of seventy, was hailed by the young modernists as their comrade-in-arms. His works were frequently performed at international festivals of modern music, and impressed the listeners as fresh and original, written in a new idiom and with a modern technique.

There were, of course, reasons for this belated recognition of Janáček by the musical world. He was extremely nationalistic in his tendencies and uncompromising in his insistence on the exclusive use of the Czech language in his vocal works. Yet in his treatment of national material he adopted a progressive, modern attitude. Through close observation of the common people and their manner of speech, Janáček developed his unique system of declamatory music — a realistic, dynamic, eruptive musical recitation, quite different from the round smoothness of the symmetrical song melody. This forceful choral music is full of dramatic flashes, emotional intensity, and psychological penetration. He even applied this type of dramatic recitation to sacred music. His *Glagolitic Mass,* to the old Slavonic text, is a powerful evocation of primeval religious feelings.

In *Jenufa* this new style was for the first time transferred to the theater and expanded to the large proportions of a real music drama. It is a village tragedy: two half-brothers love the same young woman, Jenufa. She favors the more handsome one, who leaves her after the birth of their child. To avert the scandal threatening the family, her foster mother kills the infant, and Jenufa is suspected of the crime. The conflict, despair, and turmoil arising from this situation are resolved by the enduring affection of the once rejected lover, who saves Jenufa. Janáček's declamatory music in this score is not dry or mechanical; it expands into lyrical stretches of great melodic beauty. Music of this type, of course, depends for its full effect on the original text in the Czech language, with its rolling consonants, its sonorous vowels, its musical cadences and inflections.

Jenufa is not a continuation of Smetana's folk-song operas; here folk song is replaced largely by folk speech, and Smetana's racial idealism is opposed by social realism. Yet Janáček's music is a tonal revelation of Czech national feeling, in utterance quite different from the German or Italian manner, though it has some contacts with Russian emotionalism. This is especially evident in Janáček's later operas: *Katia Kabanova,* founded on a play by the Russian dramatist Ostrovsky, and *From the House of the Dead,* a dramatization of Dostoyevsky's novel. Janáček's other operas, such as the satirical play *Mr. Brouček,* have little appeal to a cosmopolitan audience, for there are too many local allusions to characters and situations familiar only to the Czechs. In his instrumental music, Janáček's modern trend is conspicuous, in melodic material, peculiar orchestration, and terse harmony.

Between 1920 and 1935 a number of highly talented Czechoslovak composers aroused attention by performances of their music at the festivals of the International Society for Contemporary Music. Among them were the German Bohemians Egon Kornauth (born in 1891), Fidelio Finke (born in 1891), and Erwin Schulhoff (1894–1942), and the Czechs Rudolf Karel (1880–1945), Jaroslav Krička (born in 1882), Boleslav Vomáčka (born in 1887), Hans Krasa (1899–1944), and others. It was the tragic fate of Schulhoff and Karel to die in Nazi concentration camps, and of Krasa to be led to a gas chamber, for the crime of being Jewish.

Czech composers of the modern school followed the international musical trend and wrote ingenious scores abounding in devices of polytonality and atonality. The most advanced among them is Alois Hába (born in 1893), who entered a field in which he had no competition and became the champion of quarter-tone music. In this unique idiom he wrote a number of instrumental works and even an opera, *Die Mutter*, which was performed in Munich in 1931. The firm of August Foerster built a quarter-tone piano for Hába's experiments. The new musical effects that are obtained through the quarter-tone system present great technical difficulties for performers, and the introduction of third-tones and sixth-tones by Hába made these difficulties almost insuperable. Perhaps this type of music will be developed successfully when special electronic instruments are devised to secure accurate production of such minute intervals.

The Czech composer best known internationally is Bohuslav Martinu (born in 1890). Martinu is interested primarily in structural problems rather than in immediate appeal to the listener's imagination. He is therefore at his best in works of solid contrapuntal texture: symphonies, concertos, and string quartets. Yet when he applies himself to the composition of dances in the native Czech manner, he succeeds in retaining local color without too much preoccupation with technical matters. Martinu spent a great many years in Paris; in 1941 he came to America and settled in New York. His works are frequently performed by American orchestras.

The name of Boleslav Jirák (born in 1891) became familiar to the music world through his symphonies, which had successful performances in England and America. In 1949 he settled in Chicago as a teacher.

Another internationally known Czech composer is Jaromir Weinberger (born in 1896). He achieved fame through his successful opera *Schwanda, the Bagpipe Player* (1927), a musical comedy full of popular tunes and characterized by fine workmanship, which places it in the category of Smetana's masterpiece *The Bartered Bride*. In 1939 Weinberger came to America, where he continued to compose.

Thus modern Bohemian composers maintain the tradition of Smetana, Dvořák, and Janáček. The best of their music is inspired by native folkways; the characteristic Bohemian rhythms and melodic figures are strongly outlined against a background of modernistic harmonies.

Russia

As late as 1827, the year of Beethoven's death, there was no Russian music in the proper sense of the term. The common people of Russia, especially the peasants, generated a prodigiously rich folk music, but this had not yet been explored and utilized. Music was cultivated at the Imperial Court at St. Petersburg by famous guests from Italy, Germany, France, and Spain. The Neapolitan opera composers Tommaso Traetta (1727–1779), Baldassare Galuppi (1706–1785), Giuseppe Sarti (1729–1802), the Spanish composer Martín y Soler, the celebrated pianists Muzio Clementi and John Field, the French violinist Rode, and the French opera composer Boieldieu were welcomed in Russia, and they taught music to talented Russians. The early Russian composers wrote mainly in the Italian manner; some of them were sent to Italy to study. Dimitri Bortniansky (1751–1825), a pupil of Galuppi, wrote sacred music that is still performed in Russian churches. Evstigney Fomin (1761–1800), a student of Padre Martini, wrote operas which were produced in St. Petersburg; Alexei Titov (1769–1827) also had several operas produced in St. Petersburg. A serf, Ivan Khandoshkin (1747–1804), wrote violin music, and was the first Russian to give instrumental concerts.

The real birthday of Russian music was on December 9, 1836, when the opera *A Life for the Czar* by Mikhail Glinka (1804–1857) was performed for the first time in St. Petersburg. This opera, based on Russian folk music, has for over a century remained the cornerstone of Russian art music. Revered and beloved by the Russians, it is virtually ignored in other countries; it seems to lose its communicative power outside Russia.

Though Glinka spent a great part of his life in foreign countries — in Germany, Italy, France, and Spain — the substance of his art remained Russian, even when he treated the Spanish *Jota aragonesa* in a brilliant orchestral caprice. Glinka's second opera, *Russlan and Ludmilla*, did not produce so profound an impression as *A Life for the Czar*, though the music is of uncommon interest. Its melodic material supplements the Russian type of folk song by ample use of Persian, Tartar, and Turkish melodic turns, thus starting the Oriental tendency that later became so prominent in Russian music. *Russlan and Ludmilla* is based on Pushkin's poem of the same name. Here for the first time we see the alliance of Russian national music with the great poet, Alexander Pushkin — who came to be looked upon as the patron saint of Russian music.

Many years elapsed before Glinka found worthy successors in Russia. His older contemporary Alexey Verstovsky (1799–1862) wrote several operas of considerable merit, one of which,

Askold's Grave, is occasionally performed in Russian opera houses even now. But the quality of Verstovsky's music falls far below the standard established by Glinka. A new flowering of Russian music came about in the 1860's. Its pioneer was Alexander Dargomyzhsky (1813–1869), the author of the operas *Russalka* and *The Stone Guest,* after Pushkin's poems.

The decisive turning point arrived when a number of highly gifted young musicians appeared on the Russian scene, and St. Petersburg became the site of one of the most spectacular developments in the entire history of music. Almost overnight, a great Russian art came into being, and composers arose capable of creating masterpieces of Russian music comparable to the best products of European romantic art.

This new art was nurtured by two sources. It drew its first breath of life from indigenous Russian folk songs. Following Chopin, this new school strove to communicate the Slavic soul to the world by means of a musical art that had folkways for its basis. In order to accomplish this task, it was necessary to acquire an adequate technique of composition. Technical mastery, however, could be learned only from the great foreign masters of Germany and France. The mediator in developing closer intercourse between the young Russian musicians and western European art was Anton Rubinstein, whose signal service to Russian music was to open the gates to the second source of the new Russian art — great European music.

Anton Rubinstein (1829–1894) was an artist whose significance is nowadays unjustly minimized. He was a pianist of immense powers, the only rival of Liszt. Rubinstein was responsible in great measure for the organization of higher musical education and of concert life in Russia. He was the founder of the Imperial Russian Musical Society, organized in St. Petersburg in 1858, whose aim was to acquaint Russian music-lovers with great masterpieces of European music and to encourage Russian composers to emulate the achievements of the West. Rubinstein was the conductor of the society's orchestral concerts. He was also the founder and the first director of the Conservatory of Music in St. Petersburg, an institution that subsequently became one of the greatest conservatories in Europe. He entrusted his brother Nicholas Rubinstein (1835–1881), himself a pianist of the first rank, with the task of establishing a similar conservatory in Moscow.

For some forty years Anton Rubinstein enjoyed an international reputation as a great piano virtuoso. He was also regarded as a leading composer of his time. His symphonies — especially the "Ocean" Symphony — were performed throughout the musical world. His Fourth Piano Concerto in D Minor was a standard repertory piece. Rubinstein wrote a number of operas and oratorios; his opera *The Demon* still enjoys regular performances in Russia. But in the world at large, only the modest *Melody in F* survives among the hundreds of works in Rubinstein's catalogue.

The reason for this spectacular decline in Rubinstein's stature was his western allegiance. Even though he was the prime moving force in Russian musical culture in the second half of the nineteenth century, he was regarded by Russian musical nationalists as a product of Germanic culture, incapable of advancing national Russian music. In a mood of ironic self-contemplation, Rubinstein once remarked: "For the Christians I am a Jew; for the Jews, a Christian; for the Russians, a German; for the Germans, a Russian." He might have added: "For the conservatives, I am a bold revolutionary; and for the revolutionaries, a hopeless conservative."

In Rubinstein's music the real Russian element supplies only an occasional flavor, agreeable but not essential. But that national element, missing in Rubinstein's works, became the main melodic and rhythmical substance in the music of five composers who announced their determination to create a new, truly national art — the "Mighty Five" of Russia: Borodin, Cui, Balakirev, Mussorgsky, and Rimsky-Korsakov. In their technique of composition they followed the "modernists" of their day — Berlioz, Schumann, and Liszt. The lesson they had learned from the brilliant scores of these masters they applied to their own sparkling and artistic settings of the newly discovered national material.

Schumann's romantic sensitivity struck a responsive chord in the souls of the emotional Russians; Berlioz appealed to them by his colorful instrumentation; while Liszt captivated them by his dazzling virtuosity and theatrical display. From the mixture of these artistic influences, superimposed on the basic national substance, arose a new art of great fascination.

Mili Balakirev (1837–1910) was the spiritual leader of the "Mighty Five." He exercised upon his companions the great authority of a master. But after a productive beginning, he ceased to compose. To the musical world he is chiefly known by his fantasy for piano, *Islamey*, long regarded as the most difficult piece ever written for the instrument — at least before the advent of the ultramodern school. In *Islamey*, Oriental colors and rhythms were imprinted on a virtuoso piece for the first time. From then on, Russian music became the European mediator of Asiatic influences. In the history of Russian music, Balakirev is also noted for his important work in collecting Russian folk songs.

César Cui (1835–1918) had a successful career as an army officer. He was the military teacher of Czar Nicholas II. Music was to him an avocation, but he was a talented composer and an influential music critic. Of his considerable output, only the charming piece *Orientale* is known to the outside world; some of his songs are popular in Russia.

Alexander Borodin (1833–1887) was a professor of chemistry and composed only in his leisure hours. He left few works, but almost every one of them has kept its place in the international repertory. Borodin's music is remarkable for its emphasis on Asiatic colors and rhythms. The tendency of Balakirev's *Islamey* was continued by Borodin in his opera *Prince Igor*, whose gorgeous ballet music is a great favorite on concert programs. Borodin's symphonic sketch *In Central Asia* is another example of his Oriental art. His symphonies, however, lean toward the folk song of European Russia. His beautiful Second String Quartet is frequently performed, as are his poetic songs.

Of all these amazing Russian composers who combined music with professional careers, Modest Mussorgsky (1839–1881) possessed the finest natural gift. His epoch-making opera *Boris Godunov*, after Pushkin's historic drama, is usually performed not in the composer's original version but in Rimsky-Korsakov's edition, with new orchestration and with many adjustments in melody and harmony. In 1928 the Soviet government published Mussorgsky's original score of *Boris Godunov*, and there followed a protracted debate as to the relative merits of the original score and of Rimsky-Korsakov's revision. Some writers accused Rimsky-Korsakov of falsifying the composer's intentions and reducing Mussorgsky's innovations to tepid conventional harmonies. However, the opera conductors are well pleased with Rimsky-Korsakov's scoring and are reluctant to relinquish it in favor of the less colorful original. In either version, *Boris Godunov* is a powerful drama, in which the soul and sentiment of the Russian people are expressed more genuinely than in any other stage work. The chorus, representing the mass of the people, sings with pathos, grandeur, solemnity, and directness of expression; in the solo parts, the Russian spirit is communicated with great power. Psychologically, the tonal painting of the tragic part of Boris has few equals in operatic literature.

Mussorgsky's songs display a lyric talent of the first rank in the penetrating intensity of emotional expression. His song cycles *The Nursery* and *Songs and Dances of Death* paint the innocence and purity of infancy and the dark and tragic mystery of death with an equally powerful penetration to the essentials. The Russian local color is most strikingly manifest; the Oriental tones resound with a startling power of pathetic accent. Mussorgsky's piano suite entitled *Pictures at an Exhibition* is chiefly known through the brilliant orchestration of it by Ravel. It is a Russian counterpart of Schumann's *Carneval*; it paints picturesque scenes with masterly distinction and with great variety of characteristic melodies, rhythms, and harmonies.

Nicolas Rimsky-Korsakov (1844–1908) has a twofold importance in music history: as a creative composer, and as an energetic propagandist of new Russian music. He was Russia's most distinguished teacher, and many Russian composers were his pupils at the St. Petersburg Conservatory — among them Liadov, Gretchaninoff, Ippolitov-Ivanov, Glazunov, and Stravinsky. In accomplished musicianship, Rimsky-Korsakov surpassed his colleagues of the national brotherhood, who accepted his advice and help. His reorchestration of Mussorgsky's *Boris Godunov* has been mentioned; he also orchestrated the same composer's opera *Khovantshina*, Dargomyzhsky's *The Stone Guest*, and a considerable part of Borodin's *Prince Igor*.

Of Rimsky-Korsakov's own compositions, many have been absorbed into the international repertory. His operas treat episodes from Russian history, legends, and fairy tales, and scenes from Russian life. At least one of these has gained a firm place outside Russia, *Le Coq d'or* (The Golden Cockerel). With its brilliant and quite modern music, this witty satire has been acclaimed by connoisseurs and by the enlightened public in many countries. His three symphonies are hardly ever performed outside Russia; conspicuous and enduring international success, however, has rewarded his symphonic suite *Scheherazade*, based on stories from *The Thousand and One Nights*. Rimsky-Korsakov's autobiography, *My Musical Life*, gives valuable source material for a study of Russian music.

The lion's share in winning the world to Russian music fell to Peter Tchaikovsky (1840–1893). He was not a member of the national school, such as was envisioned by the "Mighty Five"; indeed, his personal relations with some of them were not always pleasant, until the eminence of his genius made his superiority clear. Though he was educated at St. Petersburg, under the direct influence of Anton Rubinstein, Tchaikovsky's career as a composer was connected with Moscow. When in 1866 Nicolas Rubinstein offered Tchaikovsky a position at the Moscow Conservatory as teacher of theory, the young composer was removed from the personal influence of the national school, which had its seat in St. Petersburg. The musical division of the two Russian capitals was emphasized: St. Petersburg was intent on extreme nationalism; the Moscow school was more internationally minded, though by no means forgetful of the national ideals.

Tchaikovsky's first work to be accepted outside Russia was the Piano Concerto in B Flat Minor. Nicolas Rubinstein had figuratively pulled the concerto to shreds when Tchaikovsky first showed it to him, and the composer, chagrined and distressed, gave the work to the famous German pianist and conductor Hans von Bülow, who played it for the first time in the world at a concert in Boston, on October 25, 1875. Later, German conductors began to include Tchaikovsky's orchestral works in their programs with ever growing success. In 1891, Tchaikovsky visited America and conducted six concerts of his works in New York, Baltimore, and Philadelphia.

The first three of Tchaikovsky's symphonies are seldom played in concerts, but the Fourth, the Fifth, and especially the Sixth ("Pathétique") evoke an enthusiasm rarely accorded to symphonic works. The Fifth and Sixth symphonies are of a cosmopolitan character, while the Fourth abounds in phrases reminiscent of Russian folk songs.

In 1876 the great Tolstoy sent Tchaikovsky a collection of folk songs. Tchaikovsky's reply is interesting in showing his attitude toward folk music. He wrote: "Your songs are symphonic material, very good material, and I shall certainly make use of them some day." As he was busy with the Fourth Symphony shortly afterwards, it is not unlikely that he made use of Tolstoy's material in this work. Tchaikovsky's benefactress Mme. von Meck, to whom the Fourth Symphony was dedicated, expressed her delight at its Russian atmosphere, and added: "Glinka is the creator of Russian music; you are its greatest builder." On

March 17, 1878, Tchaikovsky wrote to her: "Regarding the Russian element in my music, I can say that not infrequently I would start a work with the intention of using some folk song that struck my fancy. Sometimes (as for instance, in the finale of our symphony) this happens spontaneously and quite unexpectedly. The kinship between my music and the songs of the people, in melodic and harmonic inflections, is explained by the fact that I grew up in a remote part of the country, and from my earliest childhood was fascinated by the ineffable beauty of Russian popular music. I love Russian folk songs passionately in all their manifestations — in short, I am a Russian in the fullest sense of the word."

The Fourth Symphony marked a decisive turning point in Tchaikovsky's career. It was written at the time of his unfortunate marriage that lasted only three weeks; it also marked the beginning of his intellectual friendship with Mme. von Meck — that wealthy and magnanimous lady who for thirteen years supported him generously, without ever meeting him personally. With the Fourth Symphony Tchaikovsky attained full mastery in handling the national element in his music.

Tchaikovsky's violin concerto has fascinated several generations of virtuoso violinists. His overture-fantasia *Romeo and Juliet* has charmed symphony audiences in Europe and America, and his piano pieces and songs are a part of the international repertory. Less well known are his operas. Yet in Russia, his operas *Eugene Onegin* and *The Queen of Spades* are more frequently heard than any other stage works. Both draw their lifeblood from Pushkin; the story of the Byronic gentleman, Eugene Onegin, and the romantic tale of an officer who forfeits his life for gain at the card table, appealed powerfully to Tchaikovsky's imagination and evoked some of his most attractive music. Tchaikovsky's three ballets, *Swan Lake*, *The Sleeping Beauty*, and *The Nutcracker*, are favorites everywhere.

One of the most promising Russian composers of the St. Petersburg group was Alexander Glazunov (1865–1936), hailed as a worthy successor to the Mighty Five. He wrote his first symphony at the age of sixteen, and composed industriously until about 1906, when he decided to devote his life to pedagogy as director of the St. Petersburg Conservatory. Several of his eight symphonies are regarded in Russia as classical works of the national school, but they are rarely heard abroad. His brilliant violin concerto is his best known and his most frequently performed work.

To the St. Petersburg group belongs also Anatol Liadov (1855–1914), composer of several charming miniatures; his *Music Box* has become one of the most popular pieces in piano literature. His short symphonic poem *Baba-Yaga* recreates the atmosphere of Russian fairy tales in vivid colors. Liadov contributed greatly to the treasury of Russian music by his excellent arrangements of folk songs. Another member of the St. Petersburg group was Sergei Liapunov (1859–1924), known in Russia as a composer of fine piano music.

The principal exponents of the Moscow school after Tchaikovsky were Sergei Taneyev, Anton Arensky, Nicolas Medtner, Reinhold Glière, Michael Ippolitov-Ivanov, Alexander Gretchaninoff, Nicolas Tcherepnin, and Sergei Rachmaninoff. A figure apart was Alexander Scriabin, who began as a follower of the Moscow school and then became one of the most important of the Russian innovators.

Sergei Taneyev (1856–1915), a pupil of Tchaikovsky, was equally eminent as composer, pianist, theorist, and pedagogue. His symphonic and chamber music is akin to Glazunov's in solidity of structure and polyphonic strength, but the emotional inflections of his vocal music show some traces of Tchaikovsky's influence. Taneyev's great treatise *Florid Counterpoint in the Strict Style* has earned him a tremendous reputation in Russia.

Anton Arensky (1861–1906) was the closest in spirit to Tchaikovsky. He was a composer of emotional and often passionate music. His piano trio, written in the memory of Tchaikovsky, is occasionally heard outside Russia.

Nicolas Medtner (1880–1951), of German extraction, was a composer of songs and piano music in a romantic manner. He rarely used Russian national themes in his works; his ballads for piano have a cosmopolitan flavor. It is strange that despite the international character of his music, it is not better known.

Reinhold Glière (1875–1956) was a distinguished composer; his epic symphony *Ilya Murometz* (1911), depicting the spectacular deeds of the legendary Russian hero, is one of the most brilliant scores of Russian music. After the revolution Glière wrote a ballet, *Red Poppy* (1927); the "Sailor's Dance" from this ballet, based on a revolutionary song, has become extremely popular all over the musical world.

The name of Michael Ippolitov-Ivanov (1859–1935) is known to Western music lovers chiefly through his orchestral suite *Caucasian Sketches* (1894). He lived for a number of years in the Caucasus, and many of his works reflect the atmosphere of this mountain country situated on the dividing line between European Russia and Persia. Sergei Vassilenko (1872–1956) also devoted many of his symphonic and operatic works to Oriental themes, but he failed to produce even a single work of international renown.

Alexander Gretchaninoff (1864–1956) was the composer of songs familiar to every singer of international repertory. His best known song is the poetic *Lullaby*, which he wrote in 1887; he composed many hundreds of songs afterwards, none of which surpassed in popularity that early opus. After the revolution, Gretchaninoff lived in France and America.

Nicolas Tcherepnin (1873–1945) was widely known in Europe as the conductor of Diaghilev's Ballets Russes before World War I. His own ballets are little known outside Russia, but his fine songs, in the style of Mussorgsky, are occasionally heard in concert halls. His son, Alexander Tcherepnin (born in 1899), made his career in Germany, France, and America, and has established himself as a modernist composer of piano music and stage works.

The most illustrious of this group was Sergei Rachmaninoff (1873–1943). He acquired fame as one of the greatest pianists of the twentieth century. He was admired in many countries, especially in America, where he made his home for many years, until his death. Rachmaninoff the composer — perhaps the last of the great romanticists — is known to most amateurs by his piano preludes and to the concert public through his Second Piano Concerto in C Minor, which has become an international classic — the only piano concerto written by a twentieth-century composer to acquire universal popularity. Some of Rachmaninoff's beautiful Russian songs are well known abroad; among his symphonic works, the Second Symphony and the tone poem *The Isle of the Dead* are often included in concert programs.

Alexander Scriabin (1872–1915) began his career as a Russian Chopin by writing a series of brilliant piano études. He then experienced the Wagnerian influence, and finally formed his own concept of music as a synthesis of arts on a mystic plane. His symphonic works *Poème divin* and *Poème d'extase* seek to penetrate to the depths of religious consciousness. His last great score, *Prometheus*, assembles a vast tonal apparatus, including a keyboard for luminous effects, designed to project colors on a screen in order to enhance the aural perception by visual impressions. This color organ has, however, been applied only at a very few performances. It remains a paradoxical effort, disturbing to traditional musicians and frowned upon by the modernists, who regard such auxiliary means as the product of exaggerated romanticism. There is nothing of the Russian national spirit, of Russian folk-song element, to be found in Scriabin's high-strung, ecstatic, glowing, sensuous, and often demoniac inspirations. Yet, even without these outward signs of Russianism, Scriabin's art is characteristically Russian in its straining toward the unattainable, in its alternation of ecstasy and despondency, in its deep religiosity, in its mystical and pantheistic faith, which is akin to that shown in Dostoyevsky's unique literary productions.

In his piano compositions Scriabin presents ingenious problems of pianistic technique and virtuosity, progressing from a Chopinesque start to extreme modernism in harmony, structure, and expressive content. His ten sonatas are representative documents of modernism, and are, in their peculiar way, fascinating despite their problematic nature. His intricate études and preludes present a challenge to advanced pianists.

Russian orchestral and symphonic music reached western Europe first with Anton Rubinstein's symphonies and operas, and then with Tchaikovsky's concertos. Russian operas were heard much later in Europe and America. There was, however, a third art, long flourishing in Russia, which triumphed in the first decade of the twentieth century, when the famous Russian Ballet of the Imperial Theater made its spectacular European tour. What a delightful surprise it was to discover that dancing could be a fine art, when performed with technical perfection! What a feast for the eyes in the gorgeous splendor of stage setting and costumes! What wonderful music full of brilliance, vivacity, rhythmic and melodic charm!

The overwhelming impression produced by the performances of the Russian ballet must be judged in its historical perspective. In the last decades of the nineteenth century, the ballet in Germany and France had become unimaginative and old-fashioned. The great masters, spurning this "third art" in favor of symphony and opera, had abandoned the field of ballet music to inferior composers. Only exceptionally had this art produced a composer of great gifts, such as Delibes. In Russia, however, ballet had always been a privileged art, and the best national composers wrote music for it — Glinka, Borodin, Rimsky-Korsakov, Glazunov.

The culmination of this art was achieved when Sergei Diaghilev organized his ballet company and presented its unforgettably beautiful productions in Paris, London, and New York. It was Diaghilev who launched the fabulous career of young Igor Stravinsky. The brilliant scores he wrote for Diaghilev's Ballets Russes, *The Firebird, Petrouchka,* and *Le Sacre du Printemps,* laid the foundation of his international fame and have become classics of twentieth-century modernism.

Radical changes of artistic outlook followed the Russian Revolution of 1917. A cataclysm of such dimensions was bound to call forth new forces, and they shook the entire edifice of Russian art. Both positive and negative phenomena appeared in the wake of the upheaval. Vital artistic ideas were born, opening new vistas of enticing promise; but mixed with these ideas were also many short-lived fads, trumpeted abroad as great discoveries. Paradoxically, Soviet Russia, after a tremendous social revolution, failed to encourage a similar revolution in the arts. Music was summoned to serve as a propaganda medium, to promote a proletarian, as opposed to a bourgeois, art.

The greatest Russian modernist, Igor Stravinsky, remained in Europe during World War I and the Russian Revolution. Sergei Prokofiev also lived abroad for some years before returning to Russia in 1933. Both Stravinsky and Prokofiev were readily accepted by the Western musical world as representatives of the modern cosmopolitan art.

Igor Stravinsky (born in 1882), a pupil of Rimsky-Korsakov, was brought up in the nationalist traditions of the St. Petersburg school. During the first part of his career he drew his inspiration from the national treasure of folk songs and dances. Indeed, dance became the principal medium through which Stravinsky's great gifts were revealed to the world. In his first ballet written for Diaghilev, *The Firebird,* and in his opera *The Nightingale,* there are elements of traditional Russian Orientalism, in the colorful garb of the orchestral art which he had learned from Rimsky-Korsakov. Yet these scores are marked by a vitality that bears testimony to a great and original talent.

In *Petrouchka* (1911) Stravinsky gave the world his masterpiece. Here he found a subject beautifully suited to his special gifts. The drama of a wooden puppet in a Russian carnival appealed to Stravinsky because of the appearance of psychological reality in a world of unreality. The puppets assume human passions in their actions, and the resulting incongruity produces a grotesque parody of genuine folk music — the Russian popular songs and dance tunes.

During subsequent years Stravinsky, and the growing mass of his imitators in several countries, utilized the new technique of musical grotesqueness in the field of pure instrumental music, where it became a caricature of the noble art of music itself. The incessant machine-like rhythm of *Petrouchka* suits its mechanical puppet action. This type of rapid, palpitating rhythm was once a playful and pleasant characteristic of classical music; we find it in some of Bach's *partitas* for violin solo, in the finales of some of Haydn's quartets, and in Paganini's virtuoso pieces. But its modern counterpart is not jocose; it is sinister, menacing, and brutal. It has lost all amiability; indeed, the very concept of amiable music has vanished from this art.

Modernism is combined with primitive savagery in Stravinsky's third ballet score, *Le Sacre du Printemps*, which depicts the "rites of spring" in pagan Russia. This epic of primitive emotions, with its savage rhythms, anarchic harmony, and dazzling orchestration, produces an overwhelming impression. But it lacks the fine balance of component elements that makes *Petrouchka* a masterpiece. *Le Sacre* is a daring experiment, given to excess in every direction, piling up new and fantastic effects. Technically, it is immensely impressive, but it leaves the esthetic sense perturbed by its lack of form and benumbed by its brutal onslaughts on the ear.

Stravinsky must have felt that no progress was possible along the path of *Le Sacre*; it could have led only to utter chaos. So he turned about and proceeded in the opposite direction, toward a miniature ensemble and naturalistic effects. His little fairy tale *L'Histoire du soldat* (1917) represents this new development. Here is a modernistic version of the Faust legend, with

the sulphurous odor of the Devil very much in evidence, a grotesque little orchestra of village musicians playing wrong notes
off beat, with melody and accompaniment at odds, and with
unfortunate attempts at virtuosity — and all this intended not as
a joke but in dead earnest! Yet this distorted and intentionally
ugly music succeeds almost in spite of itself as a rare phenomenon of perfection born of ugliness.

In his dramatic scenes *Les Noces* (1917–1923), Stravinsky
returned once more to the fascinating Russian peasant music,
with its quaint rustic accent, and to the primitive harmony of
Russian church modes.

In his second phase Stravinsky turned from Russian nationalism to a new cosmopolitan art. Cut off from the nourishing
roots of his native soil, his music became dry and acrid in sound,
lacking eloquence and convincing power. From a technical
point of view, his works of this period, with their medley of disparate styles, are interesting, but their curious retrospective style
does not fit happily into the framework of modernistic technique.
Stravinsky conjures up the ghosts of Lully, Handel, Pergolesi,
Weber, and Tchaikovsky, either directly, by quoting their melodies without alteration, or indirectly, by fashioning them into
strange and novel patterns. This long series of stylistic experiments is not animated by inner warmth. Its emotional temperature is tepid, when not downright chilly. Stravinsky's later
music illustrates perfectly the conception of snobbishness in art.
Yet even in his snobbishness Stravinsky remains a master; snobbishness may go hand in hand with technical perfection — there
is no paradox in such an alliance.

In his search for a style, Stravinsky produced two works in a
grand manner reminiscent of the monumental art of the classical past: *Oedipus Rex* and the *Symphony of Psalms*. Although
the intellectual capacity displayed in these scores commands
respect, it cannot compensate for their lack of soulful expressiveness and of that vitality which makes Stravinsky's early scores
so electrifying in their impact. *Oedipus Rex* is a static opera,

without mimic action, for which Stravinsky substitutes Latin recitation to orchestral accompaniment. This solemn archaic work arouses curiosity, but its art is sterile.

The *Symphony of Psalms* — again in cold impersonal Latin — occupies an awkward place between the church and the concert hall. The religious sentiment in this interpretation of the psalms remains veiled. The listener cannot grasp the composer's true attitude toward religion, prayer, and faith; the impression, insofar as it reaches the soul, cannot stand comparison with Palestrina or Bach, Bruckner or Ernest Bloch. This music is stately, grave, architectural — yes; but we miss in it the warm blood, the throbbing heart, the outcry of the tormented soul, the all-important manifestations of religious music, and we ask ourselves whether this master of cool parody, of the grotesque, of mechanical music really has anything essential to communicate in his religious compositions.

Sergei Prokofiev (1891–1953) first attracted attention by a series of short piano pieces which, by their title — *Sarcasms* — and still more by their actual sound, betray their intentional musical grotesqueness. In the ballet *Chout* (The Buffoon), introduced by Diaghilev's Ballets Russes, Prokofiev continues along the path of the parodistic style of polytonal harmony and eccentric orchestration. The most brilliant example of Prokofiev's musical satire is his opera *Love for Three Oranges* (1921), with its exciting march that has become popular all over the world.

In his symphonic music and his instrumental concertos, Prokofiev has something more substantial to offer. He adheres to the formal patterns of sonata, variation, or rondo; his modernistic traits are found mainly in his use of harmony, rhythm, and orchestral color. His earliest major work, the *Scythian Suite* (1916) for orchestra, is full of barbaric strength and vitality. Here Prokofiev follows the Russian national school, but with a ruthlessly dissonant harmony and a much sharper rhythmic edge. From this fierce music it is a wide leap backwards to his *Classical Sym-*

phony (1917), which represents the obverse side of Prokofiev's nature: his predilection for plastic, delicately chiseled form, and finely wrought detail, in an intricate polyphonic texture. This little symphony revives the style of the eighteenth century, with a delightful flow of melody, a graceful swing of rhythm, and a vivacity indicating a happy mood. Prokofiev wrote seven symphonies in all; of these the Fifth is the most profound, and it has justly found a place in the permanent repertory of international music.

Of Prokofiev's five piano concertos, the Third combines classical form with modern harmony and expert treatment of the piano part. One might class it with Rachmaninoff's Second Piano Concerto in effectiveness and technical finish, but Prokofiev's work is set at a cooler temperature, owing to his eager avoidance of romantic expressiveness. Similar qualities — brilliance of technique and crispness of style — characterize his nine piano sonatas. His two violin concertos, on the other hand, are distinguished by a free flow of undisguised melody. Prokofiev's most popular work is the musical fairy tale *Peter and the Wolf* (1936), written for the Children's Theater in Moscow. This unassuming but charming work proves that excellent music can be written in a thoroughly modern idiom without sacrificing amiability and grace.

To the world outside Russia, Nicolas Miaskovsky (1881–1950) is a somewhat mysterious figure. He wrote twenty-seven symphonies, all of which have been published and performed in Russia. It is a rare occasion when a symphony by Miaskovsky appears on a program in Europe or America. Yet he was one of the most eminent symphonists of the twentieth century, not only because of the number of his symphonies but because of their quality. Miaskovsky does not strain after ultramodern harmonies; he does not resort to superfluous, unnecessary contrapuntal complications or inflated orchestration. To exercise such economy and yet produce interesting, attractive, and convincing works, one must be a master in the good old-fashioned sense of the term, one who has absorbed all the learning of the art and who applies his superior knowledge with good taste, adding something of his own, something charming and delightful, that essential trifle without which a work of art cannot be persuasive or enduring.

The name of Dmitri Shostakovitch (born in 1906) became known when his First Symphony was introduced by the Leningrad Philharmonic in 1926. It soon made the rounds of the principal symphony orchestras in Europe and America. A young composer of exceptional talent had been discovered. An industrious worker, he kept piling work upon work without repeating his first spectacular success. In the meantime, while gradually advancing to leadership in the Soviet musical world, Shostakovitch wrote music chiefly for home consumption, stressing the political aspect. His second and third symphonies are of this political type, glorifying the Soviet Revolution.

In 1936, the unexpected news came from Russia that Shostakovitch had been deposed from his high position. Official Soviet critics declared that his opera Lady Macbeth of Mzensk had relapsed into complacent bourgeois mentality, and that since this type of music was contrary to socialist ideology, it could not be tolerated. As often happens in the case of censored books, this attack on Shostakovitch created an immediate demand for his works in the West, particularly in the United States. Shostakovitch rehabilitated himself at home by producing his Fifth Symphony, which was hailed by Soviet critics as a modern masterpiece, and which is, indeed, one of his strongest scores.

When in 1942 the news was flashed across the Atlantic that Shostakovitch had written his Seventh Symphony during the siege of Leningrad, amid daily bombings and dreadful conflagrations, there was eager competition among American conductors for its first performance in the United States. The race was finally won by Toscanini, who, in July 1942, conducted it on the radio. A month later, the first American public performance was given by Koussevitzky at the Berkshire Music Center. The score had been brought to America by airplane on a roll of microfilm and enlarged to readable size in New York. Within six months, nearly fifty performances had been given in the United States. A similar stir was produced by Shostakovitch's Eighth Symphony a year later. His Ninth Symphony evoked less response; but the success of the Tenth, performed in America and in Europe in 1954, demonstrated once more that Shostakovitch had lost none of his amazing vitality.

As a symphonic composer, Shostakovitch — in breadth of design, in wealth of melodic material, in the ingenuity and dramatic intensity of symphonic development and colorful orchestration — may be nominated as the Russian heir of Gustav Mahler. His symphonies are modern but not radical. There is no indulgence in the chaotic harmony and rhythmic extravagances of extreme modernism, no attempt at evolving a cerebral scheme of atonal melody. To be sure, Shostakovitch is fully acquainted with modernistic tricks, and applies them occasionally for special effects; but he is aware that it is pernicious for a composer to cultivate eccentric, extravagant, and perverse art. Modernistic procedures may be invigorating in small doses, but they are lethal when applied indiscriminately. Shostakovitch likes to spice and flavor his music, but his innate artistic instinct guards him from taking musical drugs to excess. Singable, expressive melody in the traditional sense of the term forms the backbone of his symphonic art, and he does not resent being classified as a romantic composer, a definition that in the vocabulary of the extreme modernists is a term of contempt. The sweeping international success of Shostakovitch's symphonies and other works is also due to the fact that his music strikes a happy medium between the nationalistic Russian and the cosmopolitan European style. Like Beethoven, who is evidently his model, Shostakovitch prefers a broad, universal approach to art rather than a narrower, restricted nationalism.

Two Soviet composers of Shostakovitch's generation have become well known abroad: Khatchaturian and Kabalevsky.

Aram Khatchaturian, an Armenian born in the Caucasus in 1903, did not begin the serious study of music until he was nineteen, the age at which Shostakovitch had already written his First Symphony. From his earliest works, Khatchaturian followed the path of Russian Orientalists, such as Borodin and Balakirev. Dmitri Kabalevsky (born in 1904) has written symphonies and concertos; he is best known outside Russia by his symphonic overture *Colas Breugnon*.

In conclusion, it may be said that Russian music has satisfied the two necessary conditions for international popularity: it has both expressive content in a strongly national style and a technical method of presentation that makes it accessible to the alien ear. Tchaikovsky and Rimsky-Korsakov in the nineteenth century, Prokofiev and Shostakovitch in the twentieth century, and many other Russian composers of impressive and original music, by satisfying these basic requirements, have written their names indelibly in the annals of cosmopolitan music.

1 2

Hungary and Rumania

Hungary

Hungary has been for ages the source of vigorous and distinctive folk music. Haydn, as the house musician at the estate of the Hungarian Prince Esterhazy, heard this music at nearby villages; its echoes are found in the finale "all 'ongarese" of his Trio in G Major and in some of his string quartets. But it was not until the appearance of Liszt's *Hungarian Rhapsodies* that Hungarian music began to interest the international circles of Europe. Following Liszt's example, Brahms wrote his celebrated *Hungarian Dances* and made use of the fiery Hungarian rhythms in the finale of his Piano Quartet, opus 25. Joseph Joachim wrote the *Hungarian Violin Concerto*. All these great musicians, however, were attracted not by Hungarian peasant music but by the colorful songs and dances of the Hungarian gypsies. Yet rural Hungarian folk music and the cosmopolitan art of itinerant gypsies are widely different in their character and origin. It is only in recent years that this difference has been properly understood and analyzed.

The father of Hungarian art music was Ferenc Erkel (1810–1893). His national opera, *Hunyadi László* (1844), was to Hungary what Glinka's opera *A Life for the Czar* was to Russia. Regrettably, this national Hungarian classic and the many subsequent operas by Erkel remained products for home consumption; admirable as Erkel's music is, it fails to arouse the enthusiasm of a cosmopolitan audience.

The first Hungarian-born musician of universal fame was Franz Liszt (1811–1886). He was one of the few great artists who belong to no nation in particular and to all nations in general. Liszt was also the leader of a musical revolution, champion of new music, a giant on the musical scene, with no superior and few equals in his time. He was cosmopolitan by the universality of his gifts, by his wide travels, and by his world fame, but he was Hungarian by birth and racial origin, and it is therefore right and proper that Hungary should claim him as Poland claims Chopin.

Liszt was at home wherever he lived in Europe. During his lifetime he was, successively, a virtuoso of incomparable power, a chivalrous lover of fascinating women, a grand seigneur, and, in the end, an *abbé* of the Roman Catholic church.

For Liszt's development as a composer, the twenty years he spent in Paris were decisive. There he met poets, painters, and musicians who were in the vanguard of the flourishing romantic school in art. From Victor Hugo and Lamartine he received the poetic impulse that gave him inspiration for creating music that allied itself to literature. The painter Delacroix awakened his understanding of color and of the interrelations of painting and music; Chopin gave him the appreciation of national art.

Liszt's music was nourished by these sister arts. The works that earned him fame were inspired by great poetry, by masterworks of painting, and by the popular environment of folk songs and dances. The three albums of his piano pieces entitled *Années de pèlerinage* record travel impressions of Switzerland and Italy; in a sense, they represent the early beginning of impressionism, which grew so luxuriant in the music of Debussy half a century later.

In his twelve symphonic poems, Liszt associated music with literary themes, a relationship that is the essence of romanticism. These symphonic poems include *Tasso* (after Byron), *Les Pré-*

ludes (after Lamartine), *Mazeppa* (after Victor Hugo), *Die Ideale* (after Schiller), and *Hamlet* (after Shakespeare). His two greatest symphonic works, the "Dante" and the "Faust" symphonies, are also inspired by poetic masterpieces.

Three great musicians contributed to the formation of Liszt's mature style: Paganini, Chopin, and Berlioz. Paganini's unique and daring feats of virtuosity captivated all Europe, and the young Liszt was seized with the flaming ambition to become the Paganini of the piano. Paganini's *Caprices*, as transcribed by Liszt for the piano, and Liszt's own études demonstrate this transformation of the pianoforte into an instrument for virtuoso performance. From Chopin he learned the art of chromatic harmony, colorful, sensitive, and peculiarly suitable for pianistic treatment. Berlioz gave Liszt a new understanding of the modern orchestra and also showed him the fascinating possibilities of program music.

Among the classics, Beethoven was the artist from whom Liszt learned most. Beethoven's later sonatas, at that time scarcely intelligible to the mass of music lovers, were interpreted by Liszt at his concerts with incomparable insight and with a technical proficiency that laid bare their intricacies of design and expression. It was mainly through Liszt that these sublime works eventually became the common property of the musical world. In his own lengthy and grandiose piano sonata, Liszt reveals the art that he learned from Beethoven, applying to it his own grandeur of conception, boldness, and novelty of execution, and that peculiarly Lisztian mixture of poetic and erotic ecstasy, colored by religious mysticism.

Relatively less well know are Liszt's sacred works — the oratorios *St. Elizabeth* and *Christus*, the Masses, and the psalms. Liszt also produced numerous arrangements of Bach's organ works, and fantasies on themes from various operas. These transcriptions show a sovereign master of the piano, who in his own playing could conjure up the deep sonorities of the organ, the brilliant instrumentation of full orchestra, and indeed, the sounds of an entire opera, with soloists, chorus, and ballet assembled on the stage. Liszt's transcriptions helped to translate all types of music into the idiom of the piano, with a wealth of striking, graceful, elegant, and novel ornamentation.

Liszt's two companions in the "Music of the Future," Berlioz and Wagner, may have surpassed him in the sheer impressiveness of their mighty works. But Liszt is superior to both Wagner and Berlioz in his ideas of style and in technique of composition. Together with Chopin, Liszt brought out the colorful art of chromatic harmony. He created a cyclic sonata form, whose different themes all evolve from one main theme. This formal idea had first appeared in the instrumental suites of the seventeenth century, and it had been dormant for nearly two hundred years. Beethoven had used a cyclic construction to some extent in his last piano sonatas and string quartets, and it was from these artistic antecedents that Liszt developed his own form.

During the twelve years that Liszt spent at Weimar (1848–1860), he made that city a veritable garden of the Muses, reviving the glory it had known during Goethe's residence there. Poetry and drama were now replaced by music and opera, with the Grand Duke Karl Alexander acting as a generous patron of arts and Liszt as musical commander-in-chief. In Liszt's castle-like mansion Europe's most distinguished personalities gathered. Princess Caroline Wittgenstein presided over this unique court of art, with reverence and deep affection for the master. Liszt, the champion of progress, was most generous in promoting works by other deserving composers. As conductor of the Weimar Court Opera, he had ample means at his disposal: a well-organized opera theater, a good orchestra, and pianists, violinists, and singers from many lands, who regarded it as a great honor to take part in Weimar's wonderful artistic activities.

Liszt's influence on modern concert life, especially on the art of piano-playing, is immense. There was no comparable virtuoso before him, and one can hardly expect the appearance of one equal to him in the future, so long as the piano remains essentially the same instrument it is today. Liszt was also a great teacher. The roster of his pupils includes celebrated names of all nationalities.

Though Hungary was always full of musical talent, a specific and purposeful Hungarian school of composers did not come into existence until the twentieth century. The modern champions of this national renaissance in Hungarian music were Béla Bartók and Zoltán Kodály.

It is difficult to decide whether Bartók (1881–1945) was more eminent as a composer or as a scholar. He devoted long years to collecting Magyar, Rumanian, and Slavic songs and dance tunes in his native Transylvania. He discovered a world of Eastern rustic music unaffected by civilization. The fruits of this research provided the thematic material for Bartók's own music, through stylistic assimilation and development.

Bartók's instrumental arrangements of Hungarian and Rumanian dances, with their curious, almost barbaric harmonization, suit to perfection the primitive character of these melodies. Indeed, he is at his best as a composer of dance music inspired by the rhythms of the people. Bartók's modernistic harmonies are quite palatable in such stylizations when applied in small doses. But the spice of his dance music grows bitter in his quartets and sonatas, where stimulating accentuation is turned into a series of hard-hitting blows, and plausible discords are compounded into protracted and ear-splitting cacophony. In this music he laboriously avoids anything that might suggest amiable, sweet, and euphonious sounds; it thrives on acoustical violence, moving from one yelling outcry to another.

Bartók's research demonstratesd that Hungarian music has preserved many Oriental traits, as exemplified by its so-called "gypsy" scale (a super-minor scale with two augmented seconds), its asymmetric melodic structure, its coloristic figurations, its primitive syncopated rhythms, its fitful alternation of mood from inexpressible sadness to passionate joy, its emotional intensity. In the picturesque villages of the Hungarian plains, in the fertile Danubian flatlands, in the wild mountainous regions of Transylvania, music flows freely, like the effervescent wine produced by the golden Tokay grape, so justly prized by connoisseurs.

Zoltán Kodály (born in 1882), Bartók's collaborator in the exploration of Hungarian folk music, is less austere in his compositions than Bartók and less uncompromising in his attitude, but just as strongly nationalistic. At least one of his works, the *Psalmus Hungaricus*, has had a remarkable international success; another composition by Kodály that has become a modern masterpiece is the suite *Háry János*, full of merry Magyar tunes and rhythms.

The eminent Hungarian pianist Ernst von Dohnányi (born in 1877) belongs, as a composer, to the Brahms school rather than to the representatives of the Hungarian national trends. After World War II he settled in America.

World-famous Hungarian virtuosos include the violinists Joseph Joachim (1831–1907) and Leopold Auer (1845–1930). More recently the school of Jenö Hubay (1858–1937) has sent forth many excellent violinists, of whom Joseph Szigeti (born in 1892) is best known.

Rumania

Though politically the Hungarians and the Rumanians have often been at odds, in their popular music they have many points in common. The Rumanians have so far produced only one composer of international stature, Georges Enesco (1881–1955). An exceptionally versatile musician, Enesco was a great violinist, a fine pianist, an excellent conductor, and a composer of decided individuality. But this enormously gifted man failed to fulfil the expectations raised by his early works, the two *Rumanian Rhapsodies* for orchestra, which are his only scores to gain a permanent place in the international repertory.

1 3

Latin America

A century ago, a mighty movement of musical self-determination arose in Europe, leading to the emergence of national music in many musically young lands. Russia, Poland, Bohemia, and the Scandinavian countries produced music that astonished the world by its vitality. We are now witnessing a similar process in the Latin American republics. Until very recently, these picturesque lands were regarded by European musicians merely as purveyors of popular songs and dances of a tropical sensuous nature — the habanera, the tango, the maxixe, and the rumba. But now, the musical world is being made aware of the formation in South America, Central America, and the West Indies of music that is not only colorful and enticing but also valuable from a purely musical point of view. These local national phenomena are gradually acquiring supranational value.

At the dawn of the twentieth century, Latin America was still going through a period of musical adolescence. Creative musicians were determined to acquire a European technique of composition. The older generation went to study in Germany; younger men looked to Paris for musical enlightenment. To them, modern French music presented more allure than German romantic academism, which had exercised so profound an influence on the early developments in North American music.

Three principal racial strains contibuted to the building of Latin American folk music: Spanish, Indian, and Negro. The

Indian influences survive only in remote villages of the Andes and in some isolated parts of Central America, where the natives still retain their traditional songs and dances in their original purity. The African influence is strong in the Negro republic of Haiti, and also in Cuba and Brazil, where Negro populations are large.

The most important element of Latin American music is the Spanish strain, introduced by the conquistadores in the sixteenth century. Mexico, Argentina, Chile, and Peru reflect the Spanish character in their folk music. Brazil is in the realm of Portuguese popular art. National composers in all Latin American countries have freely utilized this prime cultural material in their works, adding a native inflection and a peculiar rhythmic stress to the imported European elements, so that the final product is quite different from the original.

The first South American composer of serious music whose works were performed in Europe was Carlos Gomes (1836–1896), a Brazilian. For many decades, the overture to his Indian opera *Il Guarany* was a popular number on programs of orchestral music. But although the subject of this opera was Latin American, the music was entirely Italian in style; the native rhythms in *Il Guarany* are used simply as spice, in the same manner that European composers have used such materials in operas dealing with exotic subjects.

The most important contributions to art music in Latin America have been made by Mexico, Brazil, Argentina, and Chile. Among Mexican composers, the name of Carlos Chávez is well known. Born in 1899 of an Indian mother and a mestizo father, he was immersed in the atmosphere of Mexican folk music from early childhood. He had the good fortune to have for his teacher a musician of remarkable ability and inspiration, Manuel Ponce, the founder of the national school of Mexican music. Chávez evolved his particular style in a roundabout way, passing through the stages of European romanticism, French impressionism, and cosmopolitan neoclassicism. During the years spent in Paris and New York, Chávez established contact with modern musicians, and under their influence adopted a method of musical constructivism corresponding to the Cubist school in painting.

His most representative work is *Sinfonia India*. Generally speaking, Chávez avoids using folk songs in their original form, but he makes an exception here, employing three Indian melodies as thematic material. He also uses Mexican percussion instruments — Indian drums, a water gourd, rattles, rasps, and cymbals — in addition to the customary instruments of the symphonic orchestra.

The Mexican government honored Chávez by appointing him director of the National Conservatory and head of the Department of Fine Arts and of the Secretariat of Public Education. As founder and conductor of the Symphony Orchestra of Mexico, he has done much to advance the art of music in his country and to support and encourage native talent.

Manuel Ponce (1882–1948) is known to the outside world through his charming little song *Estrellita*. He was forty years old when he took courses with Paul Dukas in Paris, and he applied the Parisian impressionist technique to his Mexican music. In 1941, Ponce went on a tour of South America, conducting his own works, one of which has been heard in North America — a concerto for guitar and small orchestra, written for the world-famous Spanish guitar player, Andrés Segovia.

Prominent in the Mexican national group was Silvestre Revueltas (1899–1940). He started his career as a violinist and conductor before turning seriously to composition, in which he was encouraged by Chávez. Primitive rhythms and peculiar Mexican sonorities impart to his music a strange and fascinating flavor.

A unique figure in Mexican music is Julian Carrillo (born in 1875). A full-blooded Indian, he was the first modernist of Mexico. He received a thorough academic education at the Leipzig Conservatory, and wrote symphonies in traditional style.

Then he developed a system of composition in quarter-tones and even smaller divisions. To perform his works written in this microscopic technique, he constructed special instruments. Several of these extraordinary pieces have been played in the United States.

Brazil has produced at least one composer who has attained world fame, Heitor Villa-Lobos (born in 1887), the author of hundreds of works in every conceivable genre. In this mass of music, embracing the most diversified species, two forms have a special significance: the *chôros* and the *Bachianas Brasileiras*.

The term *chôro* has but a remote relation to a chorus of singers; rather, it is the name of a popular Brazilian street dance, which has been extended to denote a band playing the peculiar tunes for this particular dance. Villa-Lobos uses the term in a still broader sense — to denote a composition in a large form, combining the essential peculiarities of popular Brazilian music in its various aspects. He has written a dozen *chôros*, some of them for a solo instrument — such as the guitar or the piano; others for a large orchestra reinforced by a whole battery of Brazilian percussion instruments.

The *Bachianas Brasileiras* by Villa-Lobos combine Bach's contrapuntal style with Brazilian thematic material. From the stylistic point of view, this appears to be a rather doubtful venture, but there is a certain charm in its practical realization.

One feature common to both Chávez and Villa-Lobos is their genuine interest in the education of young musicians. When Chávez was director of the Mexican National Conservatory, his program was remarkably comprehensive, and his students became acquainted with all styles, old as well as new, classical, romantic, and modern. Bach's fugues and Beethoven's sonatas thus became neighbors to Indian pentatonic music, Gregorian chant, and Protestant chorales.

Villa-Lobos pursued a similar educational program. In 1932, when he was appointed General Director of Music Education of Brazil, he launched a vigorous campaign of reform, organizing public-school music in a curriculum embracing *califasia* (good speech) and *califonia* (good singing). Furthermore, he has collected and arranged hundreds of Brazilian songs for use in schools. He also devised a variant of the medieval Guidonian hand, teaching the elements of music to school children by associating the tones of the scale with the five fingers.

Oscar Lorenzo Fernandez (1897–1948), one of Brazil's most remarkable composers, is known outside Brazil through his brilliant orchestral dances in the Brazilian style and through his poetic songs. Less extravagant in his modernistic practices than the fiery Villa-Lobos, Fernandez represents the neoromantic trends in Brazilian music.

Francisco Mignone (born in 1897) is a very versatile and prolific composer, highly esteemed in Brazil although little known elsewhere. He writes colorful orchestral music in the Brazilian style, and also chamber music in a neoclassical idiom.

Camargo Guarnieri (born in 1907) represents the international school of Brazilian music. Most of his works, particularly the effective orchestral dances, reflect the native rhythm, but in his more recent compositions he tends toward neoclassicism, with emphasis on contrapuntal procedures.

Eleazar de Carvalho (born in 1912) has attained considerable success in America and in Europe as a conductor of exceptional gifts. He is also the composer of a Brazilian opera and of symphonic and chamber music.

Argentina possesses a wealth of folk music, both songs and dances, originating mostly among the Gauchos, the hardy cowboys who roam the vast pampas of Argentina. Ballad-singing, guitar-playing, and dancing are the Gaucho's pastime.

This wealth of folk music gives artistic nourishment to native composers. The dean of Argentinian music was Alberto Williams (1862–1952) whose grandfather was an Englishman. Alberto Williams studied with César Franck and acquired a thorough technique of composition which he put to service in his nine symphonies and a great number of piano pieces and songs. In many of these works he artfully applied the native Argentinian melodies and rhythms.

Among other well-known composers of Argentina are the brothers Castro, José María Castro (born in 1892) and Juan José Castro (born in 1895), who write music of a romantic nature. Juan Carlos Paz (born in 1897) represents the modernist wing of Argentinian music. His pieces are set in a hard atonal idiom, following the precepts of Schönberg.

The best known Argentinian composer of the younger generation is Alberto Ginastera (born in 1916), who combines fine native inspiration with consummate modern technique. His chamber music often appears on the programs of international festivals.

Several hundred other composers of all countries in Central and South America have been listed in special works. For the purposes of the present book, a brief catalogue of the most prominent composers of the various countries must suffice. Here follows a list in alphabetical order.

Bolivia. Indian folklore predominates. The leading composer is José Maria Velasco Maidana (born in 1899). His main work is the ballet *Amerindia*, intended to extol "the new Indian of tomorrow."

Chile. Spanish folklore prevails, the Araucanian Indians being too small a part of the population to influence the national scene. The two best-known composers are Humberto Allende (born in 1885) and Domingo Santa Cruz (born in 1899). Allende, though hardly known in the United States, has been acclaimed in Paris and at various international festivals in Europe. Felipe Pedrell, the famous Spanish historian, called Allende "the first modern composer of his country." Santa Cruz, famous at home as composer and educator, pursued his professional studies in Spain. As professor at the Chilean National Conservatory and as president of the Instituto de Extensión Musical, he has done a great deal for Chilean national music. A prolific composer in the neoclassical manner, he is considered an outstanding modernist. His most ambitious work is *Cantata de los ríos de Chile* for chorus and orchestra, depicting musically the grandiose scenery of Chile's streams and mountains.

Colombia. The music of Colombia is nurtured mainly by Spanish sources. The leading composer is Guillermo Uribe-Holguín (born in 1880), a pupil of Vincent d'Indy in Paris. His numerous compositions have been influenced by French impressionism.

Costa Rica. The music of Costa Rica is least influenced of all Latin American countries by exotic Indian and Negro factors. The country has not yet produced an outstanding composer.

Cuba. The music of Cuba, though not much performed in the United States, is well known to the many North American visitors to Havana. North American night clubs have taken over Cuban popular dances: the habanera, *danzón*, rumba, and conga. Spanish and Negro features dominate in Cuban music, and Cuban composers utilize popular music to a great extent. Alejandro García Caturla (1906–1940) mixed Negro rhythms and sonorities with modernistic harmony. Amadeo Roldán (1900–1939) won fame as a composer of genuinely Cuban-African music in a modern idiom. His most sensational work is the ballet *La Rebambaramba*. Ernesto Lecuona (born in 1896) is the conductor of a famous rumba band and composer of several Cuban dances that have become greatly popular.

Dominican Republic. The Indian music of the Dominican Republic has the distinction of being the earliest American music to claim the attention of European historians — as early as the sixteenth century. None of the modern Dominican composers have so far obtained a position of rank.

Ecuador. This country possesses a rich and interesting folk music combining Indian and Spanish features, but so far it has produced little modern music.

Guatemala. With a large aboriginal population, Guatemala is rich in Indian folklore. Jesús Castillo (1877–1946) dedicated his life to collecting and exploring native Indian melodies. His half-brother, Ricardo Castillo (born in 1891) was educated in Paris; he makes use of Indian themes and rhythms in his works. Salvador Ley (born in 1907), a pianist and composer, was a pupil of the author of this book in Berlin. He has written a number of works for piano.

Haiti. This French Negro republic has preserved in its popular songs the rhythms of the African jungle. The polyrhythmic drum music of Haiti has magical connotations, powerful impulses being attributed to it by the natives. Modern influences are found mainly in the urban tunes. No composer of more than average gifts has as yet emerged in Haiti.

Honduras. This is the least progressive of all the Latin American countries in regard to music.

Nicaragua. Much old Indian folklore has been preserved in Nicaragua, but of modern musical culture there is little to be found. Luis A. Delgadillo (born in 1887), educated in Milan, is the ablest composer. But in order to secure performances for his symphonic music, in which Indian themes predominate, he has to go to other, more advanced countries.

Panama. With its mixed population — Indians, Negroes, Spaniards, Americans — Panama has interesting folk music: songs, dances, and primitive instruments. There is no serious music of distinction.

Paraguay. There are no composers of note, but much Indian folk music is preserved in its original state.

Peru. Possessing considerable culture, Peru keeps its Inca music alive, with the original instruments. But Spanish music has also left its traces. The country has a musical history that is centuries old and a growing modern musical life. The most gifted composer is Andrés Sas, born in Paris in 1900, who at the age of twenty-four came to Peru as a teacher. A modernist, he knew how to accommodate himself to the Peruvian milieu. Inca music was explored by M. and Mme. Raoul d'Harcourt in their monumental publication *La Musique des Incas et ses survivances*.

El Salvador. This small country, inhabited mainly by mestizos, still maintains its traditional Indian fiestas.

Uruguay. In its music, Uruguay has much in common with its neighbor Argentina. Spanish and Italian influences are strong. Most of the modern composers pursued their professional studies in France or in Italy. Eduardo Fabini (1883–1950) was the country's most respected composer. Alfonso Broqua (1876–1946) and Carlos Pedrell (1878–1941) were born in Uruguay, but their activities were mostly connected with Paris, where they spent most of their lives. Much of their vocal music has been published.

Venezuela. In this country Spanish music abounds with Negro and Indian traits mixed. The history of Venezuelan music can be traced back for well over two centuries. Lately, the capital, Caracas, has become an important center of the arts. Venezuela's most eminent musician was the world-famous pianist Teresa Carreño (1853–1917). Vicente Emilio Sojo (born in 1887), conductor of the Symphony Orchestra of Caracas, is an experienced composer of vocal music.

14

The United States

The history of American music may be roughly divided into four distinct periods: the English tradition in the eighteenth century; the German tradition dominating the nineteenth century; the French impressionistic influence, from World War I to about 1930; and finally the quest for an American style and for modernism, together with the discovery of American folk music.

Among the forerunners, who were mostly amateurs brought up in the English tradition, the Philadelphia lawyer Francis Hopkinson (1737–1791), a signer of the Declaration of Independence and a man of high culture and considerable political importance, made history as the earliest American-born composer. In 1788 he published *Seven Songs for the Harpsichord or Piano-forte*, dedicated to George Washington. In this dedication he claims to be "the first native of the United States who has produced a Musical Composition." Hopkinson had a close competitor in William Billings (1746–1800), the Boston tanner, whose collections of his own choral hymn tunes and anthems — *The New England Psalm Singer*, and others — published between 1770 and 1794, have recently been revived. Though unpretentious and immature in their effort at "fugueing," they are not without a certain charm.

For a long time Boston remained the center of religious music. The first book printed in the colonies was *The Bay Psalm Book* (Cambridge, 1640), which in its earlier editions contained only the texts. In a later edition, published in 1698, thirteen tunes were added. Secular music had its home mainly in Philadelphia. Alexander Reinagle (1756–1809), a native of England and the first professional musician in America, was active there for many years.

At the time when representatives of the English school were still active in the American colonies, the first builders of the German tradition began to make inroads into American musical life. The German organist Karl Theodore Pachelbel (1690–1750), son of an organist from Nuremberg, settled in Boston in 1730. He brought the great German organ art to America. Johann Friedrich Peter (1746–1813), a German Moravian missionary, became the founder of a Moravian group in Bethlehem, Pennsylvania, and established a musical tradition that was centered on Bach. Even today the Bethlehem Bach Festivals rank high among American musical institutions. Johann Christian Gottlieb Graupner (1767–1836) was a player in Haydn's orchestra in London, and emigrated to America in 1795. He organized modest orchestral activities in Boston. They were taken up later on a larger scale by the Harvard Musical Association, and led eventually to the founding of the Boston Symphony Orchestra.

The phenomenal rise of German symphonic music since Haydn, Mozart, and Beethoven had its effect in America, awakening the desire to hear those far-famed masterpieces. The most important event in the nineteenth century was the founding of professional symphony orchestras after the German model. As early as 1842, the Philharmonic Society of New York began its activities. A few years later a group of German musicians formed a little orchestra in New York on a cooperative basis. This group became known as the "Germania Orchestra" and was remarkably successful as a traveling ensemble during its six years of existence (1848–1854). For the first time, symphonic music became known to many cities in the eastern and southern states. Celebrated soloists, like Jenny Lind, Henriette Sontag, and the

Norwegian violinist Ole Bull were heard at the Germania concerts. They prepared the ground for the still more important activities of the German-born conductor Theodore Thomas (1835–1905), who in 1864 began symphony concerts with his orchestra in the principal American cities. For a time he was conductor of the New York Philharmonic Orchestra, and he spent the last years of his life as conductor of the Chicago Orchestra. His propaganda for the Germanic symphonic art bore rich fruit. In 1881 Henry L. Higginson founded the Boston Symphony Orchestra, the direction of which he entrusted to successive German conductors: Georg Henschel, Wilhelm Gericke, Artur Nikisch, Emil Paur, Max Fiedler, and Karl Muck. Only after World War I was the German monopoly broken, with the French conductors Henri Rabaud and Pierre Monteux, the Russian, Serge Koussevitzky, and the Alsatian Charles Munch.

The influence of German music on American composers in the nineteenth century was almost monopolistic. The older generation of American musicians did their professional studying in Germany: at the Leipzig Conservatory, at the Klindworth-Scharwenka Conservatory in Berlin, in Munich with Rheinberger, and at the Frankfurt Conservatory with Joachim Raff.

During the long period of German hegemony, native American musicians seldom rose above the rank of talented pupils. The first to maintain independence in a limited field was Lowell Mason of Boston (1792–1872), a pioneer of church and school music. He was the senior member of a family conspicuous in American music through several generations.

The first truly American composer, as far as native inspiration goes, was Stephen Foster (1826–1864). He created a number of simple songs that have become an imperishable treasure of American music, as genuine as national music of any country in the world.

Louis Moreau Gottschalk (1829–1869), a contemporary of Foster, represented an Americanism of a different type. The first full-fledged American virtuoso, educated in Paris, he attracted the attention of Berlioz and Chopin by his brilliant pianism; as a composer, he was the first to give a voice to the American South. He was born in New Orleans; Creole tunes and rhythms dominate his music, which belongs more to the Spanish orbit of the Antilles and Central and South America than to the United States. Much of his piano music is of a brilliant salon type, exploiting picturesque programmatic titles.

In symphonic and chamber music also, Americans gradually acquired skill and competence. For about half a century the Boston school of composition held the front ranks. John Knowles Paine (1839–1906) brought back from his studies in Berlin a remarkable technical equipment. As the first Professor of Music at Harvard, he became a leading personality in American music. His solidly constructed works show only faint traces of the American spirit, but in the history of American music he has a secure and respected place as the first man who brought to America real technical proficiency in the structural art of composition.

Paine was the leader of the New England school of composition, the group which comprised the most important American composers at the turn of the century; MacDowell, Foote, Chadwick, Kelley, Horatio Parker, Hadley, Daniel Gregory Mason, Converse, and Hill. To the same group belongs the first important American woman composer Mrs. H. H. A. Beach (1867–1944). As a young woman she attracted attention by her piano concerto, which she played with the Boston Symphony Orchestra, and also by her choral works. But after initial success, her music disappeared from the repertory.

Of American composers in this group, Edward MacDowell (1861–1908) was by far the most important. Although born in New York and educated in Paris and in Germany, he was intimately connected with New England, by residence and artistic sympathy. His *New England Idyls* for piano are characteristic of this aspect of the composer's personality. MacDowell did not make use of real folk songs, yet he caught the spirit of New England in the peculiar accents, the suggestive sound of his music. This American flavor eludes analysis, yet the music exhales it like the fragrance of a flower. MacDowell wrote a number of scores in larger form. His two piano concertos and several piano sonatas, though less American than the *New England Idyls,* have been the only compositions by any American composer accepted to a certain extent in Europe as a noteworthy contribution to the neoromantic literature. They follow the line of Schumann and Grieg, while maintaining their individual nature.

MacDowell's mental illness and his premature death deprived American music of its pioneer, not only in composition but also in education. He was the first Professor of Music at Columbia University, and many American musicians studied under him. As a fitting memorial to his great achievement, the MacDowell Colony was organized in Peterborough, New Hampshire, for the benefit of composers and other creative artists; it has special facilities enabling them to work in an agreeable environment during the summer months. Mrs. Marian MacDowell, the composer's widow, was until her death in 1956, at the age of ninety-eight, actively engaged in the affairs of the MacDowell Colony, as its president.

A challenge to American composers to use their folk materials came from Dvořák, who spent three seasons in New York (1892–1895) as the head of the National Conservatory there. He was charmed by American Negro spirituals, and emulated this idiom in his celebrated symphony *From the New World.* It is interesting to note that many of the leading American musicians and composers objected to Dvořák's idea of using Negro themes. The *Boston Herald* of May 28, 1893, published several of these opinions. Paine wrote that "American music, more than any other, should be all-embracing and universal," as American civilization was a fusion of various European nationalities. Benjamin J. Lang, conductor of the Cecilia Society, said that it was "not natural for a white man to write a symphony using real plantation melodies." Chadwick made the narrow-minded statement: "Such Negro melodies as I have heard I should be sorry to see become the basis of an American school of composition." Only Mrs. H. H. A. Beach took a positive stand, expressing the opinion that Negro melodies were "the legitimate domain of a talented and sufficiently trained Negro composer." She also called attention to other important regional music of America, "the ballads of the North and South, which more fully represent the feeling of our entire country than those of any of its component nationalities could possibly do, whether African, German, or Chinese."

Other composers of the New England group variously contributed to the modest beginnings of musical Americanism. Arthur Foote (1853–1937) was the first composer of rank educated entirely in America. His numerous works are akin to those of Paine, with a stronger leaning, however, toward Brahms. Though filled with the German romantic spirit, his art has in its very restraint something of the Puritan attitude. For this reason, as well as for their intrinsic qualities, his best works have a fair chance of becoming American classics.

George W. Chadwick (1854–1931), educated at the Leipzig Conservatory and under Rheinberger in Munich, spent his entire career in Boston, directing the New England Conservatory from 1897 until his death. His melodious music has more popular appeal but less nobility and formal finish than Foote's distinguished art. Chadwick's symphonic works and chamber music are now forgotten; only his effective *Melpomene Overture* is still heard.

Edgar Stillman Kelley (1857–1944), a prolific and resourceful composer, belongs to the generation of Foote and Chadwick. With the technical equipment of German late romanticism, he strove to instill an American spirit into his music. His *New England Symphony* (1913) and the miracle play *The Pilgrim's Progress* (1917) belong to the most substantial American achievements of their time. Years spent in San Francisco made him acquainted with Chinese music, and in his *Aladdin Suite* for orchestra he utilized this knowledge. For nearly a decade he resided in Berlin, where several of his pieces of chamber music were heard with respect.

Horatio W. Parker (1863–1919) was educated in Boston and in Munich. At the age of thirty he reached the climax of his career with his oratorio *Hora Novissima*, which obtained a sensational success at its first performances in New York and Boston. This masterpiece of choral composition was the first American work ever given at choral festivals in England. Cambridge University honored Parker by conferring upon him the degree of Doctor of Music, and on later occasions his *Legend of St. Christopher* was performed at the Worcester and the Bristol festivals. For twenty-five years he held the professorship of music at Yale. His opera *Mona* won the prize of $10,000 offered by the New York Metropolitan Opera Association. Performed in New York in 1912, this opera has now sunk into oblivion; nor have any of his more than eighty works, except *Hora Novissima*, survived. Yet Parker was an important musician, and one wonders how, honored as he was during his lifetime, he could be so quickly forgotten. His music certainly deserves a better fate.

David Stanley Smith (1877–1949) was the heir to Horatio Parker's ideals and his successor at Yale University. His music has often been belittled because of its supposedly antiquated romantic tendencies. Yet it commands sincere respect for its mastery of form and its melodic invention — valuable qualities which are often absent from the works of the assailants of romanticism. Smith's strength lay in his chamber music, grown upon Brahmsian soil, which became none the less an Americanized and somewhat modernized product.

Henry Hadley (1871–1937), who studied with Chadwick and at the Vienna Conservatory, was a versatile and skillful composer. He wrote half a dozen operas and four symphonies, apart from numerous overtures, symphonic poems, choral and chamber music, concertos, and songs. His music, too, was derived from the German sphere, but it has a more modern sound than that of his older colleagues, as Hadley was not insensitive to the charms of Wagner and Richard Strauss. The Henry Hadley Society, founded after his death, keeps alive much of his music through annual performances.

Frederick Converse (1871–1940) went from Harvard University to Munich to study with Rheinberger. After his return he became dean of the New England Conservatory. His opera *The Pipe of Desire* was the first by an American composer to be given at the Metropolitan Opera House (1910). In later works Converse progressed from his German beginnings to the more brilliant neoromantic effects of modern Russian and French composers. Another aspect of Converse's art lay in his quest for outspoken Americanism.

Daniel Gregory Mason (1873–1953), a member of the famous Mason family, belongs to the Boston school by birth and as a pupil of Paine and Chadwick, from whom he received some indirect German influences. As a pupil of Vincent d'Indy in Paris, his music also shows some French traits. Yet the German character prevails. Mason's carefully elaborated compositions are relatively little known, since American works are now generally neglected unless they participate in the nationalistic and modernistic trend.

Geographically, Henry Franklin Gilbert (1868–1928) belongs to the New England group, for he was born near Boston and spent most of his life there. But he differs from the rest of his regional colleagues in two important respects: from the very first he pursued the ideal of musical Americanism, and his music lacks the European polish of his contemporaries. As a result, his works give the impression of spontaneous composition in the native style, but his harmonies appear at times uncouth. Of his works, the most significant are the *Comedy Overture on Negro Themes* and *Dance in Place Congo*. In American music history Gilbert is an important figure, but his music is seldom performed.

Charles Sanford Skilton (1868–1941), also a New Englander, cultivated musical Americanism by his investigations of Indian music. He wrote several orchestral suites on Indian themes that are occasionally performed.

Charles Wakefield Cadman (1881–1946), a native of Pennsylvania, was also attracted by Indian lore. His Indian opera *Shanewis* was successfully performed by the Metropolitan Opera in 1918, and several arias from this opera are still heard in the concert hall. Cadman also published a number of highly successful songs.

Most of these composers who were active at the threshold of the twentieth century had been trained in Germany. But the German phase of American music was gradually superseded by French influences, particularly by the impressionist movement. The first American representative of this style was Charles Martin Loeffler (1861–1935). An Alsatian by birth, he was half German and half French, by descent as well as by training. As a youth he spent several years in Russia and became familiar with Russian folk music. In America, he started his career as a violinist of the Boston Symphony Orchestra, but later devoted himself entirely to composition. His music superimposes French impressionistic devices on a basis of Germanic linear solidity, tempering the combination with Russian reminiscences. This triple coalition produces something distinctly original. The brilliant color in Loeffler's orchestral works stems from French and Russian sources; the plastic melodic material and the stimulating rhythms lead back to German and Russian classical models as well as to folk song. As to American traits, one would scarcely expect to find them in the international music of this enlightened European. Loeffler's most important work is a *Pagan Poem* (after Virgil) for piano and orchestra, which still enjoys frequent performances.

Edward Burlingame Hill (born in 1872), a New Englander, studied in Boston and Paris. He became an outspoken champion of French music and published a book on the subject. In his own orchestral works, he carries out the precepts of French art with brilliance and lucidity. His symphonic poem *Lilacs* evokes impressionistic colors with great subtlety. Hill is one of the greatest masters of orchestration among American composers; as a Harvard professor, he taught a generation of young American musicians.

Charles T. Griffes (1884–1920) became fascinated by French music of the modern school when he first heard the piano pieces of Debussy and Ravel. Griffes found his natural medium in the impressionistic technique, and adapted it to his own taste. His most significant work is the symphonic tone poem *The Pleasure Dome of Kubla Khan* (after Coleridge), suffused with Eastern imagery and exotic charm. Of his piano music, *The White Peacock*, a product of his infatuation with impressionism, has become a modern classic.

Emerson Whithorne (born in 1884) also fell under the French influence and followed the impressionistic predilection for Oriental color. Although he had never been to China or Japan, he used Oriental themes in many of his works, employing the congenial methods of French art.

The picturesque program music of Griffes and Whithorne is thus concerned not with American but rather with Oriental themes. Other composers applied this impressionist technique to American subjects, and added the realistic touch of twentieth-century modernism. Frederick Converse wrote a symphonic score, *Flivver Ten Million,* in which he glorified and at the same time ridiculed the assembly line of the Ford industry. Philip James (born in 1890) produced radio tone poem entitled *Station WGZBX.* James Philip Dunn (1884–1936) wrote the symphonic work *We*, depicting Lindbergh's translantic flight. One of the most successful American scores in the realistic vein was the ballet *Skyscrapers* by John Alden Carpenter (1876–1951), a Chicago businessman who studied at Harvard with Paine and adopted music as a pleasant avocation. The materialistic aspects of the American scene prevail in this score, with its description of the noisy hubbub of New York life. Many other brilliant scores might be added to this list of realistic American music.

A special brand of Americanism is represented by the remarkable output of Charles Ives (1874–1954). An amateur in the sense that he did not depend on his art for a livelihood, Ives published his music at his own expense. America, the land of unlimited possibilities, is reflected in these unique scores, in the seemingly chaotic harmony and the very intricate system of asymmetrical rhythms. In his technique, Ives anticipated the extreme developments of the ultramodern idiom. Yet his Americanism is evident in the tuneful melodic essence underlying his music. Born and brought up in New England, Ives was a student of Horatio Parker at Yale University. His inspiration derives from the traditional New England hymns and American folk music. In his own songs a subtle declamation prevails, with a free rhythm resulting in great difficulties for the singer, who finds little support in the entirely independent, harmonically dissonant accompaniment. The titles of his pieces and the texts of his songs suggest the American scene: *Three Places in New England, Concord Sonata, Washington's Birthday.* Ives lived long enough to be recognized by American society; he was awarded a Pulitzer Prize for one of his symphonies, which had been written nearly forty years before.

Carl Ruggles (born in 1876) is a companion and a comrade-in-arms of Ives. A native of Vermont, he is a visionary, embodying the passionate Puritan energy of his ancestors and despising academic regulations and conservative traditions. Typical of his strange music is the "symphonic ensemble" *Men and Mountains.* Prefixed to the score is a quotation from William Blake: "Great things are done when men and mountains meet." Another work by Ruggles, *Portals* for string orchestra, carries a motto from Whitman: "What are those of the known but to ascend and enter the Unknown?" This expresses an idea not dissimilar to that underlying Lamartine's poem which inspired Liszt's *Pré-*

ludes. But what a difference between Liszt and Ruggles! At the international festival in Venice in 1925 a score by Ruggles for six trumpets, entitled *Angels*, was performed. Does it refer (like the brass choir in Berlioz' *Requiem*) to the Last Judgment — to the angels of the Apocalypse — or to the angelic hosts shining in dazzling splendor? The listener is not told. Will the public of the future ignore Ruggles as a musical hermit or pay tribute to him as an American genius?

Charles Ives and Carl Ruggles are pioneers of ultramodern music in America. Wallingford Riegger, Edgar Varèse, Henry Cowell, and George Antheil have gone still further in the direction of musical experimentation.

Wallingford Riegger (born in 1885) received a solid academic training in Germany; upon his return to America, he became interested in acoustical research in his desire to justify dissonant harmony by scientific argument. The titles of his works — *Studies in Sonority* and *Dichotomy* — indicate his abstract pursuits. In his later works, he adopted a more tractable idiom.

Edgar Varèse (born in 1885), a visitor from Paris, became a leader of the modern movement in New York by founding the International Composers Guild. In 1926 Leopold Stokowski, always a supporter of daring experiments, performed with the Philadelphia Orchestra Varèse's symphonic poem *Amériques*, a title referring not to the United States in particular but to all the Americas of the mind — imaginary free countries open to bold, novel ideas and enterprises. The scientific turn of Varèse's inspiration is indicated by his *Intégrales* for chamber orchestra, and particularly by *Ionization*, written in 1931 for an orchestra of percussion instruments of all types, including some forty drums and two sirens, without making use of melody or harmony. These works have hardly anything in common with what is generally called music. It would perhaps be more fair to Varèse to consider him not a composer but an ingenious experimenter bent on research into new sonorities and rhythmical effects.

Henry Cowell (born in 1897) created a sensation with his

"tone clusters," played with the fist or the forearm on the piano. His achievements are twofold: he is an inventor of new technical devices, and a composer in quest of the old, primitive sources of Americanism in music. Among his inventions is the rhythmicon (an instrument devised in collaboration with the famous Russian engineer Theremin), meant to facilitate an otherwise hardly attainable complexity of rhythm. Of late, Cowell has devoted much attention to the quaint eighteenth-century "fugueing tunes" of William Billings, and to the early southern rural hymn tunes.

George Antheil (born in 1900) calls himself in his autobiography the "bad boy of music." His most sensational work was a *Ballet mécanique*, scored for ten mechanical pianos and several airplane propellers, which rocked the roof of Carnegie Hall in 1927. His next work was *Transatlantic*, "an opera of the machine age," given by the intrepid Frankfurt Opera in 1930. In his later compositions, Antheil became mellow and abandoned his ear-splitting machine music in favor of regularly constructed symphonies and operas.

Shortly after World War I, an American Conservatory was founded in Fontainebleau. Nadia Boulanger, a highly gifted teacher of composition, became a dominating influence at this conservatory; many American composers who have since won distinction were her pupils. Among them we find Aaron Copland, Walter Piston, Roy Harris, Virgil Thomson, and many others. What they learned from Nadia Boulanger, however, was certainly not Americanism, but modernism of the Stravinsky brand — not the vigorous, young, elemental Stravinsky, but the austere Stravinsky of the neoclassical period. These young Americans learned the formal elements, but they were not encouraged to give their music an American accent and content. Later they solved their national problems in their individual fashions. Copland and Harris have to a considerable extent based their art on American folk music. Walter Piston has opposed the ostentatious use of American tunes, believing that, in music by Americans, American accent, color, and flavor will become apparent without intentional effort on the part of the composer.

Walter Piston (born in 1894) is one of America's most accomplished craftsmen. A master of counterpoint and logical structure, he practices neoclassicism of the Stravinsky type in a variant all his own, distinguished by sharply defined rhythm, colorful, tangy, modern harmony, and vigor of thematic invention. He has written several symphonies and many pieces of chamber music; as professor at Harvard University he exercises considerable influence on the rising generations of American musicians. Although he places considerations of structure above those of programmatic content, his music nevertheless conveys a vivid impression of specific moods. Particularly in his ballet *The Incredible Flutist*, Piston reveals a capacity for tone painting that is almost romantic in style.

Roy Harris, born in Oklahoma in 1898, grew up in a region where people still sang ballads that had lingered there from the days of the pioneers. His early experiences were not forgotten by Harris, in spite of the sophisticated schooling he received from Nadia Boulanger and the severe counterpoint he learned from her. He refused to allow his innate Americanism to be frozen in the chilly atmosphere of the cult of Stravinsky's neoclassicism, which engulfed so many young American students in Paris. The music of Harris is distinguished by the simple melodic inflection of American folk songs. This popular tendency is particularly evident in his overture *Johnny Comes Marching Home*, based on a Civil War song. The Third Symphony, his best-known work, also abounds in plain, strong American thematic material. It shows the composer's respect for tonality, his predilection for contrapuntal forms, for modal writing, as opposed to the impressionistic, ornamental, and rhapsodic melody. His Fourth Symphony is a glorification of folk song, in its treatment of several popular tunes sung by a chorus.

For Harris, Americanism is a source of inspiration, the deepest well of his music. Commenting on his Fifth Symphony, he makes this confession of faith: "I hoped to express qualities of our people which our popular dance music, because of its very nature, cannot reveal. Our people are more than pleasure-loving. We also have qualities of heroic strength — determination — will to struggle — faith in our destiny. We are possessed of a fierce driving power — optimistic, young, rough and ready — and I am convinced that our mechanistic age has not destroyed an appreciation of more tender moods." Few composers have outlined their aims and the nature of their art with such determination.

The music of Aaron Copland (born in 1900) encompasses many fields. It draws on folk music in the score of *Billy the Kid* and in his masterpiece, the ballet *Appalachian Spring*; on jazz in his early piano concerto; on Mexican songs in *El Salón México*. In his instrumental works, Copland shows great interest in cosmopolitan ideas of structure and modern technique.

Outstanding among Copland's works inspired by Americanism is *A Lincoln Portrait*. Extracts from Lincoln's speeches and writings are recited by a speaker, while the orchestral music surrounds them with an atmosphere of sound characteristic of their spirit and expressive of their content. The intention of the composer was, as he stated, "to suggest something of the mysterious sense of fatality about Lincoln's personality . . . also something of his gentleness and simplicity of spirit."

There is a strange, self-contradictory diversity in Copland's musical style. He accentuates his Americanism; but he also feels obliged to demonstrate how up-to-date he is. In some of his works a plain, tuneful melody reigns supreme. Others, like his piano variations and to some extent the piano sonata, abound in hideous, discordant harmonies and machine-like rhythms, with an utter absence of singable melody, as if this music had been designed to beat Stravinsky at his own game. These are concessions to a temporary fad, such as a number of American composers eager to exhibit their moden mentality have made.

Virgil Thomson (born in 1896) has absorbed, more than any

American composer, the veneer of Parisian sophistication. His music is a blend of Gallic *esprit* and tuneful melodies of American extraction — all this put to the service of parody. His most famous work is an opera to an especially written text by Gertrude Stein, entitled *Four Saints in Three Acts* and obviously designed to "épater le bourgeois." It was given for the first time in 1934 at Hartford, Connecticut, appropriately enough under the auspices of the Society of Friends and Enemies of Modern Music.

To the modern wing of American composers of the same generation belongs Roger Sessions (born in 1896). He rejects any idea of geographical Americanism and adopts in his music a style that is austere and detached from all programmatic meaning. He has written relatively few works — two symphonies, a violin concerto, a string quartet, a piano sonata, and a number of smaller pieces — which have earned him the reputation as a scholarly musician of great integrity. The tremendous difficulties posed by his scores, which are usually constructed according to the linear principle, unfortunately preclude their frequent performance.

Quite different from the modernist tendencies of composers associated with the Parisian-American group is the music of Howard Hanson (born 1896). He has declared himself an uncompromising champion of the much-maligned romanticism; in fact he gave the title "Romantic" to his second symphony. His basic inspiration is derived from the Nordic elements inherent in his Scandinavian ancestry, and for this reason he has been called "the American Sibelius." Yet his music abounds in modern technical devices of considerable stringency. As the director of the Eastman School of Music at Rochester, and as a conductor, Hanson has done a great deal for American music by giving annual festivals of works by his colleagues, regardless of their schools or stylistic persuasions.

Quincy Porter (born in 1897) studied with Horatio Parker at Yale University and also in Paris with Vincent d'Indy. The influences of American academism and Gallic impressionism became fused in his music so as to produce a distinctive style. He occupies the middle of the road among American composers, and is equally competent in symphonic and chamber music.

Randall Thompson (born in 1899) attracted considerable attention with his Second Symphony, a fine work exhaling an optimistic mood. He uses modern harmonies but remains on the side of moderation. One of his most successful choral works is *The Testament of Freedom,* a setting for men's voices and orchestra of passages from Thomas Jefferson's political writings, forming an impressive edifice in a neo-Handelian manner.

Leo Sowerby (born in 1896) occupies a curious position in American music. He is well known in Chicago, where he has made his headquarters, but his works are rarely performed elsewhere. His music is solid in form and rather conservative in idiom, at least in comparison with other American composers of the same generation. The catalogue of his productions is impressive: several symphonies, a number of instrumental sonatas, and much organ music. Contrapuntal cohesion and harmonic clarity are the main characteristics of Sowerby's compositions.

Douglas Moore (born in 1893) is a serious composer who is not intent on radical and sensational modernism. His opera *The Devil and Daniel Webster* presents an interesting combination of fantasy and realism against a background of American history; the symphonic suite *Pageant of P. T. Barnum* shows Moore's ability to write music in a humorous vein. As Professor of Music at Columbia University, Moore has rendered a great service to the cause of music education in America.

Among composers of the older generation, Arthur Shepherd (born in 1880) of Idaho has been active in various parts of the country. His works depict the broad expanses of America. Typical of these is his First Symphony, subtitled "Horizons." His idiom adheres to romantic precepts, and his music is rarely heard.

Transitory fame as a composer was the destiny of Deems Taylor (born in 1885). He obtained a tremendous success with his operas *The King's Henchman* and *Peter Ibbetson,* both of which were produced by the Metropolitan Opera, a rare distinction for an American composer. His orchestral suite *Through the Looking Glass,* inspired by Lewis Carroll's children's classic, enjoyed frequent performances in concert halls. But these basically romantic works, devoid of aggressive modernism, soon went out of fashion.

Louis Gruenberg (born in 1884) wrote *The Emperor Jones,* an opera based on O'Neill's famous play, and it scored a sensational success at its production by the the Metropolitan Opera in 1933. His *Daniel Jazz,* for voice and instruments, had numerous performances at various music festivals; but his later works have been unappreciated. Gruenberg's musical idiom, which appeared to be quite modern at the beginning of his career, apparently lost its impact on a public accustomed to greater excitement.

Bernard Rogers (born in 1893) is the composer of numerous works, usually with programmatic derivation. His opera *The Warrior* was performed at the Metropolitan Opera House but proved unsuccessful. His sacred oratorio *The Passion,* on the other hand, aroused considerable praise for its high inspiration. As a teacher of composition and orchestration at the Eastman School of Music in Rochester, Rogers has rendered valuable service to a whole generation of young American composers.

Philip James (born in 1890) has written a number of admirable works in all genres, but they are rarely performed. His First Symphony is particularly strong in its astringent harmonies and rhythms.

Otto Luening (born in 1900), who studied with Busoni in Europe, has developed a style that is neoromantic in essence, with a strong contrapuntal fabric. His numerous works, including the opera *Evangeline,* are, however, infrequently heard. In recent years he became interested in experimental music with electronic instruments.

Werner Janssen (born in 1899) joined the camp of the modernists with his symphonic piece *New Year's Eve in New York*

(1930), which reflected the tendencies of ultrarealistic music; but after a few performances, this work was forgotten as a passing curiosity. He eventually settled in Hollywood as a conductor.

Paul Creston (born in 1906), of Italian ancestry (his real name is Joseph Guttoveggio), gained considerable success with his effective symphonic and instrumental works. They are marked by dissonant harmony, without, however, overstepping the bounds of acoustical perceptions. His Second Symphony has had numerous performances.

Another composer of Italian ancestry, Norman Dello Joio (born in 1913) of New York, has become extremely successful through his orchestral and chamber music, written in an accessible idiom of international currency. He also has a flair for choral writing.

Harold Morris (born in 1890) of Texas is a composer of high-strung music in an emotional and almost passionate vein. This style is at odds with the prevailing tendencies among American composers, and it must be for this reason that Morris has failed to obtain many performances for his music. His musical language is international in essence, even though his subject matter is often ostentatiously American.

Herbert Elwell (born in 1898) of Minnesota studied with Nadia Boulanger in Paris but has not joined the neoclassical school. He stops short of experimental dissonance, but he feels free to use modern harmony, characteristic of neoromanticism. His ballet *The Happy Hypocrite* has had numerous performances; he has also written many instrumental compositions, which are, however, little known to the general public.

Ernst Bacon (born in 1898) has pursued the ideal of musical Americanism in his symphonic and other works, such as his orchestral suite *From These States*. His musical play *A Tree on the Plains* has had several performances, but few of his other works have been heard.

Theodore Chanler (born in 1902) studied with Nadia Boulanger in Paris and has acquired a taste for neoclassical types of composition. He has written few works, mostly for small instrumental groups and for vocal combinations, but they are marked by a certain attractive quality.

Isadore Freed (born in 1900), of Russian parentage, came to America as a child and studied with Ernest Bloch. In his music there are reflections of two national strains, Jewish and American, as far as the subject matter is concerned; the general idiom is moderately advanced. Freed's choral works are often heard, but he has been unable to gain wide acceptance in the international arena of contemporary music.

Marc Blitzstein (born in 1905) composes mainly for the theater. He is fascinated by the possibilities of opera with spoken dialogue, of the type that was popular in Germany between the two wars. He writes his own texts for his operas, of which *The Cradle will Rock*, a sharp social satire, aroused much discussion when it was performed in 1936. In a more solemn vein is his *Airborne Symphony* for speaker, voices, and orchestra, written during the war to glorify the heroes of aviation.

William Schuman (born in 1910) is one of the most successful American musicians. Not only as a composer but as an organizer and educator he has attained the highest honors. As the head of the famous Juilliard School of Music, he wields great influence in American musical education. In his music, Schuman has a definitely American tone and accent, but he is not free from indulgence in the reckless procedures of ultramodern harmony. The logic of dissonance is not sufficiently understood by American modernists, and Schuman is no exception. In his Third Symphony, however, he applies dissonance more judiciously, and it has become his best-known work. He is lucky in having earned the admiration of musicians as well as of sophisticated audiences. Yet this good fortune has its dangers as well as its satisfactions. Schuman is forced to defend his title for a high place in modern American music continually, in order to justify the speedy recognition of his talent.

Samuel Barber (born in 1910) is of all American modernists

the only one who is genuinely liked by the public, for he avoids the repellent procedures of the ultraradicals and apparently regards singable melody as indispensable even in our century. Furthermore, he is not afraid to yield to romantic sentiment and lyric effusion. His earliest works, the overture to *The School for Scandal*, the *Adagio for Strings*, and the *Essay for Orchestra*, have become the most frequently performed orchestral pieces by any contemporary American composer. Yet it must be admitted that there is little of the element of outspoken Americanism in Barber's music.

Gardner Read (born in 1913) candidly subscribes to the romantic school. He did not hesitate to take such a time-honored subject as *The Temptation of St. Anthony* for his ballet suite. His music takes its point of departure from Sibelius, but he goes far beyond conventional harmony into highly dissonant polytonal combinations. Read is not insensible to the lure of impressionism, as is proved by his symphonic evocation *Night Flight*.

Robert Palmer (born in 1915) tends toward neoclassicism, but he is also interested in the experimental possibilities of new music. He excels in chamber works, which are occasionally heard at music festivals.

Vincent Persichetti (born in 1915) is a modernist by conviction, but he is sufficiently careful not to overstep the limits of workable complications in harmony and in counterpoint. His predilection lies in chamber music, in which he can develop his sense for the clear contrapuntal line. His works are becoming increasingly known in musical circles.

David Diamond (born in 1915), a pupil of Nadia Boulanger in Paris, had experimented a great deal in the domain of highly dissonant harmony, before evolving a style that is decidedly romantic. His highly ingenious *Rounds* for string orchestra enjoys frequent performances; an orchestral suite from his music to *Romeo and Juliet* has also proved popular. He has written several symphonies and concertos, and has been generally fortunate in securing performances for his works.

The generation of American composers born at the outbreak of World War I symbolically marks the rise of a national American school of composition. To this generation belong Irving Fine, Gail Kubik, Leonard Bernstein, Harold Shapero, William Bergsma, and Peter Mennin. Lukas Foss, although born in Berlin, has identified himself with the cause of American music.

Irving Fine (born in 1914) may be described as a neoromanticist. But there is no rhapsodic vagueness in his close-knit music, with its carefully worked out contrapuntal fabric. He is at his best in chamber music.

Gail Kubik (born in 1914) wrote some successful film music before he attracted attention by his more ambitious works. He does not flaunt his musical Americanism, maintaining the level of internationally acceptable tonal painting.

Leonard Bernstein (born in 1918) leaped into fame almost overnight as a symphonic conductor. His career of uninterrupted successes in Europe and America has not, however, deflected him from composition. He has written two enormous works, the "Jeremiah" Symphony and *The Age of Anxiety*. He has also revealed an uncommon talent for popular musical comedy. His is a success story rare in the annals of American music.

Harold Shapero (born in 1920) has earned a reputation as a composer of great gifts, although he has written relatively little. His music is almost austere in its emphatic classicism. He calculates his effects with fine discrimination, caring more for the perfection of the line than for appeal to the public. He resolutely rejects any superficial references to American subject matter in his works.

William Bergsma (born in 1921) has written works on American subjects, but his Americanism consists of broad thematic allusions rather than of literal quotation from folk music. In his tonal texture he adheres to classical lines, enhanced by a certain admixture of modern harmonies.

Peter Mennin (born in 1923) composed seven symphonies in ten years. Contrapuntal considerations predominate in his writing. Such American traits as Mennin's music possesses are revealed in rhythmic inflections rather than in folklike melody. He has been successful in attracting attention to his music and securing speedy performances.

Lukas Foss (born in 1922) came to America at the age of fifteen. Almost at once he established himself as a pianist of unusual gifts and as a precocious composer. Despite the sharp criticism directed against some of his scores in the press, he continued to compose with great energy, driving toward the ideal he had set for himself — that of creating music of clear line, singing melody, and transparent harmonic texture. Some of his scores have a mystic quality, relating him to Mahler, as does his oratorio *The Parable of Death*. But he has also written music of distinctly American quality, like his highly effective opera after Mark Twain, *The Jumping Frog of Calaveras County*.

A complete list of American composers of serious music would include a thousand names. Even a selective list must necessarily omit many composers well known in their particular localities. Elliott Carter (born in 1908) of New York certainly deserves greater appreciation, and his music merits more performances than it actually receives. Burrill Phillips (born in 1907) of Nebraska enjoys a fine reputation, although little of his music has been heard; it has a distinctive flavor, gaiety, and rhythmic verve, giving the impression of a latter-day Rossini. Paul Bowles (born in 1911) began his career as a composer of highly sophisticated music in a Parisian-American style. He then lived in North Africa for a number of years, wrote several successful novels, and gradually withdrew from musical activities. Bernard Herrmann (born in 1911) is mainly known as the composer of excellent film music. He is also a determined modernist, familiar with all the intricacies of the twentieth-century idiom. His most ambitious score, the dramatic cantata *Moby Dick* (1937), failed to win favor with the public or the press. Everett Helm (born in 1913) of Minnesota has traveled a great deal in South America and Europe. A cultured musician, he has written a number of works in a style that represents a compromise between neoromantic and neoclassical music. Because of this adaptability, his works have frequently been performed at international festivals. Vittorio Giannini (born in 1903) is an American of Italian origin. He did not attract general attention until the production of his opera *The Taming of the Shrew* on television in 1954.

Among American women composers the names of Mabel Daniels, Marion Bauer, Ruth Crawford, and Louise Talma are well known. Mabel Daniels (born in 1878) has written some fine choral works; her cantata *Song of Jael* has been successfully performed. Her symphonic prelude *Deep Forest*, somewhat impressionistic in style, has also been favorably received. Marion Bauer (1887–1955) showed consistent interest in twentieth-century music and published a book on the subject. Her chamber music had occasional hearings in New York. Ruth Crawford (1901–1953) was a conspicuous member of the modernist group of American composers. She wrote music in a highly advanced idiom; at the same time she was active in folklore research and published several collections of American folk songs. Louise Talma (born in 1906) is a neoclassicist who believes in the artistic supremacy of logical structure and the continuity of diatonic music, in which dissonance is the incidental product of well-planned contrapuntal development. In this respect she belongs to the group of American composers inspired by Stravinsky's successful experience in transmuting traditional elements into new sounds.

In the melting pot of American racial diversity, Negro influences have played a significant role through the emergence of the so-called spirituals — the religious songs of the slaves in the Southern plantations. Many of these songs were arranged and published by Henry Thacker Burleigh (1866–1949). Negro strains have been used in the works of many American composers along with Southern ballads and Western cowboy songs. The earliest symphonic works by Negro composers were produced almost simultaneously, by William Grant Still (born in 1895) and by William Levi Dawson (born in 1898). It is sufficient to give the titles of some of Still's works to point out their sources of inspiration: *Darker America, From the Black Belt, Afro-American Symphony, The Black Man Dances, Pages from Negro History.* Dawson's *Negro Folk Symphony* is regarded as the first full-fledged symphony by a Negro composer explicitly derived from Negro folk music.

Negro composers of a later generation show less dependence on purely racial subjects. Ulysses Kay (born in 1917) has written music in the characteristic neoclassical manner that has tempted so many composers of his generation. Howard Swanson (born in 1909) is the composer of an effective work entitled *Short Symphony*, which obtained immediate success after its first performance in New York in 1950 and has been since included in the repertory of many orchestras. Among Negro artists, the singers Roland Hayes, Marian Anderson, and Dorothy Maynor have achieved international distinction by their soulful interpretation of Negro spirituals, as well as of the traditional classical songs.

On the international scene the most popular product of American culture is undoubtedly jazz. The term "jazz" first appeared in 1916, indicating a new type of night club music. Soon jazz became the rage of America. In November 1918, an American jazz band appeared in Paris and gave the Parisian public its first taste of this strongly spiced specialty. European musicians were not slow in making use of this exciting product. One can see jazz influences in the works of Ravel, Honegger, Stravinsky, and many others. Jazz even became the subject of a scholarly investigation in a book entitled *Le Jazz hot*, by Hugues Panassié. In Germany, jazz made its entrance several years later. The "Chocolate Kiddies," a band of colored dancers and players, were the first to acquaint Berlin with the distorted rhythms, the grotesque antics, the peculiar sound effects of saxophones, and the trombone glissandi that are the main features of jazz.

It should be noted that jazz is not the achievement of one or of several composers, but rather a special method of ensemble playing that might be applied to almost any music. In fact, many classical compositions have been translated into the jargon of jazz. The notes are not meant to be played with rigorous exactitude; they serve as a general directive for the players, who decorate them with fanciful improvisations so that the same piece is never heard twice in quite the same manner. With this technique of improvised variation, the best jazz bands have obtained a high degree of efficiency. The inventiveness of talented players has also led to the discovery of many new tricks on almost every instrument.

Jazz has produced at least one master who, with profound artistic intelligence, discovered how the vulgar burlesque of ordinary jazz could be subjected to the more refined methods of real art. The man who made jazz the foundation of inspired music in traditional symphonic forms was the American Jew, George Gershwin (1898–1937). The first product of this symphonic jazz was his *Rhapsody in Blue*, which he performed with Paul Whiteman's orchestra in 1924. The "blue" in the title is a reference to the songs of a nostalgic nature called "blues," originated by the Negro composer William Christopher Handy (born in 1873).

Gershwin combined the melodic inflection of the Negro spirituals with the dynamic swing music of jazz, bringing to this synthesis the resources of modern harmony, a superior sense of form and structure, and a more discriminating taste than the rest of the jazz fraternity put together. His Jewish sensitivity, coupled with the rhythmic force and vitality of the jazz idiom, created an authentic style of Americanism, full of vital energy. In his opera *Porgy and Bess*, Gershwin presented a Negro folk drama in a framework of jazz rhythms and modern harmony that bids fair to make it the first American grand opera. The increasing success of *Porgy and Bess* not only in America but also in Europe testifies to the enduring strength of this native master-piece.

Quite different from Gershwin's art is that of another American Jew, Irving Berlin (born in 1888). While Gershwin acquired a complete mastery of modern composition, Irving Berlin, through-out his highly successful career, never even learned to write notes on paper. Starting as a newsboy in New York, he earned a living as a "singing waiter" in Chinatown, improvising tunes by in-stinct, without any musical education. Berlin's first success was the song "Alexander's Ragtime Band." Hundreds of others fol-lowed. His patriotic song "God Bless America" nearly gained the status of a national hymn during World War II. Irving Berlin, like Stephen Foster, has a flair for the simple sentiment of the people, and his unaffected songs have found their way into the hearts of millions.

Still another aspect of popular musical Americanism is the production of Philip Sousa (1854–1932), the famous American bandmaster whose march "Stars and Stripes Forever" has become an American classic of its genre.

There are several American composers who have made their careers primarily in popular music but who have worked in the field of symphonic composition as well. Such is Morton Gould (born in 1913), who has created the new forms, the "sympho-nette" and "concertette," reproducing in miniature the classical prototypes of the symphony and the concerto but filled with a substance that is purely American in its swinging rhythms and jazzy syncopation. He has also written some orchestral music of considerable complexity.

A history of American musical comedy would fill a large volume. Its sources are by necessity European. The first impor-tant composer of musical comedy in America was Victor Herbert (1859–1924), an Irishman who came to the United States as a cello player. His tuneful operettas continue to enchant succes-sive generations of American music lovers. The American-born composer Jerome Kern (1885–1945) created in his *Showboat* a genre that approaches a true folk opera. Richard Rodgers (born in 1902) produced in the score of his *Oklahoma!* another American classic in musical comedy.

It is curious that the only successful composer of American modern opera is an Italian, Gian-Carlo Menotti (born in 1911). He came to the United States in 1928 and studied at the Curtis Institute of Music in Philadelphia. He thoroughly mastered the English language, and his most successful operas, *The Medium*, *The Telephone*, and *The Consul*, are written to his own librettos. His feeling for drama is shown by the variety of his subjects. *The Medium* is a tragic story of a fraudulent spiritualist who falls victim to her own imagination; Menotti's score to this opera abounds in effects of sinister expectations, reminiscent of Puccini's *Tosca*. *The Telephone* is, on the other hand, a merry interlude from American urban life, and here Menotti gives a fine caricature of the *opera buffa*. *The Consul* creates a feeling of drama by the unique device of presenting the consul himself *in absentia*, while the characters of the drama seek refuge from imminent peril in the vain hope of receiving a visa. The musical accompaniment to this dramatic situation is extremely vivid. It has been said that Menotti's music as a whole represents a compromise between traditional and modern currents of Italian music, with an admixture of Russian influences. That may be so, but Menotti's success is nevertheless a positive factor in the American lyric theater. Menotti also had the historic distinction of writing the first television opera, *Amahl and the Night Visitors*, an imaginative Christmas tale to his own text.

The political turmoil in Europe drove a great many famous composers to the United States. It is sufficient to list their names to gauge the significance of this emigration: Rachmaninoff, Gretchaninoff, Stravinsky, Schönberg, Bartók, Hindemith, Bloch, Toch, Krenek, Martinu, Weinberger, Weill. With their reputations firmly established in Europe, they did not attempt to make a deliberate entry on the scene of musical Americanism, and occasional works, such as Bloch's symphonic poem *America,* have been merely complimentary tributes to their adoptive country.

Kurt Weill (1900–1950) in particular succeeded in adapting himself to the American musical needs as soon as he arrived in the United States. At least one of his works, the American folk opera, *Down in the Valley,* was successfully produced before his untimely death.

A few brief sketches of some of the many naturalized American composers may be offered here. Bernard Wagenaar (born in 1894), formerly of Holland, is the son of the eminent Dutch composer, Johan Wagenaar, with whom he also studied before coming to New York in 1921. Bernard Wagenaar has written several symphonies and many pieces of chamber music. His modernism is of an international stamp, but he has been unable to secure much attention from the general public.

Paul Pisk (born in 1893), formerly of Vienna, emigrated to the United States in 1937 and has devoted himself primarily to teaching. His works often appeared at the international festivals between the two wars and achieved a respected place in the musical world.

Mario Castelnuovo-Tedesco (born in 1895) came to America as a foremost Italian composer, and was received with the respect commensurate with his rank. He settled in Hollywood and continued to compose prolifically. He has not changed his style during his American period, and has maintained his characteristic traits — a broad melodic line against a rich harmonic background, illuminated by fine instrumental color.

Miklós Rózsa (born in 1907), formerly of Hungary, has made his fortune in Hollywood as a composer for films. This lucrative source of income allows him to continue to compose the kind of music that he wrote in Europe — intricate, dissonant, and difficult to perform. Some of his symphonic music has been featured on the programs of American orchestras.

Jenö Takacs (born in 1902) came to the United States from his native Hungary after a world-wide peregrination. After World War II he settled in Cincinnati. Much of his music is inspired by Hungarian folk elements, but he has also experimented in highly dissonant, modernistic forms.

Karol Rathaus (1895–1955) lived in Austrian Poland, Vienna, Berlin, and London before coming to New York in 1938. His chamber music was often featured at international music festivals.

Felix Labunski (born in 1892) was active in Polish music in Warsaw and in Paris before coming to America in 1936. Settling in Cincinnati as a teacher, he took part in local music festivals and also presented his new works there.

Stefan Wolpe (born in 1902), formerly of Berlin, lived in Palestine for several years but eventually decided to come to America. His style is a curious synthesis of extreme modernism and simple melodic writing, while the subject matter of his cantatas and ballets ranges from Israel to sport, capitalism, and Chinese poetry.

Vittorio Rieti (born in 1898) earned a reputation as one of the leading European modernists. His ballets were performed by Diaghilev; his symphonies and chamber music were often features at the music festivals. Although an American citizen, he spends much of his time in Europe.

Ernst Lévy (born in 1895) of Switzerland has written twelve symphonies and a great number of other works of large dimensions, distinguished by fine culture and precision of logical development, in a style that is basically romantic with some harmonic ramifications that lead into regions bordering on polytonality. Lévy came to America during World War II and occupied various teaching positions. He also gave piano recitals. Apart from a few sporadic performances, his music has remained practically unknown to the American public.

A number of Russian composers came to the United States in the wake of the revolution, among them Saminsky, Achron,

Dubensky, Berezowsky, Nabokov, Dukelsky, Lopatnikoff, and Haieff.

Lazare Saminsky (born in 1882) studied with Rimsky-Korsakov. He has written five symphonies, several operas, oratorios, and other music. His sources of inspiration are manifold: there is the original romantic yearning to express emotional moods and philosophical concepts along grandiose lines, and there is a quest for new tone colors. Remote culture and archaic evocations are also the object of Saminsky's interests. But above all, Saminsky cultivates Jewish music, from the modern type of Biblical oratorio to vocal settings of contemporary Jewish poetry.

Joseph Achron (1886–1943) is known to the musical world mainly through his earliest work, *Hebrew Melody* for violin. But he was also the composer of some highly intricate instrumental works which are of great interest to historians of modern music.

Arcady Dubensky (born in 1890) has frankly embraced the conservative style as far as melody and harmony are concerned. In his instrumentation, however, he is anything but old-fashioned: among his works is a quartet for bassoons, a tuba concerto, and a fugue for eighteen violins, which has had numerous successful performances.

Nicolai Berezowsky (1900–1952) established himself as a successful composer of symphonic and chamber music in a style that comprises elements of neoclassicism and impressionism, with melodic lines often suggesting a Russian background. Just before his death he produced an effective children's opera, *Babar*.

Nicolas Nabokov (born in 1903) was connected with the Diaghilev ballet in Paris. Upon his arrival in America he produced several works on native subjects, such as the railroad ballet *Union Pacific*. His music has a poetic quality, and his modernism is not too aggressive. Nabokov has also been active as organizer of international music festivals.

Vladimir Dukelsky (born in 1903) began his career auspiciously as a composer of ballet music for Diaghilev and of symphonies that were performed by Koussevitzky. He also has an innate talent for popular music and, under the name of Vernon Duke, he has produced numerous musical comedies. At least one of his songs, "April in Paris," has become a perennial hit. His success as a popular composer progressed in inverse ratio to his luck with regard to performances of his serious works. He has published an autobiography in which he describes the vicissitudes of a "double" composer with disarming candor.

Nikolai Lopatnikoff (born in 1903) lived in Finland and Germany before coming to America on the eve of World War II. His works for orchestra and smaller groups were constantly featured at European music festivals, and he has been fortunate enough to maintain this popularity in the United States. Lopatnikoff writes in classical forms, and his most ingratiating characteristics are a lyric melody and propulsive rhythm.

Alexei Haieff (born in 1914) studied with Nadia Boulanger and joined the ranks of American neoclassicists. His works are set in traditional forms, and he writes with the economy of means typical of that school of composers. But Haieff is not reluctant to make use of national allusions; there are, for instance, definite jazz rhythms in his piano concerto. He has been eminently successful in performances of his works in America and in Europe, and indeed his style has all the elements calculated to please the classicists at heart as well as the sophisticated modernists of nonromantic persuasions.

It is hardly necessary to emphasize that America has for a century been the goal of European artists seeking fame and monetary rewards. In the nineteenth century, European celebrities were imported by American impresarios with great fanfare of publicity. Jenny Lind, the "Swedish Nightingale" was presented as a circus attraction by the celebrated P. T. Barnum. Paderewski's tour of the United States in the 1890's was accompanied by a tremendous publicity campaign. Celebrated composers — Tchaikovsky, Dvořák, Saint-Saëns, Puccini, Ravel — have visited America. American orchestral conductors were, until very recently, practically all foreigners. The Damrosch family — especially Leopold and Walter, father and son — have played a decisive role in spreading symphonic music in America, as did Theodore Thomas before them. The names of Toscanini, Koussevitzky, Stokowski, and Bruno Walter have become household words for American music-lovers. As to pianists and violinists, the roster of their tours in the United States comprises practically the entire sum of virtuoso achievements.

In the field of musical scholarship, America has gradually emancipated itself from the hegemony of German *Musikwissenschaft*. The American Musicological Society, founded in 1935, is publishing its own magazine. The Music Library Association brings out the quarterly, *Notes*, giving a comprehensive bibliographical survey of new publications. *The Musical Quarterly*, founded in 1915, largely took over the functions of the *Sammelbände* issued by the old International Society, which was disbanded at the outbreak of World War I. Many European scholars who found refuge in the United States — Alfred Einstein, Curt Sachs, Willi Apel, Karl Geiringer, and others — have contributed to these American journals.

The music departments of the great American libraries — the Library of Congress, the New York Public Library, the Boston Public Library — have accumulated valuable collections of musical source materials. The music schools of American universities have undertaken various programs of research and have published important books on music through their university presses.

Richly endowed musical institutions, such as the Juilliard School of Music in New York, the Curtis Institute in Philadelphia, the Eastman School in Rochester, and the Berkshire Music Center, have offered precious advantages to talented students, while the older institutions, such as the New England Conservatory in Boston, have modernized their courses. Renowned European teachers have taken up permanent residence in the United States, thus providing opportunities for private study.

No parallel to European complete editions of works by great masters exists in America, because no American composer of classical stature has arisen. Yet native composers are not left without a modicum of glory. Their works are published by the renowned firms of G. Schirmer, Carl Fischer, C. C. Birchard, and others. Their rights are protected by the American Society of Composers, Authors, and Publishers and by Broadcast Music Incorporated. The Union of American Musicians has extended protective rights to performing musicians, from the most famous to the most humble.

The rise of the phonograph, particularly since the introduction of the long-playing recordings, has spread musical education far and wide in America. Radio stations broadcasting classical music over the frequency modulation networks reach a select audience of music-lovers, while transcontinental networks broadcast symphony and opera to the remotest parts of North and South America.

In this book, the author has endeavored to describe how musical leadership has been held by one nation after another: by France, the Netherlands, Italy, Germany. There is a probability that the next dominion of music may be established in America. At present, the United States is the vast basin into which all others pour their musical surplus. The great task is to insure proper utilization of these multifarious resources, as a prerequisite for the creation of a truly American school of composition, possessing native inspiration and cosmopolitan knowledge.

Index